Study Guide

to accompany

Psychology
Making Connections

Gregory J. Feist
San Jose State University

Erika L. Rosenberg
University of California, Davis

Prepared by
Susan Snycerski
San Jose State University

Mc Graw Hill

Boston   Burr Ridge, IL   Dubuque, IA   Madison, WI   New York   San Francisco   St. Louis
Bangkok   Bogotá   Caracas   Kuala Lumpur   Lisbon   London   Madrid   Mexico City
Milan   Montreal   New Delhi   Santiago   Seoul   Singapore   Sydney   Taipei   Toronto

The McGraw·Hill Companies

McGraw-Hill Higher Education

Study Guide to accompany
PSYCHOLOGY: MAKING CONNECTIONS
Gregory J. Feist and Erika L. Rosenberg

2 3 4 5 6 7 8 9 0 QWD/QWD 0 9

ISBN 978-0-07-728751-1
MHID   0-07-728751-7

www.mhhe.com

Contents

Page

Chapter 1   Introduction to Psychology   1

Chapter 2   Conducting Psychological Research   12

Chapter 3   The Biology of Behavior   26

Chapter 4   Sensing and Perceiving Our World   42

Chapter 5   The Developing Human   59

Chapter 6   Consciousness   73

Chapter 7   Memory   87

Chapter 8   Learning   99

Chapter 9   Language and Thought   114

Chapter 10   Intelligence, Problem-Solving, and Creativity   126

Chapter 11   Motivation and Emotion   139

Chapter 12   Stress and Coping   153

Chapter 13   Personality: the Uniqueness of the Individual   164

Chapter 14   Social Behavior   178

Chapter 15   Psychological Disorders   190

Chapter 16   Treatment of Psychological Disorders   211

Chapter 1
INTRODUCTION TO PSYCHOLOGY

KEY TERMS

Psychology
Cognitive psychology
Developmental psychology
Behavioral neuroscience
Biological psychology
Health psychologists
Personality psychology
Social psychology
Clinical psychology
Educational psychology
Industrial/organizational (I/O) psychology
Sports psychology
Forensic psychology
Shamans
Asylums
Moral treatment

Psychoanalysis
Empiricism
Psychophysics
Structuralism
Introspection
Functionalists
Behaviorism
Humanistic psychology
Positive psychology
Gestalt psychology
Cognitive science
Nature through nurture
Evolution
Natural selection
Adaptations
Evolutionary psychology

OUTLINE

I. What is Psychology? (p.5)

A. *Psychology* defined: the scientific study of thought and behavior.
1. Psychology is a science that is often considered a social science but is increasingly called a biological science.

B. Why Should You Study Psychology?
1. Psychology is a good addition to a general education. Furthermore, not only do you learn about what makes other people work, it also makes you aware of how *you* work.
a. The study of psychology offers a very practical knowledge that can be beneficial in many settings.

II. Subdisciplines of Psychology (p. 8)

A. Psychology, as both a science and a practice, is divided into many areas of investigation. The field is divided into more than 25 distinct subdisciplines.
1. *Cognitive psychology* is the study of how we perceive, how we learn and remember, how we learn and use language, and how we solve problems.
2. *Developmental psychology* explores how thought and behavior change and show stability across the lifetime.

3. *Behavioral neuroscience* studies links among the brain, mind, and behavior. In this field, for example, one could stuffy brain functions involved in learning, emotion, social behavior, and mental illness, or many other areas.

4. *Biological psychology* examines the relationship between bodily systems and chemicals and their influence on behavior and thought.

a. There is much overlap between biological psychology and neuroscience.

5. *Health psychology* examines the role of psychological factors in physical health and illness.

6. *Personality psychology* examines what makes people unique as well as the consistencies in people's behavior across time and situation.

7. *Social psychology* examines how the real or imagined presence of others influences thought, feeling, and behavior.

8. *Clinical psychology* focuses on the treatment of mental, emotional, and behavioral disorders and ways to promote psychological health.

9. *Educational psychology* examines how students learn, the effectiveness of particular teaching techniques, the dynamics of school populations, and the psychology of teaching. It draws from cognitive, developmental, and social psychology.

10. *Industrial/organizational (I/O) psychology* applies a broad array of psychological concepts and questions to work settings and problems.

11. *Sports psychology* examines the psychological factors in sports and exercise (Weinberg & Gould, 1999).

12. *Forensic psychology* is a blend of psychology, law, and criminal justice (Adler, 2004).

a. Forensic psychologists make legal evaluations of a person's mental competency to stand trial, the state of mind of a defendant at the time of the crime, the fitness of a parent to have custody of their children, or allegations of child abuse.

III. The Origins of Psychology (p. 12)

A. A Brief History of the Practice of Clinical Psychology

1. Prehistoric Views: Humans have tried to cure their fellow humans of mental problems from as far back as the Stone Age (7,000 to maybe as much as 50,000 years ago).

a. Most prehistoric cultures has medicine women or men called *shamans* who treated the "possessed" by driving out the "demons" with elaborate rituals such as exorcisms, incantations, and prayers.

b. Some shamans practiced *trephination* which involved drilling a small hole in a person's skull (Alt et al., 1997; Weber & Whal, 2006) in an effort to release spirits and demons thought to be possessing the individual.

2. Ancient Views: The Egyptians and the Greeks (2600 B.C.E.) were the first cultures to focus on natural and physical explanations for disorders.

3. Medieval Views: There was a retreat in the study of psychology in the Medieval Ages (400–1400 C.E.) because people believe others were possessed by demons and spirits or the devil.

a. The era of witches and witchcraft produced such extreme views. One way to test if a person were a witch was the *float test*. The person's hands and feet were bound and he or she was thrown into a lake or river. If they floated they were a witch (because only the devil could make one float). If they drowned they were not a witch—but they drowned instead (Witch trial, n.d.).

b. *Asylums* were the first facilities for the mentally ill and were built in Europe during the time of the witch hunts of the 16th century.

   i. The conditions were terrible and chaotic. The rooms were filthy and people were chained and shackled to the walls.

c. Due to the conditions of these facilities, people began to advocate for more humane conditions. This became known as the *moral treatment*.

4. Modern Views: The last decades of the 1800s saw the emergence of the first truly modern views of psychological disorders; that is, the view that disorders were simply one form of illness and that is should be treated as other illnesses with appropriate diagnosis and therapy.

   a. *Psychoanalysis* is a clinically based approach to understanding and treating psychological disorders developed by Sigmund Freud at the turn of the 20th century.

   b. The development of the *Diagnostic and Statistical Manual* offered a standardized manual for diagnosing psychological disorders. It is now in its fourth edition (abbreviated *DSM-IV-TR)*.

      i. This edition describes objectively the behaviors and symptoms of each disorder so that psychologists from all perspectives can agree on a single diagnosis for an individual with a given set of symptoms.

E. A Brief History of Scientific Psychology: Psychology's parents can be thought of as philosophy and physiology.

   1. The Philosophy of Empiricism: Perhaps the most important philosophical question for psychology is the nature of knowledge and how human beings formed knowledge.

      a. John Locke stated that knowledge and thoughts come from experience. This view is termed *empiricism.*

F. The Psychophysics of Human Perception

   1. The first researchers in psychological science examined the subjective experience of physical sensations, in a field called *psychophysics.*

      a. One important principle of psychophysics is that perception of physical properties is not the same as the physical properties themselves.

         i. Ernst Weber, Gustav Fechner, and Hermann von Hemholtz were the first experimental psychologists.

         ii. Psychology became a full-fledge science when Wilhelm Wundt, in 1879, set up the first psychology laboratory in Leipzig, Germany. He is credited with giving psychology its independence from philosophy and physiology (Benjamin, 2007; Fancher, 1996).

iii. By establishing a laboratory, Wundt created a place where the best young minds could learn the science of psychology. He, himself, trained 180 students in his laboratory.

b. G. Stanley Hall learned from Wundt in Germany and then studied with William James at Harvard. Hall earned the first Ph.D. in psychology as James's student.

i. Hall opened the first U.S. psychology laboratory at John Hopkins University and also founded the American Psychological Association (APA).

ii. Hall also started the first scientific American psychology journal, the *American Journal of Psychology.*

iii. Mary Whiton Calkins became the first woman president of the APA in 1905. Harvard would not grant her a Ph.D. (even though she completed the coursework) simply because she was a woman!

2. Structuralism-Functionalism

a. *Structuralism* argues that breaking down experience into its elemental parts offers the best way to understand thought and behavior.

i. Structuralism used *introspection* as a method to looking into one's own mind for information about the nature of conscious experience. Structuralists divided each experience into its smallest parts.

b. *Functionalism* looked at why the mind worked the way it did, rather than to describe its parts. The functionalists asked "Why do people think, feel, or perceive and how did these abilities come to be?"

i. The functionalists also used introspection as a primary method of understanding how the mind worked.

3. Behaviorism

a. In 1913 John Watson founded the field of *behaviorism,* which proposes that psychology could be a true science only if it examined observable behavior, not ideas, thoughts, feelings, or motives.

b. The most prominent figure in behaviorism was B. F. Skinner, who was largely responsible for making behaviorism the major view in experimental psychology for almost 50 years.

i. Skinner modified and expanded on Watson's ideas suggesting that rewards and reinforcement shape and maintain behavior.

4. Humanistic and Positive Psychology

a. in the 1940s and 1950s, Abraham Maslow and Carl Rogers offered a new alternative to psychology called *humanistic psychology,* which focused on personal growth and meaning as a way of reaching one's highest potential. The humanistic movement waned in the 1970s.

b. The movement resurfaced in the 1990s when Martin Seligman and Mihalyi Csikszentmihalyi began a movement called *positive psychology.*

5. Cognitivism

a. The field of *cognitive science* that made use of the new modern metaphor "the computer" freed itself from the label *mental.*

         i. Because computers store, retrieve, and process information, just as the brain stores, retrieves, and stores information and processes sensations, memories, and ideas, these connections seemed to aid in the notion of inputs (environment) and outputs (behavior).

   6. Biological Psychology and Behavioral Neuroscience

     a. Psychologists, by the 1980s, became receptive to the idea that who we are, how we got here, and what we do and think are very much a result of brain activity, are influenced by genetic factors, and have a long evolutionary past.

        i. The developments of behavioral neuroscience, behavioral genetics, and the emergence of evolutionary psychology began to shift psychology toward a view of origins of human thought and behavior. This was enhanced by new technologies for brain imagine and sequencing of the human genome.

IV. Ways of Thinking about Mind, Body, and Experience (p. 23)

A. The Nature-Nurture Debate: For millennia thinkers have argued over which factor determines our personality: *innate biology* or *life experience.* This factor is known as the *nature-nurture debate.*

   1. The nature-only view is that who we are comes from inborn tendency and genetically-based traits.

   2. The nurture-only view states that we are all born essentially the same, and we are a product of our experience.

   3. Pitting nature against nurture gets us nowhere as it creates a false dichotomy that works against understanding the mind and behavior.

     i. Your text will point throughout the many cases in which environmental and genetic forces work together to shape who we are. Your text also provides an example in which babies whose mothers fought infection during pregnancy are more likely to develop schizophrenia later in life than babies whose mothers were healthy during pregnancy (Brown, 2006).

B. Mind-Body Dualism

   1. In the 17th century, Rene Descartes stated that the mind and body are separate entities. This idea is referred to as *mind-body dualism.*

     a. By contrast, Eastern philosophy and thought systems from other parts of the world have emphasized the interdependence of body and mind (Begley, 2007; Tulku, 1984).

     b. After more than a century, psychological science is beginning to arrive at this same conclusion.

C. The Evolution of Behavior

   1. *Evolution* is the change over time in the frequency with which specific genes occur within a breeding species (Buss, 1999).

a. Behaviors have genetic bases that are affected by many environmental factors. Human interaction with the world influences which genes are passed on to future generations, and these in turn shape human behavior.

      i. *Natural selection* is the mechanism by which the changes describe above take place.

      ii. Natural selection defined: a feedback process whereby nature favors one design over another, depending on whether it has an impact on reproduction.

      iii. The key for natural selection to work is that the behaviors have to increase reproductive success, because reproduction and passing of genes drives the whole process.

b. *Adaptations* are inherited solutions to ancestral problems that have been naturally selected because they directly contribute in some way to reproductive success (Tooby & Cosmides, 1992).

2. *Evolutionary psychology* is the branch of psychology that attempts to understand the functions of the human mind rather than just describing what it does.

Making Connections in Psychology (p. 29)

A. From neural to conceptual to social connections, the field of psychology lends itself to making connections. For example, how would psychologists from different areas of psychology study how we behave with electronic forms of communicating such as e-mail, blogs, cell phones, texting, instant messaging, social network sites, and so forth?

B. Behavioral Neuroscience

    1. These psychologists might ask, "Does the brain respond in the same way to electronic interactions as it does to face-to-face interactions?"

C. Cognitive Psychology

    1. These psychologist might be interested in how drivers pay attention to driving while talking on their cell phones.

D. Developmental Psychology

    1. These psychologists may ask, "At what age is a person too young to form electronic social networks? At what age does usage of Internet social networks peak?," and so on.

E. Social Psychology

    1. Social psychology lends itself to a multitude of research questions regarding electronic interactions as these are essentially germane to their subject matter.

F. Personality Psychology

    1. These psychologists may ask which people interact extensively with other people via Facebook than via face-to-face interactions. Are some more extraverted or introverted?

G. Health Psychology

   1. Some programs, like that in San Francisco, allow people to call if they suspect they have a particular disease (perhaps a sexually transmitted disease). This use of electronic communication may be a way to ease the embarrassment of seeking face-to-face answers to health questions.

H. Health Psychology

   1. These psychologists might attempt to determine who might be addicted to the Internet. They may ask how many hours one spends on line and whether that is healthy behavior.

GLOSSARY TERMS

psychology: the scientific study of thought and behavior.

cognitive psychology: study of how people perceive, remember, think, speak, and solve problems.

developmental psychology: study of how thought and behavior change and remain stable across the lifespan.

behavioral neuroscience: study of the links among brain, mind, and behavior.

biological psychology: study of the relationship between bodily systems and chemicals and how they influence behavior and thought.

health psychologists: scientists who examine the role that psychological factors play in regard to physical health and illness.

personality psychology: study of what makes people unique and the consistencies in people's behavior across time and situations.

social psychology: study of how living among others influences thought, feeling, and behavior.

clinical psychology: field that deals with the treatment of mental, emotional, and behavioral disorders and the promotion of psychological health.

educational psychology: the study of how students learn, the effectiveness of particular teaching techniques, the social psychology of schools, and the psychology of teaching.

industrial/organizational (I/O) psychology: application of psychological concepts and questions to work settings and problems.

sports psychology: study of psychological factors in sports and exercise.

forensic psychology: study that combines psychology and the legal and criminal justice systems.

shamans: medicine men or women who treat the possessed by coaxing and driving out the demons with elaborate rituals, such as exorcisms, incantations, and prayers.

asylums: facilities for treating the mentally ill that existed in Europe during the Middle Ages and into the 19th century.

moral treatment: approach to treatment of the mentally ill that began in Europe during the 18th and 19th centuries; its goal was to offer dignity and care in a relaxing environment.

psychoanalysis: a clinically based approach to understanding and treating psychological disorders; assumes that the unconscious mind is the most powerful force behind thought and behavior.

empiricism: the view that all knowledge and thoughts come from experience.

psychophysics: the first scientific form of psychology; laboratory studies of the subjective experience of physical sensations.

structuralism: 19th century school of psychology that argued that breaking down experience into its elemental parts offers the best way to understand thought and behavior.

introspection: the main method of investigation for structuralists; it involves looking into one's own mind for information about the nature of conscious experience.

functionalists: a school of psychology that argued that it was better to look at why the mind worked the way it did than to describe its parts.

behaviorism: a school of psychology that proposed that psychology can be a true science only if it examines observable behavior, not ideas, thoughts, feelings, or motives.

humanistic psychology: a theory of psychology that focuses on personal growth and meaning as a way of reaching one's highest potential.

positive psychology: a theory of psychology that shares with humanism a belief that psychology should focus on studying, understanding, and promoting healthy and positive psychological functioning, but does so from a scientific rather than theoretical perspective.

Gestalt psychology: a theory of psychology that proposes that we perceive things as wholes rather than a compilation of parts.

cognitive science: a theory of psychology discipline that focuses on the scientific study of human thought.

nature through nurture: the position that the environment – be it the womb or the home or the entire world – constantly interacts with biology to shape who we are and what we do.

evolution: the change over time in the frequency with which specific genes occur within a breeding species.

natural selection: a feedback process whereby nature favors one design over another, depending on whether it has an impact on reproduction.

adaptations: inherited solutions to ancestral problems that have been selected for because they directly contribute in some way to reproductive success; they continue to perform that function though the problem that required the adaptation no longer exists.

evolutionary psychology: the branch of psychology that aims to understand the functions of the human mind by looking at and understanding what adaptive problems it may have solved earlier in its ancestral past.

PRACTICE STUDY QUESTIONS

Match the letter to the corresponding numbered definition:

a. cognitive psychology
b. evolutionary psychology
c. humanistic psychology
d. biological psychology
e. developmental psychology
f. social psychology
g. clinical psychology
h. forensic psychology
i. social psychology
j. industrial/organizational psychology
k. clinical psychology

1. The study of how thought and behavior change show stability across the life span.

2. The study of how the real and imagined presence of others influences thought, feeling, and behavior.

3. The study of treatment of mental, emotional, and behavioral disorders and ways to promote psychological health.

4. The study of how we perceive, how we learn and remember, how we learn and use language, and how we solve problems.

5. A blend of psychology, law, and criminal justice.

6. An area of psychology that focused on personal growth and meaning as a way of reaching one' highest potential.

7. The study of the relationship between bodily systems and chemicals and their influence on behavior and thought.

8. The branch of psychology that is about understanding the functions of the human mind rather than just describing what it does.

9. The study of a broad array of psychological concepts and questions to work settings and problems.

10. The mind-body dualism idea was proposed by:
    a.   Descartes.
    b.   Hall.
    c.   Skinner.
    d.   Wundt.

11. In the Medieval Ages, some people actually believed that spirits, demons, or the devil possessed people.
    a. true
    b. false

12. ____ is the field of examining the subjective experience of physical sensations.
    a.   Psychoanalysis
    b.   Behavioral neuroscience
    c.   Evolutionary psychology
    d.   Psychophysics

13. _____ founded the American Psychological Association and also the first U.S. laboratory of psychology at Johns Hopkins.
    a.   G. Stanley Hall

b.   G. Gordon Liddy
c.   Mary Whiton Calkins
d.   Charles Darwin

14. _____ is the idea of breaking down experience into its elemental parts, which, in turn, was argued to offer the best way to understand thought and behavior.
     a.   Functionalism
     b.   Cognitive psychology
     c.   Mind-dualism
     d.   Structuralism

15. _____ was the most famous behaviorist and argued for the importance of reward and reinforcement in the maintenance of behavior.
     a.   Watson
     b.   Rogers
     c.   Maslow
     d.   Skinner

ANSWERS TO PRACTICE STUDY QUESTIONS

1. e
2. f
3. k
4. a
5. h
6. c
7. d
8. b
9. j
10. a
11. a
12. d
13. a
14. d
15. d

Chapter 2
CONDUCTING PSYCHOLOGICAL RESEARCH

KEY TERMS

Scientific method
Theory
Hypothesis
Replication
Pseudoscience
Research design variable
Population
Samples
Social desirability bias
Descriptive designs
Case study
Naturalistic observation
Representative sample
Correlational designs
Correlation coefficient
Experiment
Independent variable
Dependent variable
Random assignment
Experimental group
Control group
Placebo

Confounding variable
Single-blind studies
Double-blind studies
Experimenter expectancy effects
Self-fulfilling prophecy
Meta-analysis
Effect size
Self-reports
Behavioral measures
Physiological measures
Multiple measurement
Statistics
Descriptive statistics
Mean
Median
Mode
Standard deviation
Ethics
Debriefing
Institutional Review Boards (IRBs)
Quasi-experimental design

OUTLINE

I. The Nature of Science (p. 37)

A. Science is testing assumptions of how the world works. It involves collecting data from the real world and then evaluating those data to determine whether they support our assumptions.

1. Science is more than common sense, logic, and pure observation. Logic tells us how things *should* work, but until an experiment is conducted, we cannot be certain. Your text provides an example of Aristotle's mistaken logic regarding the rate at which objects fall to the ground. Thus, science combines logic with research and experimentation to determine how things work.

B. The Problem with Observation

1. Although science relies on observation, sometimes our observations can be faulty. One reason is due the fact that our knowledge of the world comes to us via our five senses, which can be tricked at times. For example, our perception of visual stimuli can be distorted as demonstrated by magicians.

C. What is Science?

    1. Science comprises at least three distinct areas: physical, biological, and social (Feist, 2006).

        a. *Physical* sciences examine the world of things such as physics, astronomy, chemistry, and geology.

        b. *Biological* sciences examine plant and animals such as biology, zoology, genetics, and botany.

        c. *Social* sciences examine humans, both individually and in groups, such as anthropology, sociology, economics, and psychology.

    2. B.F. Skinner (1953) stated that science is: (a) cumulative, (b) a process more than a product, and (c) an attitude.

D. The Scientific Method

    1. The scientific method by which scientists conduct research consists of five basic processes: *O*bserve, *P*redict, *T*est, *I*nterpret, and *C*ommunicate (O-P-T-I-C).

    2. During the *observation* and *prediction* stages, scientists develop theories from which they will generate testable predictions termed hypotheses.

    3. *Theory* defined: a set of related assumptions from which testable predictions will be made.

    4. *Hypothesis* defined: a specific, informed, testable prediction of what kind of outcome should occur under a particular condition.

    5. The next step in the scientific method, *test*, involves using established research methods and appropriate measurement techniques to test the hypothesis.

    6. In the forth step, scientists use statistical techniques to *interpret* the results from their study to determine if their predictions were correct.

    7. The last step is *communicate,* in which scientists share their results by publishing their studies in peer-reviewed professional journals. Using a standardized format published by the American Psychological Association (2000) scientists provide their hypothesis, the design of the study and methods employed, the results, and conclusions.

    8. *Replication* defined: the repetition of a study to confirm the results. To confirm results from a study, scientists often repeat the study. If results from a study cannot be reliably replicated we must assume they must have been accidental. This demonstrates how scientific discovery is cumulative.

E. What Science Is Not: Pseudoscience

    1. *Pseudoscience* defined: practices that appear to be and claim to be science, but in fact do not sue the scientific method to come to their conclusions.

    2. According to Derry (1999), pseudoscience practitioners:

        a. make no real advances in knowledge

        b. disregard well-known and established facts that contradict their claims

        c. do not challenge or question their own assumptions

        d. tend to offer vague or incomplete explanations of how they come to their conclusions

e. tend to use unsound logic in making their arguments

II. Research Methods in Psychology (p. 45)

A. Principles of Research Design: Psychologists can choose from several different research designs, or plans, for how to conduct a study. The type of design utilized depends upon the question being asked.

B. *Variable* defined: anything that changes or "varies" within or between people. For example, age, height, weight, anxiety, and gender vary from person to person. A psychologist might choose to study how and when variables influence each other. Your text provides the example of a psychologist who is interested in whether girls develop verbal skills at a different rate than boys. In this case there are two variables: gender and vocabulary.

C. *Population* defined: an entire group of population in which a psychologist is interested in studying.
    1. Examples of populations include: all girls, all college students, all children with autism.

D. *Sample* defined: a subset of a population.
    1. For example, all college students (population) might include a sample of college students from three Midwestern universities.
    2. If researchers want to draw valid conclusions or make accurate predictions about the population, they need to have samples that accurately represent those populations. That is, their *samples must be representative* of the general population with regard to age, gender, ethnicity, or any other variable that may be of interest.

E. Social desirability bias defined: The tendency toward favorable self-presentation. That is, people may give answers that are socially desirable but not true because they do not want to be perceived as prejudiced.

F. Descriptive Studies: In descriptive designs the researcher makes no predictions and does not control or manipulate any variables. Instead, in this exploratory phase of research, one looks for meaningful patterns that might lead to predictions in the future. The three most common types of descriptive methods utilized in psychology are *case studies*, *naturalistic observations*, and *interviews/surveys*.
    1. *Case studies* involve a psychologist who observes one person across a long period of time. Hypotheses are not tested in case studies, but case studies may generate possible hypotheses to be studies later.
    2. *Naturalistic observation* involves a researcher observing and recording behavior in the real world (i.e., a natural setting). This can be advantageous as a psychologist can see behavior occurring under natural conditions and not contrived conditions, such as those found in laboratory settings.

3. *Interview and survey* research are two related and widely used techniques for obtaining information on peoples' thoughts and behaviors. They both involve asking people what they have done or how they feel about a particular issue. Questions are usually asked in the same way and can be either open-ended (i.e., people can answer however they choose to do) or restricted (e.g., a person may check a Yes or No, or provide a response via a rating scale such as 1 = disagree, 3 = neither disagree or agree, or 5 = agree).

    a. Two main disadvantages for this type of research are: (a) including people who are not representative of the group and large, and (b) biased responses.

G. Correlational studies utilize correlational designs in which a researcher tests a hypothesis by measuring variables and determining the extent to which they are related. That is, they measure two or more variables and their relationship to one another.

    1. Correlational studies are useful when the variables of interest cannot be manipulated. For example, it would be unethical for a psychologist to give infants alcohol to see if alcohol consumption as an infant is related to low IQ scores later in life. However, one could find infants who had been exposed to alcohol in the womb and gather their IQ scores later in life.

    2. Correlational designs ask: Is X related to Y? Thus, using our example above we would be asking: Is exposure to alcohol in the womb related to low IQ scores later in life?

    3. A major limitation of this design is that it does not establish a causal relationship. That is, correlation is necessary for causation but not sufficient by itself to establish causation. There is always the possibility of a third (or other) variable being the causal factor.

    4. *Correlation coefficient* defined: a statistic that ranges from -1.0 to $+1.0$ and assesses the strength and direction of association between two variables. As noted, correlation variables can be positive or negative. If the correlation is positive, then a group's score on X goes up, their score on Y also goes up. As the coefficient approaches $+1.0$ the strength of the relationship increases.

H. Experimental studies

    1. A true experiment has two crucial characteristics:

        a. Experimental manipulation of a predicted cause, the *independent variable*, and measurement of the response, the *dependent variable*.

        b. Random assignment of participants to control and experimental groups (or conditions), meaning that each participant has an equal chance of being placed in either group.

    2. The *independent variable* is an attribute that the experimenter manipulates while holding other conditions constant; it is the variable that the researcher predicts will cause a certain outcome.

    3. The dependent variable is the outcome, or response to the experimental manipulation; it is what is being measured by the researcher. It is the behavior of interest (i.e., target behavior).

a. Think of the independent variable as the *cause* and the dependent variable as the *effect*.

4. *Random assignment* defined: the method used to assign participants to different research conditions so that each person has the same chance of being in one group as another.

5. The *experimental group* comprises those participants who will receive the treatment, or whatever is thought to change behavior; whereas the *control group* comprises those participants will be treated in exactly the same manner as the experimental group, except that *they will not receive the independent variable or treatment.*

> a. The control group may receive a *placebo,* which is a substance or treatment that appears to be identical to the actual treatment, but lacks the active substance.

6. *Confounding variable* defined: any additional or outside variable whose influence cannot be separated from the independent variable; an unintended influence from a variable not manipulated by the experimenter.

7. In *single-blind* studies, participants do not know the experimental condition to which they are assigned (i.e., either the experimental or control condition). In *double-blind* studies, neither the participants nor the researchers (at least the one's administering the treatment) know in which group the participant has been assigned.

> a. These two experimental techniques are meant to reduce any biases from either the experimenter or the participants.
> b. Double-blind studies are preferred because they better prevent experimenter expectancy effects.

8. *Experimenter expectancy effects* occur when the behavior of participants is influenced by the experimenter's knowledge of who is in which condition (Rosenthal, 1976, 1994).

Breaking New Ground: Discovery of Experimenter Affects and How It Changed Psychology (p. 56)

A. Robert Rosenthal, thorough his research, found that the experimenter can influence the outcome of a study simply by his or her own expectations of the outcome.

B. When working on his dissertation research, Rosenthal hypothesized that individuals who had been told they performed well, or believed they were successful, would be more likely to see success in others.

To test this, he randomly assigned participants to one of three conditions: (a) those whom were told they performed well on an IQ test, (b) those whom were told they performed poorly on an IQ test, or (c) those whom did not receive any feedback regarding their performance on the IQ test.

> a. Each group looked at photographs of people doing various tasks and then rated how successful they thought the people in the photos were.
> b. However, because he was a careful researcher, he decided to compare the average scores of the participants assigned to the different conditions *before* he

had them do anything. He did this to ensure that the groups were equivalent at the start of the study, so that if there were differences at the end of the study (differences for the dependent variable which was the amount of success the participants rated seeing in the photographs) he could be sure they were due to his independent variable (what they were told regarding their performance).

c. Rosenthal found that, not only were his groups different at the beginning of the study, but that they were different in the same way that favored or supported his hypothesis.

d. Given that Rosenthal used random assignment, the groups should have been equivalent; however, somehow the knowledge Rosenthal had about who was in each group had unintentionally created behaviors that favored his hypothesis. With this outcome, Rosenthal had discovered experimenter expectancy effects.

C. Rosenthal also discovered *self-fulfilling prophecy* which can be defined as a statement that changes events to cause a belief or prediction to come true.

a. For example, if you tell yourself, "I am going to fail this exam" and then you do not study, then that belief has become self-fulfilling when you fail the exam.

b. Self-fulfilling prophecies can be used in a positive way as well. For example, if you tell yourself, "I am going to do well on this exam" and you prepare for the exam, then that belief or prediction comes true when you score well on the exam.

III. Commonly Used Measures in Psychological Research (p. 59)

A. Self-report measures are people's written or oral accounts of their thoughts, feelings, or actions.

1. Two common self-reports used in psychology are interviews and questionnaires.

B. Behavioral measures are based on systematic observations of people's actions either in their normal environment (i.e., naturalistic observation) or in a laboratory setting.

1. These measures provide more objective, direct measurements and they are less susceptible to social desirability bias than are self-report measures.

C. Physiological measures are used to collect data on bodily responses.

1. Common measures might include heartbeat, galvanic skin response (i.e., sweating), respiration, and temperature.

D. Multiple measurement, or the use of several measures to acquire data on a single aspect of behavior, avoids some of the limitations of using the individual measures.

IV. Making Sense of Data with Statistics (p. 63)

A. *Statistics* are mathematical procedures for collecting, analyzing, interpreting, and presenting numerical data.

1. *Descriptive statistics* provide a way of summarizing and organizing data. One common way to describe data is to graph it, as graphs provide an easy visual way of determining, for example, what scores occur most frequently.
2. Another way to describe data is to calculate where the center of the scores is or its average.

     a. The *mean* is the arithmetic average of a series of numbers.

     b. The *standard deviation* is a statistical measure of variability. It is a measure of how much scores in a sample vary around the mean. A higher standard deviation means more variability (or more spread); whereas a lower standard deviation means less variability or less spread.

Psychology in the Real World: Advertising and How to Lie With Statistics (p. 64)

A. By becoming a wise consumer of research and statistical methodology, one can be more critical of claims made by advertisers or others trying to use science and statistics to sell something or to influence other's opinions or attitudes.

     1. Figures 2.12A–B demonstrates how graphic displays can be misleading. The wise consumer will see how the way in which data are graphed can change one's perception.

V. Research Ethics (p. 66)

A. *Ethics* defined: rules governing the conduct of person or group in general or in a specific situation; they are standards of right and wrong.

     a. Today, all behavioral, psychological, and medical research must be approved by an Institutional Review Board (IRB) or an Institutional Animal Care and Use Committee (IACUC). If the study does not meet the Board's approval then it cannot be conducted.

B. A historical study that would not meet ethical standards today is the Milgram Obedience experiment.

     a. Milgram's studies on obedience consisted of a "learner" (who was, in fact, a confederate who was in on the experiment), and a "teacher" (who was the real, naïve, participant). The participant thought he was in an experiment studying learning (this was deception, because Milgram was actually studying obedience).

     b. The teachers thought they were administering increasingly intense electrical shocks to the learners for incorrect responses. The teacher thought the shocks were real because the confederate often yelled out in pain and asked the teacher to stop. Although some people withdrew from the study, most participants continued to deliver shocks. However, many asked to stop participating but Milgram instructed them that they had to continue with the experiment.

     c. Only after the study had ended, did Milgram tell the participants that no shocks had actually been delivered and that the learner was a confederate working in the experiment. Although much has been learned about social behavior from these experiments, some question whether that knowledge was acceptable given the distress it caused the participants. It is now considered unethical to prevent someone from ending his or her voluntary participation in an experiment.

VI. Ethical Research with Humans (p. 67)

A. All behavioral, psychological, and medical research must adhere to the following guidelines:
1. Informed consent: Participants are informed of the nature of the experiment, their right to withdraw from the study at any time, and any known risks or benefits that might occur as a result of the experiment.
2. Respect for persons: Safeguard the dignity and autonomy of the individual and take extra precautions when dealing with study participants are less likely to understand that their participation is voluntary (e.g., children).
3. Beneficence: Inform participants of costs and benefits of participation; minimize costs for participants and maximize benefits.
4. Privacy and confidentiality: Protect the privacy of the participants, generally by keeping responses and identities of participants confidential.
5. Justice: Benefits and costs must be distributed equally among participants.

B. *Debriefing* defined: The process of informing participants of the exact purposes of the study (including hypotheses) revealing any and all deceptive practices and explaining why there were necessary to conduct the study. Results of the study are also included.

VII. Ethical Research with Animals (p. 68)

A. Humane treatment of animal subjects is the key to ethical use of animals. Federal, state, and local laws, as well as institutional policies, exist for the protection of research animals.
1. Such laws require clean, sanitary, and adequately sized structures. Proposals for animal research must ensure that the animals are comfortable, healthy, and receive humane treatment.

Making Connections: Can Experience Change the Brain? (p. 70)

A. Researchers at the University of California, Berkeley, in the 1960s, investigated whether different environments could literally (physically) change the brain. In a series of studies, they randomly assigned rats to one of several conditions, for example: (a) an enriched condition that had running wheels for exercise, toys, climbing structures, and food and water; or (b) impoverished environments with only food and water (Bennett, Diamond, Krech, & Rosenzweig, 1964; Rosenzweig, Krech, Bennett, & Diamond, 1962).
1. The level of enrichment was the independent variable and the changes in brain size or brain cell growth were the dependent variables.

2. They found that rats raised in the enriched environment showed evidence of growth in brain tissue compared to the animals raised in the impoverished environment. They replicated this finding many times under similar conditions.

B. One of the main reasons these researchers used rats was because it was unethical to use humans in such research. The animals serve as models of how human brain organization and function might be modified by experience in humans.

C. The most rigorous design one could use to study neurogenesis in humans is a *quasi-experimental design*, which is like an experimental design expect that is makes use of naturally occurring groups rather than randomly assigning participants to groups.
   1. Findings from such quasi-experimental studies are correlational NOT causal because groups were not formed via random assignment.

GLOSSARY TERMS

scientific method: the procedures by which scientists conduct research, consisting of five basic processes: observation, prediction, testing, interpretation, and communication.

theory: a set of related assumptions from which scientists can make testable predictions.

hypothesis: a specific, informed, and testable prediction of the outcome of a particular set of conditions in a research design.

replication: the repetition of a study to confirm the results; essential to the scientific process.

pseudoscience: claims presented as scientific that are not supported by evidence obtained by the scientific method.

research design: plans of action for how to conduct a scientific study.

variable: a characteristic that changes of "varies", such as age, gender, weight, intelligence, anxiety, and extraversion.

population: the entire group a researcher is interested in; for example, all humans, all adolescents, all boys, all girls, all college students.

samples: subsets of the population studied in a research project.

social desirability bias: the tendency toward favorable self-presentation that could lead to inaccurate self-reports.

descriptive designs: study designs in which the researcher defines a problem and variable of interest but makes no prediction and does not control or manipulate anything.

case study: a study design in which a psychologist, often a therapist, observes one person over a long period of time.

naturalistic observation: a study in which the researcher unobtrusively observes and records behavior in the real world.

representative sample: a research sample that accurately reflects the population of people one is studying.

correlational designs: studies that measure two or more variables and their relationship to one another; not designed to show causation.

correlation coefficient: a statistic that ranges from −1.0 to +1.0 and assesses the strength and direction of association between two variables.

experiment: a research design that includes independent and dependent variables and random assignments of participants to control and experimental groups or conditions.

independent variable: a property that is manipulated by the experimenter under controlled conditions to determine whether it causes the predicted outcome of an experiment.

dependent variable: in an experiment, the outcome or response to the experimental manipulation.

random assignment: the method used to assign participants to different research conditions so that all participants have the same chance of being in any specific group.

experimental group: a group consisting of those participants who will receive the treatment or whatever is predicated to change behavior

control group: a group of research participants who are treated in exactly the same manner as the experimental group, except that they do not receive the independent variable or treatment.

placebo: a substance or treatment that appears identical to the actual treatment but lacks the active substance.

confounding variable: variable whose influence on the dependent variable cannot be separated from the independent variable being examined

single-blind studies: studies in which participants do not know the experimental condition (group) to which they have been assigned.

double-blind studies: studies in which neither the participants nor the researchers administering the treatment know who has been assigned to the experimental or control group.

experimenter expectancy effects: result that occurs when the behavior of the participants is influenced by the experimenter's knowledge of who is in the control group and who is the experimental group.

self-fulfilling prophecy: a statement that affects events to cause the prediction to become true.

meta-analysis: research technique for combining all research results on one question and drawing a conclusion

effect size: a measure of the strength of the relationship between two variables or the extent of an experimental effect.

self-reports: written or oral accounts of a person's thoughts, feelings, or actions.

behavioral measures: measures based on systematic observation of people's actions either in their normal environment or in a laboratory setting.

physiological measures: measures of bodily responses, such as blood pressure or heart rate, used to determine changes in psychological state.

multiple measurement: the use of several measures to acquire data on one aspect of behavior.

statistics: collection, analysis, interpretation, and presentation of numerical data.

descriptive statistics: techniques that show what observations collected in research actually look like, by summarizing and describing data.

mean: the arithmetic average of a series of numbers

median: the score that separates the lower half of scores from the upper half.

mode: a statistic that represents the most commonly occurring score or value.

standard deviation: a statistical measure of how much scores in a sample vary around the mean.

ethics: the rules governing the conduct of a person or group in general or in a specific situation— or more simply, standards of right and wrong.

debriefing: the explanation of the purposes of a study following data collection.

institutional review boards (IRBs): organizations that evaluate proposed research before it is conducted to make sure research involving humans does not cause undue harm or distress.

quasi-experimental design: research method similar to an experimental design except that it makes use of naturally occurring groups rather than randomly assigning subjects to groups.

PRACTICE STUDY QUESTIONS

1. A(n) _____ is a specific, informed, and testable prediction of what kind of outcome one might expect in a certain situation, such as in an experiment.
    a. theory
    b. method
    c. hypothesis
    d. procedure

2. The _____ is a way in which scientists conduct research to ensure sound data.
    a. theory
    b. self-fulfilling prophecy
    c. scientific method
    d. hypothesis

3. Science, common sense, and pseudoscience are all the same; that is, they provide equivalent ways of knowing and understanding natural phenomena.
    a. true
    b. false

4. In psychological research, subsets of the population of interest are known as:
    a. random selection.
    b. samples.
    c. control participant.
    d. independent variables.

5. You see a researcher standing on the corner of a busy intersection and collecting data. When you ask her what she is writing down, she tells you she is counting the number of people who are driving and talking on their cell phone at the same time. This type of study is known as a(n)
    a. experimental design
    b. self-report procedure
    c. inferential design
    d. naturalistic observation

6. The P in the acronym OPTIC refers to:
    a. predict.
    b. participants.
    c. placebo.
    d. procedure.

7. Dr. Bowman, a sports psychologist, conducted a study in which he wanted to know if playing hockey games on home ice was related to winning games. What type of study or design is it?
    a. experimental

b.   double-blind

c.   correlational

d.   quasi-experimental

8.   In his study, Dr. Bowman found a correlation coefficient of +1.08. What is wrong with scenario?

     a.   +1.08 is a negative correlation, not positive

     b.   correlation coefficients are only found in true experiments

     c.   correlation coefficients cannot exceed ± 1.0

     d.   nothing is wrong with the scenario

9.   The _____ variable is the variable that is measured, or expected to change; whereas the _____ variable is the variable that the experimenter manipulates.

     a.   confounding; independent

     b.   independent; dependent

     c.   independent; confounding

     d.   dependent; independent

10.   Dr. Babcock randomly assigned 100 participants to either a group that received 10 mg of a stimulant drug or a group that received an identical looking 0 mg nonactive dose. One hour after participants in both groups took their pills they took a memory test. In this case, the 10 mg group is the _____ condition, and the 0 mg group is the _____ condition.

     a.   placebo, experimental

     b.   control, experimental

     c.   experimental, control

     d.   quasi-experimental, control

11.   In the question above (#10), the independent variable is _____; whereas the dependent variable is _____.

     a.   the dose of drug (0 or 10 mg); the scores on the memory test

     b.   the scores on the memory tests; the dose of drug (0 or 10 mg)

     c.   the people taking the drug; the experimenter

     d.   the experimenter; the people taking the drug

12.   _____ is when the behavior of participants is influenced by the experimenter's knowledge of who is in which condition.

     a.   Self-fulfilling prophecy.

     b.   Experimenter expectancy effects

     c.   Selection bias

     d.   Placebo control

13.   _____ measures are based on systematic observation of people's actions either in the natural environment or in a laboratory setting.

     a.   Self-report

     b.   Physiological

     c.   Behavioral

d.	Independent

14.	In regard to research ethics, _____ is a process in which participants are told what the study is about, what they will have to do and for how long, any known risks or benefits, and their right to withdraw from the study at any time.
	a.	beneficence
	b.	justice
	c.	respect for persons
	d.	informed consent

15.	Rosenzweig and colleagues demonstrated that when rats were exposed to enriched environments, the rats had _____ compared to rats that were exposed to impoverished environments.
	a.	greater brain cell growth
	b.	less brain cell growth
	c.	no difference in brain cell growth
	d.	None of the above

ANSWERS TO PRACTICE STUDY QUESTIONS

1. c
2. c
3. b
4. b
5. d
6. a
7. c
8. c
9. d
10. c
11. a
12. b
13. c
14. d
15. a

Chapter 3
THE BIOLOGY OF BEHAVIOR

KEY TERMS

DNA (deoxyribonucleic acid)
Chromosomes
Genes
Genome
Alleles
Dominant gene
Recessive genes
Behavioral genetics
Monogenic transmission
Polygenic transmission
Heritability
Fraternal twins
Identical twins
Twin studies
Adoption studies
Twin-adoption studies
Gene-by-environment interaction research
Epigenesis
Central nervous system (CNS)
Peripheral nervous system
Somatic nervous system
Autonomic nervous system (ANS)
Sympathetic nervous system
Parasympathetic nervous system
Glial cells
Neurons
Neurotransmitters
Soma
Axon
Dendrites
Myelin sheath
Synapse
Terminal button
Sensory neurons
Motor neurons
Mirror neurons
Interneurons
Action potential
Ions
Resting potential
Refractory period

All-or-none principle
Synaptic vesicles
Enzymatic degradation
Reuptake
Graded potentials
Acetylcholine (Ach)
Dopamine
Epinephrine
Norepinephrine
Serotonin
GABA (gamma-aminobutyric acid)
Glutamate
Medulla
Reflexes
Pons
Cerebellum
Reticular formation
Thalamus
Hypothalamus
Hippocampus
Amygdala
Cingulate gyrus
Basal ganglia
Cerebrum
Cerebral cortex
Contralaterality
Insula
Corpus callosum
Aphasia
Broca's area
Wernicke's area
Neuroplasticity
Neurogenesis
Aborization
Synaptogenesis
Electroencephalography (EEG)
Event-related potential (ERP)
Magnetic resonance imaging (MRI)
Functional MRI (fMRI)
Positron emission tomography (PET)
Endocrine system

Hormones   Catecholamines
Adrenal glands   Coritsol
Pituitary gland

OUTLINE

I. Genes and Behavior (p. 77)

   A. *Deoxyribonucleic acid (DNA):* is a large coiled molecule that resides in every cell (except red blood cells) and contains all the information needed for human development and function. DNA is packaged with proteins to form structures called *chromosomes.*
      1. *Genes* are small segments of DNA that contain the blueprints or plans for the production of proteins.
         a. All of the genetic information contained on most of our cells make up our *genome.*
         b. Genes occur in pairs of *alleles.* We inherit one allele from each of our parents.

   B. The Complex Connection between Genes and Behavior
      1. Genes seldom make behavior a certainty; instead, a specific gene plays only a small part in creating a specific behavior. Environmental events may interact with gene to make a particular behavior more or less likely.

   C. Polyeneic Influence on Behavior
      1. *Monogenic transmission* refers to hereditary passing on of traits that is determined by a single gene; whereas *polygenic transmission* is when many genes interact to create a single characteristic.

   D. Genes and Environment
      1. *Heritability* is the extent to which a characteristic is influenced by genetics. Researchers use several methods to study heritability:
         a. Twin studies: Studies comparing pairs of *fraternal* (twins develop from two different eggs fertilized by two different sperm) and *identical* (twins develop from a single fertilized egg that splits into two independent cells).
            i. If a trait is genetically influenced, identical twins should be more similar in that trait than will fraternal twins. However, if genetics play no role than identical twins will be nor more alike than fraternal twins in that particular trait.
         b. Adoption studies: Studies comparing adopted individuals to their biological and adoptive parents.
         c. Twin-Adoption studies: Studies of twins, both identical and fraternal, who were raised apart (adopted) and those raised together.
         e. Gene-by-Environment studies: Studies that directly measure genetic similarity in parts of the genome itself.

　　　　i. *Polymorphism* is the phenomenon that genes take on different
　　　　forms (i.e., some DNA sequences can be long in some people and
　　　　short in others).

　　E. Epigenesis: How the Environment Changes Gene Expression
　　　　1. Environmental events influence how and when genes are activated or
　　　　deactivated. That is, genes can be changed by an individual's behaviors and
　　　　experiences, and behaviors can be modified by genetic differences.
　　　　　　a. *Epigenesis* occurs when there is a change in the way genes get
　　　　　　expressed (activated or deactivated) without changing the sequence of
　　　　　　DNA.

II. The Nervous System (p. 83)

　　A. Organization of the Nervous System
　　　　1. The nervous system is comprised of the *central nervous system (CNS),* which
　　　　consists of the brain and spinal cord and the *peripheral nervous system,* which
　　　　consists of all the other nerve cells in the body.
　　　　　　a. The peripheral nervous systems if further divided into the: (a) *somatic
　　　　　　nervous system,* which transmits sensory information to the brain and
　　　　　　spinal cord and from the brain and spinal cord to the skeletal muscles, and
　　　　　　(b) the *autonomic nervous system (ANS)* which serves the involuntary
　　　　　　systems of the body, such as the internal organs and glands.
　　　　　　　　i. The ANS has two main branches: the *sympathetic nervous
　　　　　　　　system* and the *parasympathetic nervous system.*
　　　　　　　　ii. The sympathetic nervous system activates the body in
　　　　　　　　emergency situations; it is referred to as the *fight-or-flight response.*
　　　　　　　　iii. The function of the parasympathetic nervous system is to return
　　　　　　　　the body to a state of relaxation.

　　B. The Cells of the Nervous System: Glial Cells and Neurons
　　　　1. *Glial cells* provide structural support, promote efficient communication
　　　　between neurons, and remove cellular debris (Kandel, 2000).
　　　　2. *Neurons* are cells that process and transmit information throughout the nervous
　　　　system.
　　　　　　a. There are more than 10 billion neurons in the human brain.
　　　　　　b. Three major principles of neurons and neuronal communication:
　　　　　　　　i. Neurons are the building blocks of the nervous system. All the
　　　　　　　　major structures of the brain are composed of neurons.
　　　　　　　　ii. Information travels within a neuron in the form of an electrical
　　　　　　　　signal by action potentials.
　　　　　　　　iii. Information is transmitted between neurons by chemicals called
　　　　　　　　neurotransmitters.
　　　　3. The Structure and Types of Neurons

a. The *soma* or cell body of the neuron contains a nucleus and other components need for cell maintenance and function (see Figure 3.5 of your text).

b. Extending from the soma is a long projection called the *axon*, which transmits electrical impulses toward adjacent neurons. *Dendrites* are branch-like structures that receive incoming messages from other neurons.

    i. Some axons are wrapped in a fatty *myelin sheath* that allows the impulse to travel more efficiently.

c. The *synapse* is the junction between the axon and the adjacent neuron and at the end of each synapse is a *terminal button* that contains tiny sacs of neurotransmitters.

d. There are three types of neurons: *sensory, motor,* and *interneurons.*

    i. *Sensory neurons* receive incoming sensory information from the sense organs.

    ii. *Motor neurons* take commands from the brain and carry them to muscles of the body.

    iii. *Interneurons* are those that communicate only with other neurons.

4. Neural Communication: The Action Potential

a. The *action potential* involves two steps: (a) an impulse travels one way from the dendrites along the anon and away from the soma [a process that is both chemical and electrical], and (b) the impulse releases chemicals at the tips of neurons that are then released into the synaptic cleft to transit the message to another neuron.

5. Communication between Neurons: Neurotransmission

a. When an action potential arrives, neurotransmitters packed into tiny synaptic vesicles are released in the terminal buttons into the synaptic cleft. There the neurotransmitters can bind with receptors on another neuron or they can be taken back up into the neuron.

b. Two ways to remove neurotransmitters are *enzymatic degradation* in which enzymes bind with a neurotransmitter and destroy it, or *reuptake* in which the neurotransmitter is taken back up by the cell.

C. Common Neurotransmitters

1. *Acetylcholine (Ach)* controls muscle movement and plays a role in mental processes such as learning, memory, attention, sleeping, and dreaming.

2. *Dopamine* is released in response to behaviors that feel good or are rewarding to the person or animal. It is also involved in controlling voluntary motor control.

    a. Many drugs of abuse result in increases of dopamine, such as cocaine and methamphetamine.

    b. Parkinson's disease is associated with low levels of dopamine, causing people with that disease to gradually lose the ability to control their muscles.

3. *Epinephrine* tends not to affect mental states, whereas *norpeinephrine* does increase mental arousal and alertness and also increases heart rate and blood pressure.

4. *Serotonin* is involved with dreaming and controlling emotional states, especially anger, anxiety, and depression.

    a. Drugs that block the reuptake of serotonin are widely used to treat anxiety and depression

    b. People who are consistently angry and/or aggressive often have abnormally low levels of serotonin.

5. *GABA* is a major inhibitory neurotransmitter in the brain; it slows CNS activity and is necessary for the regulation and control of neural activity.

    a. Without GABA, the nervous system would have no "breaks" and could run out of control.

    b. Many depressant drugs (e.g., alcohol, benzodiazepines) increase GABA activity leading to relaxing and uncoordinated states.

6. *Glutamate* is the major excitatory neurotransmitter and it is important in learning, memory, neural processing, and brain development.

III. The Brain (p. 96)

A. Evolution of the Human Brain: The brain is a collection of neurons and glial cells that control all the major functions of the body. It produces thoughts, emotions, and behavior.

    1. The human brain has been shaped, via natural selection, by the world in which humans have lived.

    2. The earliest ancestors of humans appeared in Africa about 6 million years ago.

        a. The Neanderthals lived from about 350,000 to 28,000 years ago when they were replaced by our species, *Homo Sapiens*.

        b. It is possible that the human brain took up to 100,000 years to become fully wired and complex while staying the same overall size.

B. Overview of Brain Regions

    1. *Hindbrain*: the oldest brain region which is connected to the spinal cord. This region regulates breathing, heart rate, arousal, and other basic functions of survival. See Figure 3.10 of your text.

        a. The *medulla* regulates breathing, heart rate, and blood pressure, and is also involved in reflexes such as coughing, sneezing, swallowing, and vomiting.

        b. The *pons* serves as a bridge between the lower brain regions and the higher midbrain and forebrain activity.

        c. The *cerebellum* or "little brain" contains more neurons than any other single part of the brain and is responsible for body movement, balance, coordination, and fine motor skills. It is also important in cognitive activities such as learning and language (Amaral, 2000).

    2. *Midbrain*: the next brain region to evolve after the hindbrain.

a. Different parts of the midbrain control the eye muscles, process auditory and visual information, and initiate voluntary movement of the body.

b. The *reticular formation* is a network of nerves that runs through the hindbrain and midbrain and is crucial to waking up and falling asleep.

3. *Forebrain*: the last major brain region to evolve and the largest part of the human brain.

a. The forebrain consists of the cerebrum and other structures such as the thalamus and limbic system.

b. The structures of the forebrain control cognitive, sensory, and motor function, and regulate temperature, reproductive functions, eating, sleeping, and the display of emotion.

c. The *thalamus* can be thought of as a sensory relay station.

4. The *limbic system* is comprised of the hypothalamus, hippocampus, amygdala, and cingulated gyrus. These structures are important in emotion and motivation.

a. The *hypothalamus* is the master regulator of almost all our drives and motives, including hunger, thirst, temperature, and sexual behavior. It also controls the pituitary gland which produces and controls hormone regulation.

b. The *hippocampus* is wrapped around the thalamus and plays an important role in learning and memory.

c. The *amygdala* is a small, almond shaped structure located directly in front of the hippocampus. It plays a very important role in determining emotional significance of stimuli, especially when they evoke fear (Ohman, 2002; Phelps & LeDoux, 2005).

i. Without the amygdala, we cannot learn appropriate emotional responses, especially to potentially dangerous situations.

d. The *basal ganglia* are a collection of structures surrounding the thalamus that is involved in voluntary motor control.

e. The *cingulated gyrus* is a belt-like structure in the middle of the brain of which some parts (front part) play a role in attention and cognitive control (Botvinick, Cohen, & Carter, 2004).

5. The Cerebrum and Cerebral Cortex: the uppermost portion of the brain, the *cerebrum,* is folded into convolutions and divided into two hemispheres; whereas the outer layer is called the *cerebral cortex.*

a. The cortex is where much of human thought, planning, and consciousness take place. It is the area of the brain that makes us most human.

b. The cerebrum is composed of four large areas termed the: frontal, parietal, temporal, and occipital lobes.

i. The frontal lobe carries out many important functions such as attention, holding things in mind while we solve problems, planning, abstract thinking, control of impulses, creativity and social awareness (Miller & Cummings, 1999).

ii. The parietal lobes play an important role in sensation and perception to touch. The front most portion of this lobe is the *somatosensory cortex.*

iii. The temporal lobes have many different functions; the main function is hearing. This region contains the *auditory cortex.*

iv. The occipital lobes are in the rear of the brain and it is here that the optic nerve travels from the eye to the thalamus and the to the *primary visual cortex.*

c. The *insula* is a small structure that resides deep in the cerebrum and it is active in the perception of bodily sensations, emotional states, empathy, and additive behavior (Naqvi, Rudrauf, Damasio, Bechara, 2007).

6. Cerebral Hemispheres: The human cerebrum is split down the middle into two hemispheres; although the hemispheres look similar, they differ in shape, size, and function.

a. The left hemisphere processes information in a more focused and analytic manner and the right hemisphere integrates information in a more holistic, or broader, manner (Beeman & Bowden, 2000).

i. The *corpus callosum* is a thick band of nerve fibers connecting the two hemispheres of the brain; it provides a channel for extensive communication between hemispheres in both logical and creative tasks.

b. Speech and language comprehension involve two separate regions in the left hemisphere:

i. *Broca's area* is responsible for the ability to produce speech.

ii. *Wernicke's area* is responsible for the ability to speak in meaningful sentences and to comprehend the meaning of speech.

7. Communication between Hemispheres: All communication between the two hemispheres occurs via information traveling across the corpus callosum.

a. Cutting the corpus callosum may help decrease epileptic seizures, but it can also cut the ability for information to pass from the right and left hemispheres.

C. Brain Plasticity and Neurogenesis

1. *Neuroplasticity* is the brain's ability to adopt new functions, reorganize itself, or make new neural connections throughout life, as a function of experience.

2. Almost every major structure of the neuron is capable of experience-based change.

3. Not all regions of the brain are equally plastic.

a. The hippocampus, which is involved in learning, is more plastic that almost any other part of the brain.

i. The process of developing new neurons is termed *neurogenesis.*

ii. *Aborization* refers to the growth and formation of new dendrites.

iii. The formation of entirely new synapses or connections with other neurons that is the basis of learning is referred to as *synaptogensis.*

Breaking New Ground: Death of Dogma: Neurogenesis in the Adult Brain (p. 110)

A. The prevailing wisdom had been that neurons were incapable of growth, at least after early childhood. This lead Ramón y Cajal, (who discovered that nerve cells do not grow and die on an hourly basis nor do they reproduce) to put forth the *neuron doctrine,* which declared that neurons do not regenerate.

B. Evidence of Neuron Growth
    1. In the 1960s, Joseph Altman published ground-breaking studies that demonstrated the growth of neurons in several areas important in learning and memory in rats and cats (Gross, 2000).
        a. Because Altman's findings went against the established dogma, they were almost completely ignored or discounted.
        b. Three scientific events of the 1980s and 1990s led to a change in a century old idea:
            i. Studies demonstrated that birds showed exceptional neuronal growth in many areas of the adult avian brain, including the hippocampus (Nottebohm, 1985).
            ii. Increasing evidence appeared for the formation of new synaptic connections in brains of rats when raised in enriched environments, more so than normally occurs with development (Comery, Stamoudis, Irwin, & Greenough, 1996).
            iii. In the 1990s researchers started to find solid evidence for neurogenesis in one particular part of the hippocampus in adult rats, monkeys, and humans.

C. Environmental Effects on Neuron Growth
    1. We now know that neurons and their dendrites and synapses change, grow, and die in both young and old animals—including humans—depending on the kind of stimulation they receive from the outside world.

Psychology in the Real World: Using Progesterone to Treat Brain Injury (p. 112)

A. Donald Stein found and continues to provide evidence for the fact that the female hormone, progesterone, helps the injured brain repair itself.
    1. Although Stein published in first-rate journals he was unable to get money to conduct his research until Wright and Kellerman suggested conducting a clinical trial.
        a. 100 people with traumatic brain injury who came into an emergency room were randomly assigned to get regular treatment of to get a large dose of progesterone therapy.
        b. After 30 days the researchers found that those who had received progesterone therapy were more likely to survive and recovered than those who received standard treatment (Wright, Kellermen, Stein, et al., (2007).

IV. Measuring the Brain (p. 112)

    A. Electroencephalography (EEG): is a special technique that takes electrical activity from raw EEG data to measure cognitive processes.

    B. Magnetic Resonance Imagine (MRI) and Functional MRI (fMRI): uses magnetic fields to produce very finely detailed images of the structure of the brain.

        1. fMRI tells us where activity in the brain is occurring during particular tasks by tracking blood oxygen use in the brain.

    C. Positron Emission Tomography (PET): measures blood flow to brain areas in the active brain. It shows which brain areas are active during certain situations.

V. The Endocrine System (p. 115)

    A. Glands in the *endocrine system* secrete chemicals called *hormones* which travel through the bloodstream to tissues and organs all over the body and regulate body functions.

        a. The *pituitary gland* is known as the master gland of the body because it secretes hormones that control the release of hormones elsewhere in the body.

        b. The *thyroid gland* sits in the neck region and releases hormones that control the rate of metabolism.

        c. The *pancreas* releases hormones, including insulin, that play a vital role in regulating blood sugar.

        d. The *adrenal glands* sit atop of the kidneys and release hormones in response to stress and emotions. They also help regulate heart rate, blood pressure, and blood sugar.

            i. The adrenal glands also produce *catecholamines* (the neurotransmitters dopamine, norepinephrine, and epinephrine).

            ii. The adrenal glands also release stress hormones such as *cortisol* which is responsible for maintaining the activation of bodily systems during prolonged stress.

GLOSSARY TERMS
DNA (deoxyribonucleic acid): a large molecule that contains genes.
chromosomes: coiled-up threads of DNA.
genes: small segments of DNA that contain information for producing proteins.
genome: all the genetic information in DNA
alleles: pairs or alternate forms of a gene.
dominant genes: genes that show their effect even if there is only one copy of that gene in the pair.
recessive gene: genes that show their effects only when both alleles are the same.
behavioral genetics: the scientific study of the role of heredity in behavior.
monogenic transmission: the hereditary passing on of traits determined by a single gene.
polygenic transmission: the process by which many genes interact to create a single characteristic.
heritability: the extent to which a characteristic is influenced by genetics.

fraternal twins: twins that develop from two different eggs fertilized by two different sperm.

identical twins: twins that develop from a single fertilized egg that splits into two independent cells.

twin studies: research into hereditary influence comparing pairs of fraternal and identical twins.

adoption studies: research into hereditary influence in which adopted people are compared to their biological and adoptive parents.

twin-adoption studies: research into hereditary influence on twins, both identical and fraternal, who were raised apart (adopted) and who were raised together.

gene-by-environment interaction research: a method of studying heritability by comparing genetic markers that allows researchers to assess how genetic differences interact with environment to produce certain behaviors in some people but not in others.

epigenesis: change in the way genes are turned on or off without a change in the sequence of DNA.

central nervous system (CNS): the part of the nervous system that comprises the brain and spinal cord

peripheral nervous system: the part of the nervous system that comprises all the nerve cells in the body outside of the central nervous system.

somatic nervous system: nerve cells of the peripheral nervous system that transmit sensory information to the central nervous system (CNS) and those that transmit information from the CNS to the skeletal muscles.

autonomic nervous system (ANS): all the nerves of the peripheral nervous system that serve involuntary systems of the body, such as the internal organs and glands.

sympathetic nervous system: the branch of the autonomic nervous system that activates bodily systems in times of emergency.

parasympathetic nervous system: the branch of the autonomic nervous system that usually relaxes or returns the body to a less active, restful state.

glial cells: the cells of the central nervous system that provide structural support, promote efficient communication between neurons, and serve as scavengers, removing cellular debris.

neurons: the cells that process and transmit information in the nervous system.

neurotransmitters: chemicals that transmit information between neurons, across the synapses.

soma: the cell body of the neuron.

axon: a long projection that extends from a neuron's soma; it transmits electrical impulses toward the adjacent neuron and stimulates the release of neurotransmitters.

dendrites: fingerlike projections from a neuron's soma that receive incoming messages from other neurons.

myelin sheath: the fatty substance wrapped around some axons, which insulates the axon, making the nerve impulse travel more efficiently.

synapse: the junction between an axon and the adjacent neuron, where information is transmitted from one neuron to another.

terminal button: little knobs at the end of the axon that contain tiny sacs of neurotransmitters.

sensory neurons: neurons that receive incoming sensory information from the sense organs (eye, ear, skin, tongue, nose).

motor neurons: nerve cells that carry commands for movement from the brain to the muscles of the body.

mirror neurons: nerve cells that are active when we observe others making an action as well as when we are performing the same action.

interneurons: neurons that communicate only with other neurons.

action potential: the impulse of positive charge that runs down an axon.

ions: chemically charged particles that predominate in bodily fluids; found both inside and outside cells.

resting potential: the difference in electrical charge between the inside and outside of the axon when the neuron is at rest.

refractory period: the span of time, after an action potential has been generated, when the neuron is returning to its resting state and the neuron cannot generate an action potential.

all-or-none principle: the idea that once the threshold has been crossed, an action potential either fires or it does not; there is no half-way.

synaptic vesicles: tiny sacs in the terminal buttons that contain neurotransmitters.

enzymatic degradation: a way of removing excess neurotransmitter from the synapse, in which enzymes specific for that neurotransmitter bind with the neurotransmitter and destroy it.

reuptake: a way of removing excess neurotransmitter from the synapse, in which excess neurotransmitter is returned to the sending, or pre-synaptic, neuron for storage in vesicles and future use.

graded potentials: small changes in membrane potential that by themselves are insufficient to trigger an action potential.

acetylcholine (ACh): a neurotransmitter that controls muscle movement and plays a role in mental processes such as learning, memory, attention, sleeping, and dreaming.

dopamine: a neurotransmitter released in response to behaviors that feel good or are rewarding to the person or animal; also involved in voluntary motor control.

epinephrine: also known as adrenaline, a neurotransmitter that arouses bodily systems (such as increasing heart rate).

norepinephrine: a neurotransmitter that plays an important role in the sympathetic nervous system, energizing bodily systems and increasing mental arousal and alertness.

serotonin: a neurotransmitter with wide ranging effects: involved in dreaming and in controlling emotional states, especially anger, anxiety and depression.

GABA (gamma-aminobutyric acid): a major inhibitory neurotransmitter in the brain that tells post-synaptic neurons *not* to fire; it slows CNS activity and is necessary to regulate and control neural activity.

glutamate: a major excitatory neurotransmitter in the brain that increases the likelihood that a postsynaptic neuron will fire; important in learning, memory, neural processing, and brain development.

medulla: a hindbrain structure that extends directly from the spinal cord; regulates breathing, heart rate, and blood pressure.

reflexes: inborn and involuntary behaviors—such as coughing, swallowing, sneezing, or vomiting—that are elicited by very specific stimuli.

pons: a hindbrain structure that serves as a bridge between lower brain regions and higher midbrain and forebrain activity.

cerebellum: a hindbrain structure involved in body movement, balance, coordination, fine-tuning motor skills, and cognitive activities such as learning and language.

reticular formation: a network of nerve fibers that runs up through both the hindbrain and the midbrain; it is crucial to waking up and to falling asleep.

thalamus: a forebrain structure that receives inputs from the ears, eyes, skin, or taste buds and relays sensory information to the part of cerebral cortex most involved in processing that specific kind of sensory information.

hypothalamus: a limbic structure; the master regulator of almost all major drives and motives we have, such as hunger, thirst, temperature, and sexual behavior; also controls the pituitary gland.

hippocampus: a limbic structure that wraps itself around the thalamus; plays a vital role in learning and memory.

amygdala: a small, almond shaped structure located directly in front of the hippocampus; has connections with many important brain regions and is important for processing emotional information, especially that related to fear.

cingulate gyrus: a belt-like structure around the corpus callosum that plays an important role in attention and cognitive control.

basal ganglia: a collection of structures surrounding the thalamus involved in voluntary motor control.

cerebrum: each of the large halves of the brain that are covered with convolutions, or folds.

cerebral cortex: the thin outer layer of the cerebrum, in which much of human thought, planning, perception, and consciousness takes place.

contralaterality: the fact that one side of the brain controls movement on the opposite side.

insula: a small structure inside the cerebrum that plays an important role the perception of bodily sensations, emotional states, empathy, and addictive behavior.

corpus callosum: the nerve fibers that connect the two hemispheres of the brain.

aphasia: deficit in the ability to speak or comprehend language.

Broca's area: an area in the left frontal lobe responsible for the ability to produce speech.

Wernicke's area: an area deep in the left temporal lobe responsible for the ability to speak in meaningful sentences and to comprehend the meaning of speech.

neuroplasticity: the brain's ability to adopt new functions, reorganize itself, or make new neural connections throughout life, as a function of experience

neurogenesis: the development of new neurons

aborization: the growth and formation of new dendrites.

synaptogenesis: the formation of entirely new synapses or connections with other neurons.

electroencephaolography (EEG): a method for measuring brain activity in which the electrical activity of the brain is recorded from electrodes placed on a person's scalp.

event-related potential (ERP): a special technique that extracts electrical activity from raw EEG data to measure cognitive processes

magnetic resonance imaging (MRI): a brain imaging technique that uses magnetic fields to produce very finely detailed images of the structure of the brain and other soft tissues.

functional magnetic resonance imaging (fMRI): brain imaging technique that uses magnetic fields to produce very finely detailed images of the activity of areas of the brain and other soft tissues.

positron emission tomography (PET): brain imaging technique that measures blood flow to areas in the active brain; indicates which brain areas are active during certain situations.

endocrine system: bodily system of glands that secrete and regulate hormones.

hormones: chemicals, secreted by glands, that travel in the bloodstream and carry messages to tissues and organs all over the body.

adrenal glands: structures that sit atop each kidney; they release hormones important in stress, emotions, regulation of heart rate, blood pressure, and blood sugar regulation.

pituitary gland: the master gland of the body; among the numerous hormones it secretes are hormones that control the release of hormones from glands elsewhere in the body.

catecholamines: a class of chemicals released from the adrenal glands that function as hormones and as neurotransmitters; they control ANS activation and include the neurotransmitters dopamine, norepinephrine, and epinephrine

cortisol: a hormone released by the adrenal glands; responsible for maintaining the activation of bodily systems during prolonged stress.

PRACTICE STUDY QUESTIONS

1. _____ is (are) packaged with proteins to form structures called chromosomes.
   a. Genes
   b. Alleles
   c. DNA
   d. MAO inhibitors

2. The extent to which a characteristic is influenced by genetics is known as:
   a. monogenic transmission.
   b. polygenetic transmission.
   c. the genome.
   d. heritability.

3. The _____ nervous system is comprised of the brain and spinal cord.
   a. central
   b. peripheral
   c. autonomic
   d. sympathetic

4. The _____ is comprised of the sympathetic nervous system and the autonomic nervous system.
   a. central
   b. peripheral
   c. autonomic
   d. sympathetic

5. The _____ nervous system is considered the "fight-or-flight" system.
   a. central
   b. peripheral
   c. autonomic
   d. sympathetic

6. Three types of neurons are sensory, motor, and:
   a. glial neurons.
   b. interneurons.

c.   allele neurons.

d.   None of the above are correct

7.   Another name of the cell body is called the:
a.   dendrite.
b.   soma.
c.   axon.
d.   synapse.

8.   Neurotransmitters are packaged in sacs called:
a.   synaptic clefts.
b.   reuptake transporters.
c.   synaptic vesicles.
d.   terminal buttons.

9.   _____ controls muscle movement and plays a role in mental processes such as learning, memory, attention, sleeping, and dreaming.
a.   Acetylcholine
b.   Dopamine
c.   Serotonin
d.   GABA

10.   _____ is a major inhibitory neurotransmitter and drugs such as alcohol and the benzodiazepines affect this neurotransmitter.
a.   Acetylcholine
b.   Dopamine
c.   Serotonin
d.   GABA

11.   _____ is associated with drugs of abuse such as cocaine and methamphetamine and also plays a role in Parkinson's disease.
a.   Acetylcholine
b.   Dopamine
c.   Serotonin
d.   GABA

12.   The hindbrain consists of the medulla, pons, and:
a.   Cerebral cortex.
b.   cerebellum.
c.   corpus callosum.
d.   reticular formation.

13.   The _____ is the master regulator of almost all major drives and motives we have including hunger, thirst, temperature, and sexual behavior.
a.   thalamus
b.   hippocampus

        c.   hypothalamus
        d.   amygdala

14.   _____ is the area of the left temporal lobe that is responsible for speech comprehension; whereas _____ is the area responsible for the ability to produce speech.
        a.   Broca's area; Wernicke's area
        b.   Wernicke's area; Broca's area
        c.   Skinner's area; Chomsky's area
        d.   Chomsky's area; Skinner's area

15.   The brain does not have the ability to adopt new functions, reorganize itself, or make new neural connections as a function of experience.
        a.   true
        b.   false

16.   The _____ gland is the master gland of the body because it secretes hormones that control the release of hormones from glands elsewhere in the body.
        a.   thyroid
        b.   adrenal
        c.   pituitary
        d.   endocrine

ANSWERS TO PRACTICE STUDY QUESTIONS

1. c
2. d
3. a
4. c
5. d
6. b
7. b
8. c
9. a
10. d
11. b
12. b
13. c
14. b
15. b
16. c

Chapter 4
SENSING AND PERCEIVING OUR WORLD

KEY TERMS

Sensation
Perception
Sensory adaptation
Transduction
Psychophysics
Absolute threshold
Signal detection theory
Difference threshold
Weber's law
Perceptual set
Pupil
Cornea
Iris
Lens
Accommodation
Retina
Photoreceptors
Rods
Dark adaption
Cones
Fovea
Visual acuity
Optic nerve
Optic chiasm
Feature detectors
Simple cells
Complex cells
Hypercomplex cells
Depth perception
Binocular depth cues
Convergence

Monocular depth cues
Linear perspective
Texture gradient
Atmospheric perspective
Interposition
Perceptual constancy
Gestalt law of similarity
Gestalt law of continuity
Gestalt law of proximity
Gestalt aw of closure
Bottom-up processing
Top-down processing
Trichromatic color theory
Afterimages
Opponent process theory
Tympanic membrane
Semi-circular canals
Cochlea
Basilar membrane
Hair cells
Auditory nerve
Bodily senses
Mechanoreceptors
Pain
Gate control theory of pain
Olfactory sensory neurons
Olfactory bulb
Papillae
Taste buds
Taste receptor cells
Synesthesia

OUTLINE

I. The Long Strange Trip from Sensation to Perception (p. 125)

    A. *Sensation* is the stimulation of our sense organs by the outer world; whereas *perception* is the act of organizing and interpreting sensory experience.
        1. Eyes are sensitive to light waves, ears to sounds, skin to touch and pressure, tongues to tastes, and noses to odors.

B. Basic Sensory Processes
    1. *Sensory adaption* is a process that occurs when our sensitivity diminishes to an object that constantly stimulates our senses
    2. *Transduction* refers to the conversion of physical into neural information. The sense organs convert physical stimuli into action potentials.

C. Principles of Perception
    1. *Psychophysics* is the study of how people psychologically perceive physical stimuli such as light and sound waves and touch.
    2. The lowest intensity level of a stimulus that we can detect half of the time is termed *absolute threshold.*
    3. *Signal Detection Theory* is the viewpoint that takes into account both stimulus intensity and the decision-making processes people use when saying whether they detect a stimulus.
    4. A *difference threshold* refers to the smallest amount of change between two stimuli that a person can detect half of the time.
        a. Difference thresholds are also referred to as *just noticeable differences (JND).*
        b. *Weber's law* states that size of a just noticeable difference is a constant fraction of the intensity of the stimulus.
    5. *Perceptual set* refers to the effect of frame of mind on perception. Our frame of mind, which is coded in the brain, can impact how we perceive things.

II. Vision: Most mammals rely on smell over all other senses, but humans are visual creatures. (p 130)

A. Sensing Visual Stimuli
    1. Vision and the Eye
        a. The *cornea* is a clear hard covering that protects the lens; this is where light enters the eye.
        b. The light passes through liquid until it reaches a hole called the *pupil.*
        c. The *iris* is the colored part of the eye and it adjusts the pupil to control the amount of light entering the eye.
        d. The light passes through the *lens* which bends the light rays.
        e. *Accommodation* is the process by which the muscles control the shape of the lens to adjust to viewing objects at different distances.
        f. The thin layer of nerve tissue that lines the back of the eye is termed the *retina,* which consists of several layers of cells.
            i. The deepest layer of cells where processing of light energy begins is the layer termed *photoreceptors.*
        g. *Rods* are central in the role of night vision. They are most responsive to dark and light contrast and they work well at low illumination.
            i. The process of adjustment to seeing in the dark is termed *dark adaptation.*
            ii. The process of adjusting to the dark can take up to 30 minutes (Rushton, 1961).

h. *Cones* are responsible for color vision and are most functional in conditions of bright light.

i. The *fovea* is a spot on the back of the retina which contains the highest concentration of cones.

i. Our ability to see clearly, or *visual acuity,* depends upon our cones.

2. Vision and the Brain

a. After transduction at the photoreceptor layer, the visual information is processed by a different layer of cells in the retina termed the *ganglion cells*. These are the axons that make up the optic nerve.

i. The *optic nerve* transmits the signals from the eye to the brain.

ii. The point at which the optic nerve exits the eye is termed the *blind spot* of the retina because the eye has no receptor cells at the point where the optic nerve leaves the eye.

b. The optic nerve carries impulses to the thalamus and eventually to the visual cortex of the occipital lobes.

c. The *optic chiasm* is the point at which strands of the optic nerve from half of each eye cross over to the opposite side of the brain.

Breaking New Ground: Specific Functions of Individual Neurons in Vision (p. 135)

A. Researchers had known for decades that after leaving the retina, optic fibers go to the visual portion of the thalamus, the lateral geniculate nucleus (LGN), and then travel to the visual cortex in the occipital lobes.

B. David Hubel and Torsten Wiesel won a Nobel Prize in 1981 for their work demonstrating that individual neurons fire only because of very specific visual information.

1. These researchers provided the first evidence that the neurons of the visual cortex are highly specialized when detecting features of visual stimuli.

a. They implanted electrodes into the visual cortex of cats and were able to record specialized activity of individual cells in the brain's vision area.

b. They discovered neurons called *feature detectors* in the visual cortex which analyze the retinal image and respond to aspects of shapes, such as angles and movements (Hubel & Weisel, 1962, 1979).

2. Hubel and Weisel described three types of neurons in the visual cortex that acted as feature detectors:

a. *Simple cells* respond to very specific information, such as a bar of light oriented at a particular angle (see Figure 4.8B for a picture of an example).

b. *Complex cells* receive input from many different simple cells and are receptive to particular stimuli but in different parts of the receptive field.

i. Unlike simple cells, complex cells are sensitive to an image as it moves and if it appears anywhere in the visual field.

c. *Hypercomplex cells* receive input from many complex cells and the fire in response to patterns of lines.

44

3. The cortex does not passively accept the nerve impulse from the retina and thalamus. Instead, the cortex actively transforms the signals by first breaking them down and then putting them back together.

4. Another discovery they made was that if a newborn cat had its eye closed for a week during the stage when the brain is growing the most, the visual cortex does not develop properly and the animal's vision is forever stunted.

    a. If one eye is closed early in life for an extended period of time, the part of the brain receiving messages from the closed eye soon begins to receive and process visual messages from the good eye.

    b. It is not only light that is needed for the developing brain if vision is to develop properly, instead, lines, shapes, and colors—the full visual experience—is needed.

        i. Our brains learn to see.

5. Other scientists (Quiroga, Reddy, Kreiman, Koch, & Fried, 2005) have found evidence of cortical cells in the temporal lobe that respond only to images of certain individuals (e.g., Bill Clinton or Jennifer Aniston). Based on our exposure and interest in certain things or people, *single cells* can come to represent a category of things, such as all things Brad Pitt-ish.

C. Perceiving Visual Stimuli: A number of processes work together to help us recognize objects in the world. These processes involve motion, depth, size, grouping, and color perception.

    1. Perceiving Motion: We perceive movement when an image moves across the retina. Several factors contribute to how we perceive movement:

        a. *Background*: When an object moves across a complex background, it appears to move faster than when it moves across a simple background.

        b. *Size*: Smaller objects appear to move faster than larger objects, when all else is equal.

            i. The illusion of something moving when it is not is referred to as *apparent motion* because our brains interpret images that move across our retinas as movement. The "moving" lights on a movie theater marquee are a rapid succession of bulbs lighting up in a row. We know the lights are not moving, but it we interpret is as movement.

        c. The *cerebellum* or "little brain" contains more neurons than any other single part of the brain and is responsible for body movement, balance, coordination, and fine motor skills. It is also important in cognitive activities such as learning and language (Amaral, 2000).

    2. Depth Perception: The ability to see things in three dimensions and to discriminate what is near from what is far.

        a. *Binocular Depth Cues* refers to our reliance on input from both eyes.

b. *Convergence* refers to the way that your eyes move inward as an object moves closer to you.

c. *Monocular Depth Cues* aids in our depth perception that does not require two eyes, such as linear perspective.

> i. *Linear perspective* involves parallel lines that converge or come together the further away they are from the viewer. The more they converge, the greater distance we perceive (see Figure 4.9A of your text for a visual example).
>
> ii. *Texture gradient* happens when the texture of a surface becomes more tightly packed together and denser as the surface moves to the background (see Figure 4.9B of your text).
>
> iii. *Atmospheric perspective* comes from looking across a vast space into the distance in the outdoors (see Figure 4.9C of your text for a visual example).
>
> iv. *Interposition* happens when objects closer to the viewer overlap with those further away (see Figure 4.9D for an example).

3. Perceptual Constancy: The ability of the brain to preserve perception of objects in spite of changes in retinal image.

a. *Size Constancy* is when we see things as the same size regardless of the changing size of the image on our retina because we know what the image is (see Figure 4.10A and 4.1B for a demonstration of distortions in perception of size in the Ames room).

b. *Shape Constancy* refers to the fact that people know the shapes of common things just as they know the sizes; the brain uses this knowledge to override changing retinal images that might make the world confusion (see Figure 4.11 for a demonstration).

4. Organizing Visual Information: Gestalt Laws of Grouping

a. The *law of continuity* states that we see point or lines in such a way that they follow a continuous path (see Figure 4.13A and 4.13B).

b. The *law of proximity* states that we tend to group together objects that are near one another (see Figure 4.14).

c. The *law of closure* occurs then we perceive a whole object in the absence of complete information (see Figure 4.15B).

5. Visual Perception: Bottom-Up or Top-Down?

a. The perspective known as *bottom-up processing* suggests that visual perception is a process of building a visual experience from smaller pieces; we put the pieces together and then we "see" the whole thing.

b. The perspective known as *top-down processing* suggests that perception of the whole guides perception of smaller elemental features.

> i. Which process is correct actually depends on the nature of the information being processed.

6. The Perception of Color
   a. Our perception of color varies depending on our photoreceptors, our brain, and the physical characteristics of the stimulus at which we look.
      i. Color perception is partly determined by wavelength, measured in billionths of a meter or nanometers (see Figure 4.20 for the spectrum of light visible to humans).
   b. Two Theories of Color Vision
      i. The *trichromatic color theory* states that all color that we experience must result from a mixing of three colors (red, green, and blue). Light color mixing occurs inside the eye, in terms of how different kinds of cones respond to different wavelengths of light:
         (a) red cones fire in response to longer wavelength light
         (b) green cones respond to medium wavelength light
         (c) blue cones respond to shorter wavelength light
      ii. The trichromatic color theory cannot explain some aspects of color vision, such as color *afterimages* which are visual images that remain after removal of the stimulus (see Figure 4.21 for a fun example of afterimage).
      iii. Ewarl Hering (1878) proposed the *opponent process theory* which suggests that cones are linked together in three opposing color pairs: blue/yellow, red/green, and black/white. The members of the color pairs oppose one another, whereby activation of one member of the pair inhibits activity in the other.
      iv. The opponent process theory can account for the color afterimage (seen in Figure 4.21).
   c. Deficiencies in Color Vision
      i. There are many types of color vision, but only about 10 people in a million actually fail to see color at all (Goldstein, 1984).
      ii. The most common form of color blindness results from a deficiency in red and green sensitive cones. Yellow-blue deficiencies are less common (see Figure 4.22 for a color blindness test).

II. Hearing (p. 148)

   A. The Physics of Sound and the Psychology of Hearing
      1. We perceive different shapes and sizes of sound waves as different sounds. Hearing is affected by three physical properties of the sound wave: its *amplitude, frequency,* and *purity.*

a. The height or *amplitude* of the sound wave determines what we perceive as loudness; the taller the wave is the louder the sound.
b. The *frequency* of the sound wave refers to how many waves occur in a given period of time and it is what we perceive as the sound's pitch; the higher the frequency, the higher the pitch.
c. The *purity* of sound waves refers to the complexity of the wave and we perceive purity as timbre. Musicians refer to timbre as the "color" of sound.

B. The Ear
1. Our ears (termed *pinnae*) collect and funnel sounds into the passage called the *auditory canal*. Once inside the canal, the sound vibrations travel to the eardrum or *tympanic membrane*.
a. Sound waves on the tympanic membrane set into motion the bones of the *middle ear*: the hammer, anvil, and stirrup (see Figure 4.24).
i. The hammer hits the anvil and the anvil moves the stirrup. The stirrup then sets into motion a series of important changes in the *inner ear*.
b. The inner ear includes the *cochlea* and *semi-circular canal*.
i. The *semi-circular canal* play a key role in maintaining balance.
ii. The *cochlea* is a bony tube, curled like a snail's shell and filled with fluid. The *basilar membrane* runs through the cochlea, and within the basilar membrane of the cochlea are *hair cells* which are the sensory receptors for sound.
iii. As hair cells bend they transduce the sound vibrations into electrical impulses which may generate an action potential in the *auditory nerve*.

Psychology and The Real World: Hearing Loss in the Age of the iPod (p. 152)

A. Studies divide the causes of hearing loss into age-related and noise-related, but the two are related. Nonetheless, Being exposed to loud noise levels over long-periods of time leads to a loss of hearing after 10 to 15 years.

B. In a large-scale study of exposure to noise at work, middle-age men (45–70 years old) have their threshold for high frequency sounds raised by 10dB compared to men not exposed to such noise at work (Tambs, Hoffman, Borchgrevink, Holmen, & Engdahl, 2006).
1. Factory or machine workers exposed to 90dB level noise for 8 hours a day, 5 days a week suffer permanent hearing loss after 10 years on the job (Lutman & Spencer, 1999; Taylor et al., 1965).

C. The well-documented loss of high frequency hearing with age lead to some interesting technologies. *Mosquito* technology was invented by a company to disperse young people in a crowd (because they find it annoying) while leaving older people unaffected (they cannot hear it).

1. Younger people copied a high-pitch ringtone called mosquito for their cell phones so that they can hear their phone ring when older people are not supposed to hear it (Vitello, 2006).

      a. Some 30- and 40-year-olds can hear the mosquito ring tone.

2. MP3 players, including the iPod, have maximum decibel levels of around 115–120dB, about the loudness of a jet airplane.

      a. The Center for Disease Control and Prevention (2001) reported hearing loss from loud noise in nearly 13% of Americans between the ages of 6 and 19; this translates to about 5 million young people (Knox, 2007).

A. Hearing in the Brain

    1. The auditory pathways go from the cochlea to the *inferior colliculus* in the brain stem and from there to the *medial (middle) geniculate nucleus (MGN).*

      a. In the brain is where we organize and interpret sounds from the outside world. It is here where we hear.

      b. The auditory cortex receives inputs from other cortical regions, including the visual cortex and regions involved in perceiving speech.

      c. The right auditory cortex is more active in processing nonverbal stimuli and the left auditory cortex is more active in processing speech and language (Zatorre, Evans, & Meyer, 1994).

III. The Bodily Senses (p. 152)

A. The largest contact surface area any sensory input has with our bodies is the skin, and it is carefully mapped in the somatosensory cortex in the parietal lobe of the brain (Blakeslee & Bladeslee, 2007).

    1. The senses based in the skin, body, or any membrane surfaces are known as the *bodily senses.*

    2. There are at least six distinct bodily or somatic senses: touch, temperature, pain, position/motion, balance and interoception (perception of bodily sensations).

B. Touch

    1. The top layers of skin have receptor cells, termed *mechanoreceptors,* that are sensitive to different tactile qualities. We have some receptors for shape, grooves, vibrations, and movements.

      a. Repeated sensory and motor tactile experience changes the amount of cortex involved in processing that particular sensation or movement.

         i. Researchers have found that experienced violinists have larger representations or *brain maps* of the hand and finger regions of the somatosensory cortex than nonmusicians (Pantev, Engelien, Candia & Elbert, 2001)

C. Pain

    1. Pain is important for survival. People born with no pain receptors can get seriously injured or killed because they do not know they have been harmed (Watkins & Maier, 2003).

2. *Pain* is a complex emotional and sensory experience associated with actual or potential tissue damage (Merskey & Bogduk, 1994).

    a. Physical and emotional pain involve many of the same brain structures (Singer et al., 2004).

3. Pain Perception: There are different types of pain including damage to the skin, organ tissue, and nerve damage, as well as joint inflammation.

    a. Pain from skin damage is termed *nocieptive pain.*

        i. The skin has pain receptors that are sensitive to heat, cold, chemical irritation, and pressure.

    b. Nociceptors send signals to the spinal cord and then to the brain signaling that damage has happened; the brain can then initiate an appropriate response.

    c. Some of the same brain regions that are activated when we experience physical pain are also activated during emotional pain—especially when we are rejected by others or see others receive shocks (Singer et al., 2004).

4. Explaining Pain

    a. *Gate control theory of pain* proposes that the spinal cord regulates the experience of pain by either opening or closing neural channels, called *gates*, involved in pain sensations that get sent to the brain (Melzak & Wall, 1965, 1988).

        i. Thoughts, feelings, and beliefs can influence pain sensations, which is one reason people vary so much in their perception of pain.

        ii. Different people experiencing the same level of pain may have completely different experiences of their pain.

5. Controlling Pain

    a. *Endorphins* are endogenous morphine-like substances that our bodies make; they are our own natural pain-killers.

    b. Endorphins work by stimulating the release of neurotransmitters that interfere with pain messages in the spinal cord and brain.

        i. Endorphins may help to explain why some people initially experience no pain after a horrible injury from an accident.

        ii. Soldiers and automobile accident victims often report no immediate sensations of pain (Warga, 1987).

    c. Opioids are a drug class referred to as *analgesics* which means *without pain.*

        i. Morphine, heroin, oxycodone, and hydrocodone are all opioids.

        ii. There is a high risk of dependency on opioids, thus their use must be carefully monitored.

IV. The Chemical Senses: Smell and Taste (p. 158)

A. Smell and taste are chemical senses because they respond to contact with molecules from objects we encounter in the world.

    1. Smell and taste are very important survival-related senses; that is, they govern our choices about what we take into our bodies.

B. Smell (olfaction)

1. *Olfactory sensory neurons* are the receptors for smell. These neurons contain *cilia* which convert chemical information in odor molecules to neural impulses.

    a. When chemicals come in contact with the cilia, transduction occurs, and the olfactory message travels to the *olfactory bulb* in the forebrain.

    b. The olfactory bulb sends information either directly to the smell processing areas in the cortex or indirectly to the cortex by way of the thalamus (Buck, 2000).

        i. Some fibers from the olfactory bulb go directly to the amygdala, which sends smell information to the hypothalamus, thalamus, and frontal. These connections may explain why smells can instantly evoke an emotional memory (Herz, 2004).

    c. People differ in the ability to sense odors and animals have a heightened sense of smell compared to humans.

        i. Sharks can detect one drop of blood in 25 gallons of water (Marks, 2006).

C. Taste

    1. Textured structures called *papillae* found on the tongue contain about 10,000 taste buds.

    a. *Taste cells* are the cells on the buds that process taste information.

    b. Humans can distinguish five basic taste qualities: bitter, sweet, salty, sour, and savory.

        i. The experience of flavor results from the combination of taste plus smell (Goldstein, 2007). This explains why food tastes dull when you have a cold.

D. Synesthesia

    1. *Synesthesia* occurs when a person experiences sensations in one sense when a different sense is stimulated (Cytowic, 1989; Ramachandran & Hubbard, 2003); it occurs when the senses get mixed up rather than stay separate.

    a. Some people experience yellow when they hear a tone such as middle C; others taste shapes and some experience numbers as colors, such as 5s as green and 2s as red.

        i. This may occur from a cross-wiring or cross-activation of sensory neurons in parts of the brain (Ramachandran & Hubbard, 2003).

        ii. Some hallucinogenic drugs can temporarily create synesthetic experiences, but the brain mechanisms for this are not well understood (Weil & Rosen, 1998).

Making Connections in Sensation and Perception: Differences Across Cultures (p. 162)

A. Cultural Variation in Visual Perception

    1. Differences exist across cultures in response to certain visual images that use monocular cues to depth.

a. Researchers have studied the effects of living in a *carpentered world* (an environment with buildings with many right angles) on people's perceptions of depth.

b. Pederson and Wheller (1983) found that Navajos who had lived at least 10 years in round huts were much less likely to see the lines in Figure 4.18 of your text as differing in length because they are not accustomed to rooms with edges.

  i. Experience modifies perception.

c. There are also cultural differences in perceiving and attending to foreground and background.

  i. People from Eastern cultures tend to perceive the world more as a whole, with people and objects and the context being connected and belonging together. On the other hand, Western cultures tend to focus most on foreground objects and less on background and the periphery (Nisbett, Peng, Choi, & Norenzayan, 2001).

B. Cultural Variation in Olfactory Experience

  1. Because smells elicit emotions so readily, cultures often develop strong rules or norms about which smells are okay and which are not. Cultures differ widely on the acceptability of odors based on experience, climate, and cuisine.

  a. Different places vary in their standards for cleanliness and for what is acceptable body odor (Hannigan, 1995).

  b. Sex differences also occur: Women tend to be more sensitive to smells than men (Brand & Millot, 2001).

C. Cultural Variation in Pain

  1. There are widely differing perceptions of how painful childbirth is among cultures.

  a. The Yap, who live in the South Pacific, consider childbirth to be simply a part of everyday life and women routinely work in the fields up to the day before birth and are back at work the next day. The husbands experience the pain of childbirth and they stay in bed to recover after the birth of the child (Kroeber, 1948).

GLOSSARY TERMS

sensation: a physical process: the stimulation of our sense organs by the outer world.

perception: a psychological process: the act of organizing and interpreting sensory experience.

sensory adaptation: the process by which our sensitivity diminishes when an object constantly stimulates our senses.

transduction: the conversion of physical into neural information.

psychophysics: the study of how people psychologically perceive physical stimuli such as light and sound waves and touch.

absolute threshold: the lowest intensity level of a stimulus a person can detect half of the time.

signal detection theory: the viewpoint that takes into account both stimulus intensity and the decision-making processes people use when saying whether they detect a stimulus.

difference threshold: the smallest amount of change between two stimuli that a person can detect half of the time.

Weber's law: the theory stating that size of a just noticeable difference is a constant fraction of the intensity of the stimulus.

perceptual set: the effect of frame of mind on perception; a tendency to perceive stimuli in a certain manner.

pupil: the opening in the iris through which light enters the eye.

cornea: the clear hard covering that protects the lens of the eye.

iris: the muscle that comprises the colored part of the eye; it adjusts the pupil to regulate the amount of light that enters the eye.

lens: the structure that sits behind the pupil; it bends the light rays that enter the eye to focus images on the retina.

accommodation: the process by which the muscles control the shape of the lens to adjust to viewing objects at different distances.

retina: the thin layer of nerve tissue that lines the back of the eye.

photoreceptors: cells in the retina (called rods and cones) that convert light energy into nerve energy; they are transducers.

rods: photoreceptors that function in low illumination and play a key role in night vision; response to dark and light contrast.

dark adaptation: process of adjustment to seeing in the dark

cones: photoreceptors that are responsible for color vision and are most functional in conditions of bright light.

fovea: spot on the back of the retina that contains the highest concentration of cones in the retina; place of clearest vision.

visual acuity: our ability to see clearly.

optic nerve: structure composed of the axons of ganglion cells from the retina that carry visual information from the eye to the brain.

optic chiasm: the point at which strands of the optic nerve from half of each eye cross over to the opposite side of the brain.

feature detectors: neurons in the visual cortex that analyze the retinal image and respond to specific aspects of shapes, such as angles and movements.

simple cells: cortical neurons that respond to very specific visual information, such as a bar of light oriented at a particular angle.

complex cells: cortical neurons that receive input from many different simple cells and are receptive to particular stimuli from anywhere in the receptive field.

hypercomplex cells: cortical neurons that receive inputs from many complex cells; they fire in response to patterns of lines.

depth perception: the ability to see things in three dimensions and can discriminate what is near from what is far.

binocular depth cues: aids to depth perception that rely on input from both eyes.

convergence: a binocular depth cue: the way in which the eyes move inward as an object moves closer to you.

monocular depth cues: aids to depth perception that do not require two eyes, such as linear perspective.

linear perspective: a monocular depth cue: the manner in which parallel lines converge or come together the further away they are from the viewer.

texture gradient: monocular depth cue in which the texture of a surface becomes more tightly packed together and denser as the surface moves to the background.

atmospheric perspective: monocular depth cue that results from the quality of air—making objects at a distance appear blurred.

interposition: monocular depth cue in which objects closer to the viewer often overlap with and hide those further away.

perceptual constancy: the ability of the brain to preserve perception of objects in spite of changes in retinal image when an object changes in position or distance from the viewer.

Gestalt law of similarity: the tendency to group like objects together in visual perception.

Gestalt law of continuity: the tendency to see points or lines in such a way that they follow a continuous path.

Gestalt law of proximity: the tendency to group objects together that are near one another.

Gestalt law of closure: the tendency to see a whole object even when complete information isn't available.

bottom-up processing: idea that perception is a process of building a perceptual experience from smaller pieces; putting the pieces together to see the whole.

top-down processing: idea that perception of the whole guides perception of smaller elemental features.

trichromatic color theory: the theory that all color that we experience must result from a mixing of three colors of light (red, green, and blue).

afterimages: visual images that remain after removal of or looking away from the stimulus.

opponent process theory: the theory that color vision results from the fact that cones are linked together in three color pairs: blue/yellow, red/green, and black/white. The members of the color pairs oppose one another, so that activation of one member of the pair inhibits activity in the other.

tympanic membrane: the ear drum.

semi-circular canals: structure of the inner ear involved in maintaining balance.

cochlea: a bony tube of the inner ear, which is curled like a snail's shell and filled with fluid.

basilar membrane: a membrane that runs through the cochlea; contains the hair cells.

hair cells: inner ear sensory receptors for sound; they transduce sound vibrations into neural impulses.

auditory nerve: the nerve that receives action potentials from the hair cells and transmits auditory information to the brain.

bodily senses: the senses based in the skin, body, or any membrane surfaces.

mechanoreceptors: receptor cells in the skin that are sensitive to different tactile qualities—some to shape, some to grooves, some to vibrations and movements.

pain: a complex emotional and sensory experience associated with actual or potential tissue damage.

gate control theory of pain: theory that proposes that the spinal cord regulates the experience of pain by either opening or closing neural channels, called *gates,* involved in pain sensations that get sent to the brain.

olfactory sensory neurons: the sensory receptors for smell that reside high up inside the nose.

olfactory bulb: a forebrain structure that sends information either directly to the smell processing areas in the cortex or indirectly to the cortex by way of the thalamus.

papillae: textured structures on the surface of the tongue; contain thousands of taste buds.

taste buds: structures inside the papillae of the tongue that contain the taste cells.

taste receptor cells: sensory receptors for taste that reside in the taste buds; site of transduction of chemical information to neural impulse in the processing of taste sensations.

synesthesia: an unusual sensory experience in which a person experiences sensations in one sense when a different sense is stimulated; such as experiencing sound as colors.

PRACTICE STUDY QUESTIONS

1. _____ is the stimulation of our sense organs by the outer world; whereas _____ is the act of organizing and interpreting sensory experience.
   a. Perception; sensation
   b. Transduction; perception
   c. Sensation; perception
   d. Transduction; sensation

2. The lowest intensity level of a stimulus we can detected half of the time is termed the:
   a. just noticeable difference.
   b. psychophysic difference.
   c. psychophysic threshold.
   d. absolute threshold.

3. The size of the JND is a _____ fraction of the intensity of the stimulus.
   a. increasing
   b. decreasing
   c. constant
   d. one-half

4. The _____ is a thin layer of nerve tissue that lines the back of the eye.
   a. cornea
   b. pupil
   c. lens
   d. retina

5. The _____ is the colored part of the eye and adjusts the pupil to control the amount of light entering the eye.
   a. cornea
   b. visual muscle
   c. iris
   d. retina

6. _____ work well at low illumination; whereas _____ are responsible for color vision and are functional in bright light.
   a. Cones; lenses
   b. Cones; rods
   c. Lenses; rods
   d. Rods; cones

7. There are three types of neurons in the visual cortex that act as feature detectors: simple cells, complex cells, and:
    a. transduction cells.
    b. cone cells.
    c. hypercomplex cells.
    d. hypocomplex cells.

8. The illusion that we see "moving" lights on a movie theater marquee that are moving in rapid succession of bulbs lighting up in a row is referred to as:
    a. perceptual transduction.
    b. nonapparent motion.
    c. sensational perceptions.
    d. apparent motion.

9. The ability of the brain to preserve perception of objects in spite of the changes in retinal image is known as:
    a. sensational perception.
    b. perceptual constancy.
    c. texture gradient constancy.
    d. visual acuity.

10. The law of _____ states that we tend to group together objects that are near one another.
    a. closure
    b. continuity
    c. proximity
    d. grouping

11. The law of _____ occurs when we perceive a whole object in the absence of complete formation.
    a. continuity
    b. proximity
    c. grouping
    d. closure

12. The _____ theory of the explanation of color states that colors are linked together in three opposing pairs; whereas the _____ theory of the explanation of color suggests that all color that we experience must result from a mixing of three colors of light.
    a. trichromatic color; opponent process
    b. opponent process; trichromatic color
    c. wavelength distribution; color blindness
    d. color blindness; wavelength distribution

13. The _____ of a sound wave determines what we perceive as loudness.
    a. frequency
    b. amplitude
    c. purity

     d. timbre

14. Some higher frequencies that can be heard by young people cannot be heard by many older people.
     a. true
     b. false

15. Our brains make naturally occurring _____ that mimic the effects of opioids.
     a. dopamine transmitters
     b. endorphins
     c. nocirceptors
     d. serotonin receptors

ANSWERS TO PRACTICE STUDY QUESTIONS

1. c
2. d
3. c
4. d
5. c
6. d
7. c
8. d
9. b
10. c
11. d
12. b
13. b
14. a
15. b

Chapter 5
THE DEVELOPING HUMAN

KEY TERMS

Human development	Conventional level
Germinal stage	Postconventional level
Zygote	Imprinting
Embryo	Attachment
Embryonic stage	Separation anxiety
Fetal stage	Secure attachment
Neural migration	Anxious-resistant attachment
Prenatal programming	Anxious-avoidant
Teratogens	peers
Fetal alcohol spectrum disorder	Social referencing
Critical period	Emotional competence
Pruning	Peers
Sensorimotor stage	Adolescence
Object permanence	Puberty
Preoperational stage	Menarche
Animistic thinking	Spermarche
Egocentrism	Formal operational stage
Conservation	Dementia
Concrete operational stage	Alzheimer's disease
Formal operational stage	Dementia
Theory of mind	Temperament
Preconventional level	Generativity

OUTLINE

I. The Developing Fetus (p. 171)

    A. Stages of Prenatal Development
        1. Life before birth is commonly divided into three distinct stages: the *germinal, embryonic,* and *fetal* stages.
            a. The *germinal stage* begins at conception and lasts for 2 weeks.
                i. At conception, the fertilized egg forma s single-celled *zygote.*
                ii. The *embryo* is the bundle of cells rapidly multiplying cells (the blastocyst) that has implanted in the uterus.
            b. The *embryonic stage* is marked by the formation of the major organs: the nervous system, heart, eyes, ears, arms, legs, the palate, and external genitalia.
            c. The *fetal stage* is the formation of bone cells at 8 weeks after conception. By this time all of the major organs have begun to form.

i. Between 8 and 12 weeks the heartbeat can be heard with a stethoscope.
2. Brain and Sensory Development Before Birth
a. During the fetal stage, the rate of new neural growth can be approximately three million neurons per minute at its peak (Purves & Lichtman, 1985).
i. From months 3 to 5 of pregnancy, neurons move from one part of the brain to their more permanent home in a process known as *neural migration.*
b. The major sensory systems develop at different times and different rates.
i. The fetus can respond to sound about 26 weeks (6 months) after conception (Kisilevsky, Muir, & Low, 1992).
ii. Vision is the least-well-developed sense in the fetus (Hopson 1989).
3. Environmental Influences on Fetal Development
a. *Prenatal programming* is the process by which events in the womb alter the development of physical and psychological health.
b. *Teratogens* are substances that can disrupt normal prenatal development and cause lifelong deficits.
c. Maternal Nutrition: What a pregnant woman eats and drinks in important for the health of the fetus and even for the infant and child for years
after birth.
i. Both schizophrenia and antisocial personality disorder are more likely to occur if the mother is malnourished during pregnancy (Neuebauer, Hoek, & Susser, 1999; Wahlbeck et al., 2001).
ii. Iron deficiency in the mother's dies and maternal stress predispose the infant to anemia, or low red blood cell count.
d. Known teratogens include: viruses, such as rubella (measles), and the flu; alcohol; nicotine; prescription drugs, such as Prozac and Zoloft; and radiation.
i. The timing determines how detrimental the effects of any given teratogen; in general, the earlier in pregnancy the woman is exposed, the more serious the effects (see Figure 5.2 of your text).
ii. *Fetal alcohol spectrum disorder* is a consequence of prenatal alcohol exposure that causes multiple problems, which may include damage to the central nervous systems and mental retardation.

II. The Developing Infant and Child (p. 178)

A. Physical Development in Infancy and Childhood
1. Early Motor Development

a. Motor development refers to the changes in physical movement and body control. See Figure 5.5 for major milestones of motor development in the first 15 months.

2. Early Sensory Development

a. With regard to vision, the occipital cortex of the brain has to be stimulated by visual input in order to develop the proper synaptic connections needed to process visual information.

i. Infants respond to visual stimuli within 8 to 12 inches of their face.

b. For full development of the visual sense, these early months are a *critical period* which is a specific period in biological development when individuals are most receptive to a particular kind of input from the environment.

3. Early Brain Development

a. After birth, the brain continues to grow new neurons and by the 2n year of life, the human brain has more neurons than it will ever have again.

i. *Pruning* is the degradation of synapses and dying off of neurons that are not strengthened by experience in the newborn.

ii. By adolescence up to half of the synapses that existed in early childhood have been pruned (Chechik, Meilijson, & Ruppin, 1999).

iii. Normal and enriched environments create more complex neural connections, whereas abusive, neglectful, and impoverished environments create less developed neural connections and fewer of them (Mirescu & Gould, 2006).

Psychology in the Real World: Music Training Changes the Brain (p. 182)

A. Early in life there is more opportunity for experience to leave its mark on the brain.

B. Researchers examined whether the brains of string instrument players devote more resources to the fingers of the fingering hand than to the nonfingering hand.

1. Elbert et al. (1995) applied a slight pressure to each finger on each hand of right-handed musicians and nonmusicians and used an fMRI to map the brain's responses to the pressure.

a. For musicians, the area on the somatosensory cortex devoted to those fingers on the side of the brain that controls the fingering left hand was bigger than the area that controls the nonfingering right hand.

i. Musicians who started playing before the age of 12 showed the most pronounced effects.

2. An experiment by Pascual-Leone (2001) taught people who had never played piano a one-hand-five-finger exercise that they repeated in 2-hour sessions for 5 days. Next they took a test that involved repetitions of exercise.

i. Pascual-Leone found that as skill improved, cortical representation for the finger muscles involved in the task increased.

ii. After random assignment to groups, for those who continued daily practice (compared to those who did not) their brain map changes continued, whereas the brain maps for those in the other group returned to the way they were before training within 1 week.

4. Early Cognitive Development

a. Jean Piaget outlined four phases of cognitive development from birth through adolescence: *sensorimotor, preoperational, concrete operational,* and *formal operational.*

b. The *sensorimotor* stage (0–2 years) is when infants learn about the world by using their senses and by moving their bodies in it.

i. *Object permanence* is the ability to realize that objects still exist when they are not being sensed; this ability occurs around 9 months of age.

c. The *preoperational* stage (2–5 years) begins with the emergence of symbolic thought, or the use of symbols such as words or letters to represent ideas or objects

i. In this stage children engage in *animistic thinking* which is the belief that inanimate objects are alive. They also have a view of the world known as *egocentrism* which is viewing the world from one's own perspective and not being capable of seeing things from another person's perspective.

ii. *Conservation* is the ability to recognize that when objects change shape or size, the overall amount stays the same. During the preoperational stage, children cannot recognize this (see Figure 5.14 of your text for conservation tasks).

d. The *concrete operational* stage (6–11 years) is when the child can perform mental operations—on real, or concrete, objects and events—but they still have trouble with abstract ideas and reasoning.

e. The *formal operational* stage (11–adulthood) occurs when children gain the ability to reason about abstract concepts and problems.

5. *Theory of Mind* refers to our knowledge and ideas of how other people's minds work.

a. Children under age 4 do not realize that people may believe things that are not true; adults know that people believe things that are untrue all of the time (e.g., superstitions).

i. Psychologists developed the *false-belief* task to determine when children develop theory of mind (Wimmer & Perner, 1983).

6. Development of Moral Reasoning

a. Kohlberg proposed a three-stage theory of moral reasoning: *preconventional level, conventional level,* and *postconventional.*

i. In the *preconventional level* moral reasoning involves avoiding punishment or maximizing rewards.

ii. In the *conventional level* a person values caring, trust, and relationships as well as the social order and lawfulness.

iii. In the *postconventional level* a person acknowledges both the norm and the law, but argues that there are universal moral rules that may trump unjust or immoral local rules.

B. Early Socioemotional Development
    1. Attachment
        a. *Attachment* refers to the strong emotional connection that develops early in life to keep infants close to their caregivers; it is a way to describe the relationship between infant and caregiver.
        b. John Bowlby (1969) studied how infants become emotionally attached to their caregivers and noted a sequence of reactions they to go through when separated from the caregiver.
            i. *Separation anxiety* is the distress reaction shown by babies when they are separated from their primary caregiver.
        c. Mary Ainsworth developed the *Strange Situation Test* to measure attachment and noted different attachment styles.
            i. *Secure attachment* is characterized by happy infants who initiate contact when the primary caregiver returns after separation.
            ii. *Anxious-resistant attachment* is characterized by infants who are ambivalent on separation and reuniting with the caregiver.
            iii. *Anxious-avoidant attachment* is characterized by infants who stay calm when their primary caregiver leaves and who ignore and avoid her or him upon returning.
            iv. The emotional bond or attachment that infants share with their primary caregiver may serve as a model for future relationships, even in adulthood.
    2. Developing Social Relationships and Emotions
        a. *Social referencing* is the ability to make use of social information from another person.
            i. Research on social referencing shows that babies understand the meaning of some different facial expressions of emotion much earlier than age one.
        b. Develop of Emotions: Babies show their own emotions very early in life. All humans, even babies, respond to cues in their social environments.
            i. *Emotional competence* is the ability to control emotions and know when it is appropriate to express certain emotions (Saarni, 1999; Grolnick, McMenamy, & Kurowski, 2006).
        c. Peer Interaction: Nothing influences the behavior of children like other children—their peers.
            i. *Peers* are people who share equal standing or status and are at the same level in terms of age, gender, skill, or power.
            ii. All over the world, children typically choose same-sex playmates, probably because they prefer the same type of play. Girls favor cooperative play such as dress-up and tea parties;

whereas boys like more active pursuits such as wrestling and foot races.

iii. Only in adolescence do boys and girls move toward opposite-sex interactions.

Breaking New Ground: How Touch and Comfort Influence Development (p. 194)

A. The Importance of Comfort and Physical Contact

1. Harry Harlow studied attachment and noticed that baby monkeys that he separated from their mothers became very attached to cloth diapers that lined their cage. He conducted some experiments to further examine the baby monkeys.

2. Harlow separated monkeys from their mothers and put cloth and wire mothers in cubicles attached to the infants' cages. Half the monkeys were randomly assigned to get milk from the wire mother; the other half got milk from the cloth monkey.

a. Harlow found that the contact comfort was much more important than the source of food in determining which surrogate mother the monkeys preferred (see Figure 5.18 of your text).

b. Harlow's findings suggested that the view that babies preferred being with their moms because they provided food was at least partially incorrect.

i. Harlow's work was pivotal in showing the importance of comfort in primate development.

3. A study with premature human infants found that touch therapy (gently stroking the baby with warmed hands through portholes in an isolette for 15 minutes a day, three times a week, for 10 days) resulted in a significant weight gain for those who received it; premature babies that did not receive touch therapy did not gain more weight.

B. Extending the Benefits of Touch Therapy

1. Touch therapy has been used successfully on toddlers with cerebral palsy as it improved motor movements, resulted in better muscle control, and also improved cognitive and social behaviors.

a. Message therapy also helps people with developmental disorders such as autism.

III. The Developing Adolescent (p. 200)

A. *Adolescence* is the transition period between childhood and adulthood (~11–18 years).

B. Physical Development in Adolescence

1. *Puberty* is the period when sexual maturation begins; it marks the beginning of adolescence.

a. *Menarche* is the first menstrual period.

b. *Spermarche* is the first ejaculation.

C. Cognitive and Brain Development
    1. During adolescence, children gain the ability to reason about abstract concepts and problems (Piaget's formal operational stage).
        a. The frontal lobes are the last part of the brain to develop and it continues to do so until late adolescence or early adulthood.
            i. The frontal lobes are involved in planning, attention, working memory, abstract thought, and impulse control. There is a direct relationship between cognitive development and brain development.
            ii. Because the teen brain is developing, they use more frontal lobe activity during complex and demanding tasks than do adults.
            iii. Because teenage brains are not capable of handling taxing information the way adults can it may explain why teens engage in impulsive and risky behavior.

D. Social Development in Adolescence
    1. Puberty brings profound changes not only in the body but also in relationships: Family become less central, peers and sexual relationships become paramount.
        a. Having close, intimate friends during adolescence is associated with many positive social and emotional outcomes, such as self-confidence, better relationships with parents and authority figures, and better performance in school (Bagwell, Newcomb, & Bukowski, 1999). The opposite is true for those without close peer relationships.
    2. Sexual interest and sexual relationships are an obvious change in adolescent development.
        a. A sexually mature body combined with a brain that is not fully developed can result in bad judgment, as the high rates of unplanned pregnancy and sexually transmitted diseases in teen attest (CDC, 2005).

IV. The Developing Adult (p. 204)

    A. Sensation and Perception in Adulthood
    1. Many people experience some loss of vision or hearing or both by middle adulthood.
        a. Most people need reading glasses sometime in their 40s because the lens of the eye loses flexibility (Goldstein, 2007).
        b. Hearing also declines. One large-scale study found that as much as 50% of older adults (mean age 67) experienced some degree of hearing loss (Chia et al., 2007).
            i. Age-related hearing deficits may occur from problems with the ears, auditory nerve, or various brain areas are more common in men than in women (Pearson et al., 1995; Tremblay & Ross, 2007).
        c. Almost half of the people over 65 demonstrate significant loss of smell (Doty et al., 1984).

B. Cognitive and Brain Development in Adulthood
    1. Healthy Aging
        a. Aging is not a slow decline over time (Kenyon, 2005). In fact, keeping the mind active increases neural branching, which improves cognitive performance (Churchill et al., 2002; Cotman, Berchold, & Christie, 2007).
        b. One cognitive benefit of aging is *wisdom,* which is the ability to know what matters to live well, to show good judgment (Baltes & Smith, 2008).
        c. The "use it or lose it" approach to healthy aging involves learning new skills, such a language, game, or computer activity, which, in turn, can lead to neural growth (Cotman et al., 2007).

C. Cognitive Decline in the Aging Brain
    1. *Dementia* is a loss of mental function, in which many cognitive processes are impaired, such as the ability to remember, reason, problem solve, make decisions, and use language.
        a. Several neurological conditions, including Alzheimer's disease, can lead to dementia.
            i. Strokes are a common contributor to the development of dementia in the elderly.
    2. *Alzheimer's disease* is a degenerative disease marked by progressive cognitive decline and is characterized by a collection of symptoms including confusion, memory loss, mood swings, and eventual loss of physical functions.
        a. Aerobic exercise appears to protect against a decline in higher mental processing and my actually make the brain grow (Colcombe et al., 2006; Colcomb & Kramer, 2003).
            i. Neurogenesis in the adult brain might not repair damage due to a degenerative disease, but it might provide extra resources or "reserves" for cognitive function that might help counteract the cognitive effects of neural degeneration (Steiner, Wolf, & Kemperman, 2006).

D. Socioemotional Development in Adults
    1. There are few age-related changes in emotional function. In fact, there may be emotional gains with age as people become motivated to develop more rewarding, meaningful relationships (Carstensen, Fung, & Charles, 2003).
        a. This motivation stems from the awareness of people that they have a limited amount of time and they become selective in where they expend their resources in personal and emotional relationships (Carstensen et al., 2003).

E. Death and Dying
    1. In psychological terms, death is a complex event that marks the end of life.
        a. Western culture does not place much emphasis on talking about death but some Eastern cultures take a different view.

i. In Buddhism acceptance of death and of the fact that life is not permanent condition, but it is a touchstone against which life is evaluated.

b. People in the United States are increasingly preparing for death by resolving differences with family and friends and accomplishing their goals.

i. Some people prepare special rituals or events to mark the final stage of life or to say good-bye to friends and family (Bourgeois & Johnson, 2004).

GLOSSARY TERMS

human development: the study of change and continuity in the individual across the life span.

germinal stage: the first prenatal stage of development, which begins at conception and last two weeks.

zygote: the single cell that results when a sperm fertilizes an egg.

embryo: the term for the developing organism from 2 weeks until about 8 weeks after conception.

embryonic stage: the second prenatal stage, from 2 weeks to 8 weeks after conception, when all of the major organs form.

fetal stage: the third prenatal stage, which begins with the formation of bone cells 8 weeks after conception and ends at birth.

neural migration: the movement of neurons from one part of the fetal brain to their more permanent destination; occurs during months 3-5 of the fetal stage.

prenatal programming: the process by which events in the womb alter development of physical and psychological health.

teratogens: substances that can disrupt normal prenatal development and cause lifelong deficits.

fetal alcohol spectrum disorder: a consequence of prenatal alcohol exposure that causes multiple problems, notably brain damage and mental retardation.

critical period: specific period in development when individuals are most receptive to a particular kind of input from the environment (such as visual stimulation and language).

pruning: the degradation of synapses and dying off of neurons that are not strengthened by experience.

sensorimotor stage: Piaget's first stage of cognitive development (ages 1-2), when infants learn about the world by using their senses and by moving their bodies.

object permanence: the ability to realize that objects still exist when they are not being sensed.

preoperational stage: the second major stage of cognitive development (ages 2-5), which begins with the emergence of symbolic thought.

animistic thinking: belief that inanimate objects are alive.

egocentrism: viewing the world from one's own perspective and not being capable of seeing things from another's perspective.

conservation: recognition that when some properties (such as shape) of an object change, other properties (such as volume) remain constant.

concrete operational stage: Piaget's third stage of cognitive development, which spans ages 6-11, during which the child can perform mental operations—such as reversing—on real objects or events.

formal operational stage: Piaget's final stage of cognitive development, from age 11 or 12 on through adulthood, when formal logic is possible.

theory of mind: ideas and knowledge about how other people's minds work.

preconventional level: the first level in Kohlberg's theory of moral reasoning, focusing on avoiding punishment or maximizing rewards.

conventional level: the second level in Kohlberg's theory of moral reasoning, during which the person values caring, trust, and relationships as well as the social order and lawfulness.

postconventional level: the third level in Kohlberg's theory of moral reasoning, in which the person recognizes universal moral rules that may trump unjust or immoral local rules.

imprinting: the rapid and innate learning of the characteristics of a caregiver very soon after birth.

attachment: the strong emotional connection that develops early in life between infants and their caregivers.

separation anxiety: the distress reaction shown by babies when they are separated from their primary caregiver (typically shown at around 9 months of age).

secure attachment: attachment style characterized by infants who will gradually explore new situations when the caregiver leaves, and they initiate contact when the caregiver returns after separation.

anxious-resistant attachment: attachment style characterized by infants who are ambivalent when separated and reunited.

anxious-avoidant: attachment style characterized by infants who stay calm when their primary caregiver leaves and who ignore and avoid her when she returns.

social referencing: the ability to make use of social and emotional information from another person—especially a caregiver—in an uncertain situation.

emotional competence: the ability to control emotions and know when it is appropriate to express certain emotions.

peers: people who share equal standing or status and are at the same level in terms of age, gender, skill, or power.

adolescence: the transition period between childhood and adulthood

puberty: the period when sexual maturation begins; it marks the beginning of adolescence.

menarche: the first menstrual period.

spermarche: the first ejaculation.

formal operational stage: Piaget's fourth stage of cognitive development. It begins in adolescence and consists of the ability to reason abstractly, scientifically, and philosophically.

dementia: a loss of mental function, in which many cognitive processes are impaired, such as the ability to remember, reason, solve problems, make decisions, and use language.

Alzheimer's disease: a degenerative disease marked by progressive cognitive decline and characterized by a collection of symptoms, including confusion, memory loss, mood swings, and eventual loss of physical function.

temperament: the biologically based tendency to behave in particular ways from very early in life.

generativity: a term Erik Erikson used to describe the process in adulthood of creating new ideas, products, or people.

PRACTICE STUDY QUESTIONS

1. _____ refers to the single cell that results when a sperm fertilizes an egg.
    a. Embryo
    b. Zygote
    c. Spermazota
    d. Myelination

2. The _____ stage of development begins at conception and lasts for two weeks.
    a. germinal
    b. embryonic
    c. zygotic
    d. fetal

3. Vision is the most developed sense for infants.
    a. true
    b. false

4. _____ are substances that can disrupt normal prenatal development and cause lifelong deficits.
    a. Neurotransmitters
    b. Endorphins
    c. Teratogens
    d. Vitamins

5. The _____ stage of cognitive development is characterized by infants learning about the world by using their senses and by moving their bodies in it.
    a. preoperational
    b. sensorimotor
    c. concrete operational
    d. formal operational

6. The _____ stage of cognitive development is characterized the emergence of symbolic thought, or the use of symbols such as words or letters to represent ideas or objects.
    a. preoperational
    b. sensorimotor
    c. concrete operational
    d. formal operational

7. The _____ stage of cognitive development is characterized the ability to use formal logic.
    a. preoperational
    b. sensorimotor
    c. concrete operational
    d. formal operational

8. The _____ stage of cognitive development is characterized by the ability to perform mental operations on real objects and events.
    a. preoperational
    b. sensorimotor
    c. concrete operational
    d. formal operational

9. In the _____ stage of moral reasoning, the individual values caring, trust, and relationships as well as the social order and lawfulness.
    a. postconventional
    b. preconventional
    c. conventional
    d. responsible

10. _____ occurs when a baby shows distress reactions when separated from her caregiver.
    a. Imprinting
    b. Attachment
    c. Separation anxiety
    d. Imprinting

11. The _____ style of attachment is characterized by infants who are ambivalent on separation and reuniting with the caregiver.
    a. secure
    b. anxious-resistant
    c. anxious-ambivalent
    d. anxious-avoidant

12. _____ conducted important studies on contact comfort with baby monkeys.
    a. Ainsworth
    b. Bowlby
    c. Kohlberg
    d. Harlow

13. Hearing rarely decreases as one ages.
    a. true
    b. false

14. _____ is a loss of mental function in which many cognitive processes are impaired, such as the ability to remember, reason, solve problems, and make decisions.
    a. Alzheimer's disease
    b. Dementia
    c. Depression
    d. Old age

15. _____ is the biologically based tendency to behave in particular ways from very early in life.

a. Personality
b. Temperament
c. Genetics
d. Mindfulness

ANSWERS TO PRACTICE STUDY QUESTIONS

1. b
2. a
3. b
4. c
5. b
6. a
7. d
8. c
9. c
10. c
11. b
12. d
13. a
14. b
15. b

Chapter 6
CONCIOUSNESS

KEY TERMS

Consciousness
Wakefulness
Awareness
Minimal consciousness
Coma
Vegetative state
Mindfulness
Attention
Selective attention
Sustained attention
Mediation
Circadian rhythms
Rapid eye movements (REM)
Beta waves
Alpha waves
Non-REM
Theta waves

Delta waves
Insomnia
Sleep apnea
Sleepwalking
Narcolepsy
Hypersomnia
Dreams
Manifest level
Latent level
AIM
Hypnosis
Stroop effect
Psychoactive drugs
Depressants
Stimulants
Hallucinogens
Endocannabinoids

OUTLINE

I. What Is Consciousness? (p. 217)

    A. *Consciousness* is an awareness of one's surroundings (smell, sounds, lights, temperature, etc.) and of what is in one's mind at a given moment.
        1. Many studies have been conducted on consciousness, some of which include focus on sleeping, dreaming, wakefulness, perception, sensation, responsiveness, and awareness.

II. Two Dimensions of Consciousness: Wakefulness and Awareness (p. 218)

    A. *Wakefulness* refers to the degree of alertness, resulting from whether a person is awake or asleep.
    B. *Awareness* refers to monitoring of information from the environment and from one's own thoughts (Brown & Ryan, 2003)
        1. The many variations in consciousness can be thought of a continuum of levels of consciousness between wakefulness and awareness. Figure 6.1 of your text demonstrates this by showing that all states of consciousness exist somewhere in the two dimensional space.

    C. *Minimal consciousness* refers to states when people are barely awake or aware.

D. Coma (when the eyes are closed and a person is unresponsive) is a much more severe and enduring loss of consciousness than fainting.

    1. Coma is generally a result of traumatic brain injury.

    2. The *vegetative state* is another form of minimal consciousness; a person's eyes may be open, but he or she is unresponsive.

        a. New research (Owen, et al., 2006) has shown that a woman, while in a vegetative state, was able to respond to requests made by the researchers by using her brain. Via an fMRI scan, the researchers told her to imagine things, such as playing tennis. That woman's brain areas were activated in the same way as people who are conscious and asked to imagine the same thing.

        b. This situation demonstrates that just because there is no behavioral response, that does not mean that people in vegetative states cannot process information from the outside world.

E. Moderate Consciousness

    1. *The tip-of-the-tongue phenomenon* (Galin, 1994) is the experience of knowing that you know something, like a person's name, but not being able to bring it into awareness. This is an example of *moderate consciousness.*

F. Full Consciousness

    1. One state of full consciousness has been referred to as the *flow* state (Csikszentmihalyi, 1990). Sometimes we are very alert, excited, and stimulated such that we lose track of time; you may feel as though a minute has passed when an hour has passed, or vice versa. This is called *flow.*

    2. Another state of full consciousness is *mindfulness,* which is a heightened awareness of the present moment, which can be applied to events in one's environment and events into one's own mind.

        a. A mindful person may, in general, attend to more stimuli than others. People may develop skills of mindfulness, such as meditation.

III. Attention: Focusing Consciousness (p. 221)

A. Attention is a key aspect of consciousness, it is how we direct the spotlight of awareness.

    1. *Attention* defined: the limited capacity to process information that is under conscious control (Styles, 2006).

    2. *Selective attention* is the ability to focus awareness on specific features in the environment while ignoring others.

        a. The *Cocktail Party Effect* (Moray, 1959) demonstrates selective attention. Your text provides an example of being at a large party and having a conversation with others. Your selective attention is on the conversation as you block out the other discussions going on around you. However, when you hear your name mentioned by people having a different discussion, you attend to that sound and focus on that conversation momentarily.

3. Selective attention creates gaps in attention and perception. *Inattentional blindness* is the phenomenon by which we fail to notice unexpected objects in our surroundings.

Psychology in the Real World: Hazards of Cell Phone–Induced Driver Distraction (p. 224)

A. Researchers have demonstrated the dangers of talking on the phone (both with hand-held and hands-free phones).
    1. Strayer and Drews (2007) conducted several experiments with participants driving in a simulator while either talking on the phone with a hands-free device or not using a cell phone. Those talking on the phone were more likely to miss objects that appeared on the screen while driving.
        a. In a follow-up study, the researchers found that people talking on the phone were less likely to attend to both irrelevant stimuli (e.g., billboards) and relevant safety stimuli (e.g., traffic signs, pedestrians).
    2. Kellar, and Cynkar (in press) conducted a fMRI study of people driving using hands-free devices in a simulator and that showed activity in regions of the brain involved in processing spatial information (the parietal lobe) decreased by 37% when people listened to sentences while driving, whereas activity in areas associated with language processing increased (see Figure 6.5 of your text).
        a. Using a cell phone while driving is similar to drunk driving in that the drivers follow other cars too closely, show slower braking reactions, and have more accidents (Strayer, Drews, & Couch, 2006).

IV. Training Consciousness: Meditation (p. 226)

A. *Mediation* refers to a wide variety of practices that people use to calm the mind, stabilize concentration, focus attention, and enhance awareness of the present moment. Mindfulness meditation techniques encourage attention to the details of momentary experience, such as all the thoughts, feelings, and sensations available at the moment at hand (Baer, 2003).

B. Meditation and Conscious Experience: People with high scores on questionnaires that measure mindfulness have higher scores on measures of well-being and optimism, are more in-tune with their emotional states, and are less self-conscious and anxious.

C. Meditation Training and the Brain: recent studies suggest that meditation training can change the brain, much like weightlifting can change the body.
    1. For example, in one study, researchers randomly assigned business executives to either a control group or an experimental group that received 8 weeks of meditation training. Brain activity was measured with EEG.
    2. People in the meditation group showed significant increases in activity in the left frontal cortex at the end of training and four months later, compared to the control group who received no training. Left frontal cortex activation is associated with positive emotions (Davidson, Ekman, Saron, Senulis & Friesen, 1990; Davisdon, Shackam, & Maxwell, 2004).

V. Sleeping and Dreaming (p. 228)

    A. Sleep and Circadian Rhythms: Sleep occurs in the context of a daily sleep-wake cycle, which follows a pattern known as a circadian rhythm.
        1. *Circadian rhythms* defined: variations in physiological processes that cycle within approximately a 24-hour period.
        2. Our bodies keep time via a particular part of the hypothalamus, the *superchiasmatic nucleus (SCN)* which is our most important biological clock.

    B. Sleep and the Brain: While you sleep your eyes move beneath your eyelids, this is termed *rapid eye movements (REM)*. Our brains are very active while we sleep.
        1. When we are awake our brain activity shows rapid but low-energy waves termed *beta waves;* when we are awake, but relaxed and drowsy our brain activity switches to slower and slightly higher energy waves knows as *alpha waves.*
        2. A second major form of sleep is *non-REM,* which has few eye movements and those that do occur are slow rather than fast. There are four stages of non-REM sleep, each marked by unique brain wave patterns:
            a. Theta waves
            b. Sleep spindles
            c. K-complexes
            d. Delta waves

    C. The Development of Sleep Over the Life Span: Newborns of many species, especially of humans, spend more time in REM sleep than non-REM sleep.
        1. In humans, REM sleep declines rapidly over the life span.
        2. Because newborns spend so much more time in REM sleep that adults has led some researchers to hypothesize the main function of REM sleep is to assist in brain growth and development.

    D. Functions of Sleep: Sleep supports three major restorative processes – neural growth, memory consolidation, and protection against cellular damage.

    E. Sleep Deprivation and Sleep Debt: Recent surveys show the typical adult only gets about 6 hours and 40 minutes of sleep on weekdays and 7 hours and 25 minutes on weekends (National Sleep Foundation, 2008).
        1. Sleep expert William Dement (1999) developed the concept *sleep debt* to mean how much sleep our brains owe our bodies. It is like a monetary debt that must be paid back (e.g., if you miss an hour of sleep one day, you need to pay your body back by sleeping an additional hour).
        2. The most serious and dangerous payback comes in the form of accidents.

    F. Sleep Disorders
        1. *Insomnia* defined: taking more that 20 minutes to fall asleep, having trouble staying asleep, and/or not feeling rested after a night's rest for two or more consecutive weeks (Krystal, 2005).

a. Between 15 to 20% of U.S. adults suffer from insomnia (Pearson, Johnson, & Nahin, 2006).

2. *Sleep apnea* defined: literally means "without breath" and occurs when a person stops breathing for a short amount of time. They seldom fall into REM sleep and, thus, often have insomnia. It is more common in men and in obese people.

3. *Sleepwalking* occurs when a person gets out of bed during sleep, usually during the first third of the sleep cycle, and engages in activities that normally occur during wakefulness, such as walking, eating, dressing, or bathing.

    a. People who sleepwalk are difficult to awaken and do not remember having been up at night after waking in the morning.

4. *Hypersomnia* exists when a person sleeps more than 10 hours a day for two weeks or more. It involves strong urges to nap throughout the day, often at inappropriate times such as during meals or in the middle of a conversation.

G. Dreaming

    1. *Dreams* are the succession of images, thoughts, and feelings we experience while asleep. Most of us dream numerous times each night, yet we rarely recall our dreams upon waking.

        a. Psychoanalytic Theory, according to Freud (1900; 1953), argued that impulses, thoughts, feelings, and drives that threaten the waking mind are released in distorted and disguised form by the sleeping mind. Each dream is an attempt to fulfill unacceptable desires or satisfy unconscious wishes.

            i. Dreams that we consciously recall after waking up is only the surface level, which Freud called the *manifest level.*

            ii. The deeper, unconscious level, where the true meaning of a dream lies, he labeled the *latent level.*

        b. Biological Theory, according to Hobson (2001, 2002), discusses dreams with the AIM theory which stands for three biologically based dimensions of consciousness: Activation, Input, and Mode (see Figure 6.13 of your text).

            i. *Activation* is the dimension that involves the amount of neural activation and ranges from low to high activation.

            ii. *Input* is the extent to which stimulation is internal or external.

            iii. *Mode* consists of a dimension that ranges form logical (wakeful) to loose-illogical (dreaming) states.

        c. Cognitive Theory suggests dreams are not that different from everyday thinking. Researchers have shown that some of the standard processes that we use during our waking life, such as imagery, memory, speech, and problem solving, operate in a similar manner during dreaming (Callavero & Foulkes, 1993; Kahan, 2001).

            i. Some people develop the ability to know when they are dreaming (termed *lucid dreaming*) and they can control the events and outcomes of their dreams (LaBerge, 1985).

VI. Hypnosis (p. 238)

    A. *Hypnosis* is a state of mind that occurs in compliance with instructions and is characterized by focused attention, suggestibility, absorption, lack of voluntary control over behavior, and suspension of critical faculties of mind (Raz & Shapiro, 2002; Stewart, 2005).

        1. People vary considerably in the degree to which they can be hypnotized, largely because we are not all equally suggestible.

Breaking New Ground: The Cognitive Neuroscience of Hypnosis (p. 239)

    A. Some theorists consider hypnosis to be a state in which one part of the brain operates independently, a second theory maintains that hypnosis does not alter consciousness, nor do hypnotized individuals give up control of their behavior. Instead, they behave in ways they think a hypnotized person would behave (i.e., they are role-playing).

    B. Neuroscientist Amir Raz and his colleagues (Raz, Fan, & Posner, 2005) studied whether hypnosis might help eliminate the Stroop effect. The Stroop task tests visual selective attention; it measures how people deal with conflicting verbal and color information. In a typical Stroop task, participants view words such as *green, red* or *blue* printed in different colors and must name the color in which the word is printed. People are slower to identify the color of words that are printed in a different color from those that are printed in the same color. The delay in reaction time caused by the mismatched words is known as the Stroop effect (Stroop, 1935).

        a. Sixteen participants (eight highly hypnotizable and eight less hypnotizable) were told, while hypnotized, instructions on a Stroop task that they would perform a few days later in a fMRI scanner. They were also told that during the test they would see gibberish words in different colors and they would have the simple task of pushing a button corresponding to the actual color of the letters.

        b. Highly hypnotizable people who received the "gibberish" suggestion identified the colors faster than the less hypnotizable people who received the same suggestion.

        c. Brain scans during the Stroop task showed that highly hypnotizable people had turned off the areas of the brain that normally process the meaning of words, so these areas did not interfere with color recognition.

    C. Other researchers conducted a series of brain imaging studies comparing perceptions of hypnotically induced pain, physically induced pain, and imagined pain (Derbyshire, Whalley, Stenger, & Oakley, 2004; Raij, Narvanen, Hiltunee, & Hari, 2005).

        a. All participants were highly hypnotizable. Researchers induced real pain by touching participants' skin with a hot metal rod, activating a well-known pain brain circuit. They contrasted this pattern of activation with that of participants who imagined pain. (The imagined pain did not activate the same brain areas). However, hypnotically induced pain did activate the same brain circuit as the real pain did.

b. Participants reported actually feeling pain for both the real and hypnotically induced pain, but not for the imagined pain. Hypnotic pain is not just an imitation of the real thing. That is, it is more like real pain.

D. The study of hypnotically induced pain contradicts the view of hypnosis as role-playing, and the Stroop test study shows that hypnosis can enable some people to override automatic processes. The possibility of using suggestion to de-program automatic behaviors offers promise for the treatment of problematic behavior that has become automatic, such as substance abuse and eating disorders.

VII. Altering Consciousness with Drugs (p. 241)

A. *Psychoactive drugs* are naturally occurring or synthesized substances that, when ingested or otherwise taken into the body, reliably produce qualitative changes in conscious experience.

1. The use of psychoactive drugs among humans is ubiquitous. People use such drugs for a variety of reasons, including: aiding in spiritual practice, improving health, exploring the self, regulating mood, escaping boredom and despair, enhancing sensory experience, stimulating artistic creative and performance, and promoting social interactions (Weil & Rosen, 1998).

B. *Physical dependence* occurs when the use of the drug is necessary to maintain normal function and to cope with the challenges of daily life.

1. Repeated use of the drug can lead to *tolerance* which means that more of the drug is needed to produce the same effect.

2. *Withdrawal symptoms* refer to the effects a person experiences when he or she stops using the drug once they have become physically dependent.

3. *Psychological dependence* occurs when people compulsively use a substance for various reasons, such as to alleviate boredom, to regulate mood, or to cope with the challenges of daily live.

C. Depressants: decrease or slow down central nervous system activity. Alcohol, sedatives, and opioids are all depressants.

1. Low doses of these drugs calm the body and mind; high doses can slow heart rate and brain activity to dangerously low levels.

D. Alcohol: is the most widely used depressant.

1. The absorption of alcohol depends on several factors including the presence of food in the stomach and the body mass of a person.

2. Heavy drinking (five drinks per day) over time leads to fat accumulation and blocked blood flow in the liver, which ultimately results in the inability of the liver to function. Chronic alcoholism is one of the most common causes of

cirrhosis, the accumulation of non-functional scar tissue in the liver, an irreversible and eventually fatal condition.

3. With long periods of heavy drinking the brain actually shrinks.

E. Sedatives: create a feeling of stupor similar to that of alcohol intoxication.

    1. Barbiturates and benzodiazepines (which are prescription medications) slow heart rate, relax skeletal muscles, and tranquilize the mind.

F. Opioids: applied to all drugs derived from opium or chemicals similar to opium. Morphine, heroin, codeine and hydrocodone (Vicodin®) are all opioids.

    1. Opioids depress central nervous system activity, slowing heart rate, respiration, digestion, and suppressing the cough center.

    2. Opioids have been used for centuries as pain relievers.

G. Stimulants: activate the nervous system. Two of the most widely used stimulants are caffeine and nicotine.

    1. *Caffeine* is the world's most commonly used psychoactive drug, ingested by 90% of North American adults on a daily basis (Lovett, 2005).

    2. Mild to moderate use produces effects such as increased alertness, increased heart rate, loss of motor coordination, insomnia, and nervousness. Discontinuation of regular caffeine use produces withdrawal symptoms such as headache. This demonstrates physical dependence on the drug.

H. Nicotine: is the active drug in tobacco.

    1. Tobacco is used worldwide. In 2006, approximately 21% (45.1 million) American adults smoked cigarettes regularly (Centers for Disease Control and Prevention, 2006).

    2. Nicotine increases heart rate and rate of respiration. Over time, the cardiovascular arousal associated with nicotine use increases the risk of high blood pressure and heart disease.

    3. Cigarette smoking reduces life expectancy on average by 10 years, increases the risk of lung cancer more than 10-fold, and triples the risk of death from heart disease in both men and women (CDC, 2001; Doll, Peto, Boreham, & Sutherland, 2004).

I. Cocaine: derived from the Coca leaf and is a powerful stimulant that produces feelings of invulnerability and power.

    1. It is a somewhat short-acting drug, which helps explain why people abuse it. The euphoria they experience is short lasting so they administer more of the drug to maintain the pleasurable effects.

    2. Cocaine can be smoked, snorted, and injected and it can increase heart rate, produce irregular heart beat, and result in death from heart attack.

J. Amphetamines: synthetically produced compounds that produce long-lasting excitation of the sympathetic nervous system. Three main forms of amphetamines are:

methamphetamine (meth, crystal meth), dextroamphetamine (Dexedrine®), and amphetamine sulphate (Benzedrine® or "speed").

    1. Two common uses of amphetamines for medicinal purposes are appetite suppression and the treatment of symptoms associated with attention deficit hyperactivity disorder.

    2. Some effects of these drugs include: increased heart rate, increased motivation, and excited mood; some short-term effects include insomnia, stomach distress, headaches, decreased libido, and difficulty concentrating.

K. Ecstasy: (MDMA) is both a stimulant and a hallucinogen and it produces mild sensory hallucinations and physiological arousal. It has been called the "love drug" due to its effects of increasing feelings of affection and the desire to touch and hug.

    1. Negative effects of MDMA use include increased risk of depression with repeated use, slower processing times on cognitive tasks, and greater impulsivity (Halpern et al., 2004).

    2. Long-term effects include persistent mental deficits, low mood, and serotonin deficiencies in certain areas of the brain (Thomasius et al., 2006).

L. Hallucinogens: create distorted perceptions of reality ranging from mild to extreme; they alter thought and mood.

    1. Marijuana: comes from the blossoms and leaves of the *Cannabis sativa* plant. Tetrahydrocannibinol (THC) is the active ingredient that affects the brain and body when people smoke or eat it.

    2. Marijuana is not addictive in the physiological sense; it does not lead to physical dependence and withdrawal symptoms like nicotine and heroin. However, people can become psychologically addicted to it.

    3. A recent large-scale study found no increased risk of lung cancer among heavy marijuana smokers compared to non-smokers, but researchers need to conduct more research on this topic (Tashkin, 2006).

    4. Contrary to government reports that marijuana has no medical value, marijuana and endocanabinoids offer promise for medical treatment of various physical and psychological disorders (Editors, 2004; Nicoll & Alger, 2004).

M. Lysergic acid diethylamide-25 (LSD): "acid" is a synthesized form of lysergic acid that is derived from the grain fungus, ergot. Dramatic changes in conscious experience occur with use of this drug.

    1. People experience altered visual perceptions (e.g., tracers), enhanced color perception, hallucinations, and synethesia (when one "sees" sounds or "hears" colors or visual images).

    2. Side effects of LSD include increased body temperature, increased blood pressure, insomnia, and psychosis-like symptoms in some people. Although some people experience "bad trips" others report the opposite and state that the drug produced very profound, life-altering experiences (Strassman, 1984, Weil & Rosen, 1998).

Making Connections: Can Experience Change the Brain? (p. 250)

A. Brain injury and consciousness are linked. Those with damage to the lower regions of the brain that control the basic bodily functions (e.g., sleep-wake cycles) are less likely to regain consciousness than those who sustain damage to the cerebral cortex (Laureys, 2007).

    1. Brain injury can result in distractibility that may due to problems with selective attention.

    2. Other aspects of consciousness, such as sleeping and dreaming, change with brain injury as well. It can also lead to disruptions in dreaming, probably as a consequence of disordered sleep.

GLOSSARY TERMS

consciousness: an awareness of one's surroundings and of what's in one's mind at a given moment; includes aspects of being awake and aware.

wakefulness: aspect of consciousness that is the degree of alertness, resulting from whether a person is awake or asleep.

awareness: aspect of consciousness that is the monitoring of information from the environment and from one's own thoughts.

minimal consciousness: states or phases of consciousness when people are barely awake or aware.

coma: a state of consciousness in which the eyes are closed and the person is unresponsive and unarousable; a much more severe and longer-lasting loss of consciousness than fainting.

vegetative state: a state of minimal consciousness in which the eyes might be open, but the person is otherwise unresponsive.

mindfulness: a heightened awareness of the present moment, whether of events in one's environment and in one's own mind.

attention: the limited capacity to process information that is under conscious control.

selective attention: the ability to focus awareness on specific features in the environment while ignoring others.

sustained attention: the ability to maintain focused awareness on a target or idea.

meditation: practices that people use to calm the mind, stabilize concentration, focus attention, and enhance awareness of the present moment.

circadian rhythms: the variations in physiological processes that cycle within approximately a 24-hour period, including the sleep-wake cycle.

rapid eye movements (REM): quick movements of the eye that occur during sleep, thought to mark phases of dreaming.

beta waves: pattern of brain activity when one is awake; a rapid, low-energy wave.

alpha waves: pattern of brain activity when one is relaxed and drowsy; slower, higher-energy waves than beta waves.

non-REM: form of sleep with few eye movements, which are slow rather than fast.

theta waves: pattern of brain activity during Stage 1 sleep; slower, lower-energy waves than alpha waves.

delta waves: type of brain activity that dominates Stage 2 sleep; higher energy than theta waves.

insomnia: a sleep difficulty characterized by difficulty falling and staying asleep, as well as not feeling resting.

sleep apnea: a slow difficulty that results from temporary blockage of the air passage.

sleepwalking: sleep difficulty characterized by activities occurring during non-REM sleep that usually occur when one is awake, such as walking and eating.

narcolepsy: sleep disorder characterized by excessive daytime sleepiness and weakness in facial and limb muscles.

hypersomnia: sleep difficulty characterized by sleeping more than 10 hours a day for 2 weeks or more; includes urge to nap during inappropriate times.

dreams: images, thoughts, and feelings experienced during sleep.

manifest level: Freud's surface level of dreams, recalled upon waking.

latent level: Freud's unconscious level of dreams; their meaning is found at this level.

AIM: three biologically based dimensions of consciousness—Activation, Input, and Mode.

hypnosis: state characterized by focused attention, suggestibility, absorption, lack of voluntary control over behavior, and suspension of critical faculties; occurs when instructed by someone trained in hypnosis; may be therapeutic.

Stroop effect: delay in reaction time when color of words on a test and their meaning differ.

psychoactive drugs: naturally occurring or synthesized substances that, when ingested or otherwise taken into the body, reliably produce qualitative changes in conscious experience.

depressants: substances that decrease or slow down central nervous system activity.

stimulants: substances that activate the nervous system.

hallucinogens: substances that create distorted perceptions of reality ranging from mild to extreme.

endocannabinoids: natural, marijuana-like substances produced by the body.

PRACTICE STUDY QUESTIONS

1. _____ is the ability to focus awareness on specific features in the environment while ignoring others.
   a. Consciousness
   b. Mindfulness
   c. Selective attention
   d. Minimal consciousness

2. Studies have shown that people talking on cell phones are similar to drunk drivers in that they follow cars too closely, have slower braking reaction times, and are in more accidents.
   a. true
   b. false

3. Some people can train themselves to be conscious during their dreams and can change the content and outcome of their dreams. This is referred to as:
   a. non-REM dreaming.
   b. hallucinating.
   c. K-complexes.
   d. lucid dreaming.

4. _____ is when one takes longer than 20 minutes to all asleep, has trouble staying asleep, or not feeling rested after a night's sleep for two or more consecutive weeks.
   a. Sleep apnea
   b. Insomnia
   c. Hypersomnia
   d. Circadian rhythm

5. _____ is a state of mind that occurs in compliance with instructions and is characterized by focused attention, suggestibility, absorption, lack of voluntary control over behavior, and suspension of critical faculties of mind.
   a. Hallucinations
   b. Dreaming
   c. Hypnosis
   d. Meditation

6. In a study discussed in your text, people who were hypnotically induced to pain had the same activation of the brain as people who were physically induced to pain.
   a. true
   b. false

7. Excessive drinking can shrink the brain.
   a. true
   b. false

8. When a person stops taking a drug and experiences withdrawal symptoms, that person is _____ dependent on the drug.
   a. physically
   b. psychologically
   c. both a or b could be correct
   d. neither a nor b are correct

9. Which of the following drugs does not belong with the others?
   a. alcohol
   b. diazepam
   c. pentobarbital
   d. MDMA

10. Morphine, heroin, codeine, and hydrocodone are all:
    a. stimulants.
    b. hallucinogens.
    c. opioids.
    d. None of the above

11. Which drug class produces increased heart rate, feelings of arousal, increased alertness, and concentration?
    a. depressants

b. stimulants

c. hallucinogens

d. opioids

12. This drug has both hallucinogenic and stimulant properties.

    a. MDMA

    b. alcohol

    c. heroin

    d. marijuana

13. Despite government reports, marijuana does have medicinal effects.

    a. true

    b. false

14. Marijuana is not _____ addictive; but it can be _____ addictive.

    a. psychologically; physically

    b. scientifically; metaphysically

    c. metaphysically, scientifically

    d. physically; psychologically

15. _____ is when people can "see" sounds or "hear" colors or visual images.

    a. Synethesia

    b. Mindfulness

    c. Brain injury

    d. It is not possible to "see" sounds or "hear" colors or visual images.

ANSWERS TO PRACTICE STUDY QUESTIONS

1. c
2. a
3. d
4. b
5. c
6. a
7. a
8. c
9. d
10. c
11. b
12. a
13. a
14. d
15. a

Chapter 7
MEMORY

KEY TERMS

Memory
Three-stage model of memory
Sensory memory
Short-term memory
Long-term memory
Working memory
Chunking
Rehearsal
Serial-position effect
Implicit memory
Procedural memory
Priming
Explicit memory
Semantic memory
Episodic memory
Encoding
Automatic processing
Effortful processing
Levels of processing
Mnemonic device
Consolidation
Storage

Hierarchies
Schemas
Retrieval
Long-term potentiation
Interference
Retroactive interference
Proactive interference
Forgetting
Transience
Forgetting curve
Absent-mindedness
Blocking
Repression
Misattribution
Consistency bias
Persistence
Suggestibility
False memories
Recovered memory
Amnesia
Anterograde amnesia
Retrograde amnesia

OUTLINE

I. Memory: without memory we would forever be stuck in the present, unable to learn anything or to adapt to a changing environment. The ability to remember not only makes us who we are, but it is also the foundation of intelligence, learning, and thought.

    A. Researchers agree on at least three attributes of memory:
        1. There are three types of memory (sensory, short-term, and long-term) that last for different amounts of time.
        2. Different memory systems involve different areas of the brain.
        3. We reconstruct memories from our past experiences, rather than possess accurate images of what has happened. Many psychological factors affect this reconstructive process.

II. Three Types of Memory (p. 257)

    A. The case of H. M. was the first to document evidence that there are distinct kinds of memory that operate. After doctors removed the hippocampus on both sides of

H.M.'s brain and the adjoining brain structures, H.M. lost the ability to form new memories. He lived forever in the present, but retained memories prior to the surgery.

   1. *Memory* is the ability to store and use information. It does not need to be a conscious recollection.

B. The *three-stage model of memory* classifies three types of memories based on how long they last: sensory memory, short-term memory, and long-term memory (Atkinson & Shiffrin, 1971).

   1. *Sensory memory* holds information in its original sensory form for a very brief period of time, usually about half a second or less.
   2. *Short-term memory* temporarily stores a limited amount of information before it is either transferred to long-term storage or forgotten. Information in this stage lasts for about 2 to 30 seconds.
   3. *Long-term memory* has the capacity to store a vast amount of information for as little as 30 seconds and as long as a lifetime.

C. Sensory memory

   1. Interacting with the world stimulates our sensory systems: taste, smell, sound, touch, and sight. Sensory memory is the brief traces of sensation left by the firing of neurons in the brain.
   2. Seeing (iconic) and hearing (echoic) are two important sources of sensory information for humans. As such, these have received the most attention from scientists researching memory.
      a. *Iconic memory* is a brief visual record left on the retina of the eye.
      b. *Echoic memory* is short-term memory of sounds.

D. Short-term or working memory are used interchangeably. *Short-term memory* emphasizes the duration of this type of memory, whereas the phrase *working memory* emphasizes its function.

   1. Working memories can be transferred to long-term memory if they are practiced, otherwise they are lost.

E. Short-term Memory Capacity for most people is between five and nine items or units (often referred to: 7 ± 2).

   1. *Chunking* is a process whereby one transforms what she wants to remember into a smaller set of meaningful units or chunks (Thompson & Madigan, 2005).

F. How Working Memory Works

   1. Alan Baddeley (2003, 2007) suggested that working memory consists of three distinct processes: (a) *attending* to a stimulus, (b) *storing* information about the stimulus, and (c) *rehearsing* the stored process to help solve a problem.
      a. This process is supported by three temporary storage systems:
         i. One for sounds and language—*phonological*
         ii. One for images and spatial relations—*visualspatial*

iii. One that connects the two storages systems, interacts with long-term memory and provides a temporary storage for specific events—*episodic buffer.*

2. The *central executive* decides where to focus attention and selectively focuses on specific aspects of a stimulus.

3. The three storage systems each require rehearsal if the information is to be remembered for any length of time.

a. *Rehearsal* is the process of reciting or practicing material repeatedly.

G. The *Serial Position Effect*: refers to the phenomenon of short-term memory in which people recall items at the beginning and end of a list and tend to forget the items in the middle (Calkins, 1898; Madigan & O'Hara, 1992).

1. The tendency to recall items at the beginning of a list is referred to as the *primacy effect;* whereas the tendency to recall items at the end of a list is referred to as the *recency effect* (see Figure 7.3 of your text for an illustration).

H. Long-term memory is the most complex form of memory and there are two distinct kinds of and four distinct stages of processing.

1. *Implicit memory* is also known as nondeclarative memory, because we cannot directly recall this type of memory. Like riding a bike, we *know how to do it* but it is more difficult to describe how we do it. Implicit memory includes procedural memory, priming, and learning.

a. *Procedural memory* includes knowledge for almost any behavior or physical skill we learn (e.g., playing guitar, knitting, playing hockey, making fondue, etc.).

b. *Priming* is a kind of implicit memory that occurs when recall is improved by prior exposure to the same or similar stimuli.

2. *Explicit memory* is the conscious recall of facts and events. There are two distinct types of explicit memory: semantic and episodic.

a. *Semantic memory* is our memory for facts and knowledge, such as what we learn in school.

b. *Episodic memory* is our memory for the experiences we have had (episodic memories are more personal than semantic memories).

I. Stages in Long-Term Memory: For sensory input to make the transition from sensory memory to short-term memory and then to long-term memory, it must go through four processing stages: *encoding, consolidation, storage,* and *retrieval.*

1. *Encoding* is the process of attending to, taking in, and processing new information by the brain. It is a crucial phase for storage in long-term memory.

a. *Automatic processing* happens with little effort or conscious attention to the task.

b. *Effortful processing* occurs when we carefully attend to and put conscious effort into remembering information.

c. *Levels of processing* suggests that the more deeply people encode information, the better they will recall it. There are three different levels of processing (Craik & Tulving, 1975; Hyde & Jenkins, 1973).

　　　　i. structural processing—the shallowest level
　　　　ii. phonemic processing—mid-level
　　　　iii. phonemic processing—the deepest level
　　d. *Mnemonic device* is a scheme that helps people remember information. Rhyming, chunking, and rehearsal are different types of mnemonic devices.
2. *Consolidation* is the process of establishing, stabilizing, or solidifying a memory (Kandel, 2006; McGaugh, 2000).
3. *Storage* is the retention of memory over time. There are three distinct ways of organizing and storing memories: hierarchies, schemas, and networks.
　　a. *Hierarchies* are used to organize related information from the most specific feature they have in common to the most general.
　　b. *Schemas* are ways of knowing that we develop from our experiences with particular objects or events. They are organized patterns of thoughts, behavior, or some aspect of the world.
　　c. Connectionist models use networks to explain how memory works.
4. *Retrieval* is the recovery of information stored in memory.

J. The Sensory Cortexes: sensory neurons carry information about external stimuli from our sense organs to different parts of the brain. The sensations first travel to the thalamus, which then relays the sensory information to the cerebral cortex for further processing.
　　1. The visual cortex is located in the occipital lobes.
　　2. The auditory cortex is located in the temporal lobes.
　　3. The somatosensory (touch) is located in the parietal lobes.

K. Pathways for Short-Term Memory: The encoding stage of memory formation activates the prefrontal cortex as well as the hippocampus, where memory is consolidated through rehearsal and repetition (Fields, 2005; Kandel et al., 2000).

L. Long-Term Memory Storage in the Cortex: We store different types of long-term memory in different places in the brain.
　　1. *Explicit memories* are stored in the cortex, specifically in the area where the original sensation was processed (Ji & Wilson, 2007).
　　2. *Implicit memories* are stored in structures in the subcortex, specifically in the striatum, amygdala, and cerebellum (Kandel, 2006).

M. Emotion, Memory, and the Brain: Emotional events turn on genes that build proteins that solidify the synaptic connections between neurons. These proteins also stimulate the formation of new synapses and even new neurons (Kandel, 2006). All of these structures make the memory "stick" for long periods of time.

　　a. The amygdala and hippocampus are important structures for memory.

Breaking New Ground: The Remembering Brain (p. 276)

A. Donald Hebb (1949) purposed a biological basis for learning and memory. He theorized that when the synapse of one neuron fires and excites another neuron, there is permanent change in the receiving neuron, the excitatory neuron, or both, which strengthens the synaptic connection.

1. *Long-term potentiation (LTP)* is the process of strengthening the synaptic connection (Malenka & Nicoll, 1999). When synapses fire more readily, learning becomes easier and more efficient.

2. Hebb suggested that the repeated stimulation of a group of neurons leads to the formation of cell assemblies, or networks of nerve cells that persist even after stimulation has stopped.

    a. Remember: *Neurons that fire together, wire together.*

    b. Also appropriate for this description is: *Use it or lose it.*

    c. Hebb's student, Brenda Milner, reported clinical observations of H. M. and suspected a link between the hippocampus and memory formation.

B. Kandel conducted studies with a simple organism, the sea slug, to study the biological basis of memory and learning. He administered shock to the sea slug one time and the slug's defensive response lasted about 10 minutes. After repeatedly administering shock in close succession, the slug gave the same response days later.

1. The slug demonstrated conversion of short-term memory to long-term memory in regard to the shock administrations.

2. Kandel suggested that "practice makes perfect" even in simple snails.

3. Kandel found the link that Hebb have proposed in his model and won the 2000 Nobel Prize in Physiology and Medicine.

III. Forgetting and Memory Loss: In the process of remembering we select, distort, bias, and forget events. (p. 279)

A. *Interference* is one reason why we forget; it occurs because of other information competes with the information we are trying to recall.

1. *Retroactive interference* defined: occurs when new experiences or information cause people to forget previously learned experiences or information.

2. *Proactive interference* defined: occurs when previously learned information interferes with the learning of new information.

Psychology in the Real World: Memory in a Pill (p. 280)

A. There are many pharmaceutical companies attempting to develop pills to aid in the treatment of Alzheimer's disease. The FDA has approved two such drugs: Aricept® and Reminyl®.

B. There is moderate clinical support for the herbal preparation of ground up leaves of the ginkgo biloba tree in the treatment of mild to moderate Alzheimer's disease.

B. Sins of Omission: The Act of Forgetting

      1. Herman Ebbinghaus began studying forgetting in the 1880s. He described the fact that recall shows a steady decline over time and the term *forgetting curve* is used to depict this change.

      2. Forgetting is a natural part of the aging process, but education seems to have a positive effect on age-related decline.

C. The Seven Sins of Memory: Written by Daniel Schacter (2001), this book summarizes the imperfections of memory.

      1. The first three imperfections are errors of omission because they are failures of recall. These errors are: *transience, absent-mindedness*, and *blocking*.

          a. *Transience* refers to the fleeting nature of some memories.

          b. *Absent-mindedness* is a form of forgetfulness that involves attention and memory. Divided attention is like to lead to this sin of omission.

          c. *Blocking* is the inability to retrieve some information that we once stored (e.g., a classmates name, name of a movie).

              i. The *tip-of-the-tongue* phenomenon is an example of blocking.

              ii. *Repression* in another form of blocking in which retrieval of memories that have been encoded and stored is actively inhibited.

      2. The last four imperfections are errors of commission, which occur when we recall distorted, incorrect, or unwanted memories and they are called: *misattribution, bias, persistence,* and *suggestibility.*

          a. *Misattribution* occurs when we wrongly believe the memory came from one source, when in fact, it came from another.

          b. *Consistency bias* is the selective recall of past events to fit our currents beliefs.

          c. *Persistence* is the repeated recall of pleasant or unpleasant experiences even when we actively try to forget them.

          d. *Suggestibility* occurs when memories are implanted in our minds based on leading questions, comments, or suggestions by someone else or some other source.

              i. *False memories* are memories for events that never happened, but were suggested by someone or something.

              ii. *Recovered memories* are supposedly from a real event, that were encoded and stored and were not retrieved for a long period of time but then are retrieved after some later event brings them suddenly to consciousness.

D. Memory Loss Caused by Brain Injury and Disease

      1. When people forget due to injury or disease to the brain it is termed *amnesia.*

          a. *Anterograde amnesia* is the inability to remember events and experiences that occur *after* an injury or onset of a disease.

          b. *Retrograde amnesia* is an inability to recall events or experiences that happened *before* the onset of injury or disease.

Making Connections: Memory and How to Study (p. 287)

A. Students often look for ways in which they can improve their learning and memory after being exposed to the material in a General Psychology course. To master complex new material, it may be beneficial to develop new strategies such as those that follow:
1. Go to class and pay attention.
2. Read the book before class.
3. Study deep not shallow.
4. Form a study group.
5. Devise meaningful mnemonics.

GLOSSARY TERMS

memory: the ability to store and use information; also, the store of what has been learned and remembered, no necessarily conscious.

three-stage model of memory: classification of memories based on duration as sensory, short-term, and long-term memories.

sensory memory: the part of memory that holds information in its original sensory form for a very brief period of time, usually about a half a second or less.

short-term memory: the part of memory that temporarily (for 2 to 30 seconds) stores a limited amount of information before it is either transferred to long-term storage or forgotten.

long-term memory: the part of memory that has the capacity to store a vast amount of information for as little as 30 seconds and as long as a lifetime.

working memory: the part of memory required to attend to and solve a problem at hand; often used interchangeably with *short-term memory.*

chunking: the process of breaking down a list of to-be-remembered items into a smaller set of meaningful units.

rehearsal: the process of repeatedly practicing material so that it enters into long-term memory.

serial-position effect: the tendency to have better recall for items in a list according to their position in the list.

implicit memory: kind of memory made up of knowledge based on previous experience, such as skills that we perform automatically once we have mastered them; resides outside conscious awareness.

procedural memory: kind of memory made up of implicit knowledge for almost any behavior or physical skill we have learned.

priming: a kind of implicit memory that arises when recall is improved by earlier exposure to the same or similar stimuli.

explicit memory: knowledge that consists of the conscious recall of facts and events; also known as declarative memory.

semantic memory: form of memory that recalls facts and general knowledge, such as what we learn in school.

episodic memory: form of memory that recalls the experiences we have had.

encoding: the process by which the brain attends to, takes in, and integrates new information; the first stage of long-term memory formation.

automatic processing: encoding of information that occurs with little effort or conscious attention to the task.

effortful processing: encoding of information that occurs with careful attention and conscious effort.

levels of processing: the concept that the more deeply people encode information, the better they will recall it.

Mnemonic device: a method devised to help remember information, such as a rhyme or acronym.

consolidation: the process of establishing, stabilizing, or solidifying a memory; the second stage of long-term memory formation..

storage: the retention of memory over time; the third stage of long-term memory formation.

hierarchies: a way of organizing related pieces of information from the most specific feature they have in common to the most general.

schemas: mental frameworks that develop from our experiences with particular people, objects, or events.

retrieval: the recovery of information stored in memory; the fourth stage of long-term memory.

long-term potentiation: strengthening of a synaptic connection that results when a synapse of one neuron repeatedly fires and excites another neuron, there is a permanent change in the receiving neuron, the excitatory neuron, or both.

interference: disruption of memory because other information competes with the information we are trying to recall.

retroactive interference: disruption of memory because new experiences or information cause people to forget previously learned experiences or information.

proactive interference: disruption of memory because previously learned information interferes with the learning of new information.

forgetting: the weakening or loss of memories over time.

transience: most common type of forgetfulness due to the fleeting nature of some memories.

forgetting curve: a graphic depiction of how recall steadily declines over time.

absent-mindedness: a form of forgetfulness that results from inattention.

blocking: the inability to retrieve some information once it is stored.

repression: a form of blocking in which retrieval of memories that have been encoded and stored is actively inhibited.

misattribution: belief that a memory came from one source when it fact it came from another.

consistency bias: selective recall of past events to fit our current beliefs.

persistence: the repeated recall of pleasant or unpleasant experiences even when we actively try to forget them.

suggestibility: problem with memory that occurs when memories are implanted in our minds based on leading questions, comments, or suggestions by someone else or some other source.

false memories: memories for events that never happened, but were suggested by someone or something.

recovered memory: a memory from a real event that was encoded, stored, but not retrieved for a long period of time; it is retrieved after some later event brings it suddenly to consciousness.

amnesia: memory loss due to injury or disease to the brain.

anterograde amnesia: the inability to remember events and experiences that occur after an injury or the onset of a disease.

retrograde amnesia: an inability to recall events or experiences that happened before the onset of the disease or injury.

PRACTICE STUDY QUESTIONS

1.   _____ memory is the trace memory for visual sensation; whereas _____ memory is the memory for short-term retention of sounds.
   a.   Echoic; iconic
   b.   Occipital cortex; auditory cortex
   c.   Iconic; echoic
   d.   Auditory cortex; occipital cortex.

2.   The _____ refers to the phenomenon that people are more likely to remember items at the beginning and end of a list, rather than items in the middle.
   a.   retrograde amnesia
   b.   anterograde amnesia
   c.   primacy effect
   d.   serial position effect

3.   Which of the following is NOT one of four stages of long-term memory?
   a.   consolidation
   b.   storage
   c.   encoding
   d.   repression

4.   _____ is the recall of stored information from long-term memory.
   a.   Encoding
   b.   Retrieval
   c.   Consolidation
   d.   Storage

5.   The hippocampus and the amygdala are important brain structures involved in memory.
   a.   true
   b.   false

6.   When it comes to the function of your brain, the term "Use it or lose it" is scientifically demonstrated.
   a.   true
   b.   false

7.   _____ was the first person to study memory and forgetting and developed the forgetting curve.
   a.   Ebbinghaus
   b.   Hebb
   c.   Kandel
   d.   Schacter

8.   _____ amnesia occurs when an individual cannot remember things that occurred before brain injury or disease; whereas _____ amnesia occurs when an individual cannot remember things that happened after brain injury or disease.
   a.   Primacy; recency
   b.   Recency; primacy
   c.   Anterograde; retrograde
   d.   Retrograde; anterograde

9.   _____ memories are memories for events that never happened, but were suggested by someone or something.
   a.   Sensory
   b.   Repressed
   c.   False
   d.   Recovered

10.   The visual cortex is located in the _____ lobes; whereas the auditory cortex is located in the _____ lobes.
   a.   cerebral; parietal
   b.   parietal; cerebral
   c.   temporal; occipital
   d.   occipital; temporal

11.   _____ are ways of knowing that we develop from our experiences with particular objects or events.
   a.   Mnemonic devices
   b.   Schemas
   c.   Hierarchies
   d.   ESP

12.   _____ memory includes knowledge for almost any behavior or skill we learn, such as playing electric guitar or knitting.
   a.   Implicit
   b.   Explicit
   c.   Semantic
   d.   Procedural

13.   _____ is our memory for facts and knowledge, such as math equations or state capitals.
   a.   Episodic
   b.   Semantic
   c.   Procedural
   d.   Explicit

14.   _____ memory is the conscious recall of facts and events.
   a.   Episodic
   b.   Semantic
   c.   Procedural

d. Explicit

15. _____ memory is the part of memory required to attend to and solve a problem at hand.
a. Episodic
b. Semantic
c. Procedural
d. Working

ANSWERS TO PRACTICE STUDY QUESTIONS

1. c
2. d
3. d
4. b
5. a
6. a
7. a
8. d
9. c
10. d
11. b
12. d
13. b
14. d
15. d

Chapter 8
LEARNING

KEY TERMS

Learning
Association
Conditioning
Classical conditioning
Unconditioned response (UR)
Unconditioned stimulus (US)
Conditioned stimulus (CS)
Conditioned response (CR)
Stimulus generalization
Stimulus discrimination
Extinction
Spontaneous recovery
Law of effect
Operant conditioning
Reinforcer
Primary Reinforcers
Secondary (or conditioned) reinforcers
Positive reinforcement
Negative reinforcement
Punishment
Positive punishment

Negative punishment
Skinner box
Shaping
Continuous reinforcement
Intermittent reinforcement
Schedules of reinforcement
Fixed ratio (FR) schedule
Variable ratio (VR) schedule
Fixed interval (FI) schedule
Variable interval (VI) schedule
Instinctive drift
Biological constraint model
Latent learning
Conditioned taste aversion
Observational learning
Social learning theory
Modeling
Imprinting
Ethology
Behavior modification

OUTLINE

I. Basic Processes of Learning (p. 295)

    A. *Learning* defined: enduring changes in behavior that occur with experience.
        1. Learning and memory work together. Without learning and memory we could not process, retain, or make sense of new information.
        2. Learning occurs when information moves from short-term to long-term memory.

II. Habituation and the Orienting Response

    A. *Orienting response* defined: an automatic shift of attention toward a new stimulus.

    B. *Habituation* defined: a sensory process by which organisms adapt to constant stimulation.
        1. An example of an orienting response and habituation: When the heater turns on in your apartment you hear the click of the furnace to which you then *orient* your attention to that sound; soon thereafter you *habituate* to the sound of the furnace.

C. *Association* occurs when one piece of information from the environment becomes linked repeatedly with another and the organism begins to connect the two sources of information.

    1. An example of an association: Whenever Tommy hears the garage door open in the evening his father enters the house shortly thereafter. This happens repeatedly. Now, when Tommy hears the garage door open he says "Daddy!" even before his father enters. He has *associated* the sound of the garage door opening with his father entering the house.

    2. Learning by association typically occurs by chance.

III. Conditioning Models of Learning (p. 296)

A. *Conditioning* defined: a form of associative learning in which a behavior becomes more likely as a function of a link between that behavior and certain events in one's environment.

B. There are two types of conditioning in psychology: *classical* and *operant*. Both are forms of associative learning.

IV. Classical Conditioning

A. *Classical conditioning* occurs when a neutral stimulus becomes associated with a stimulus to which one has an automatic, inborn response (i.e., a reflex, such as eye blinks when a puff of air strikes the eye, salivation, knee jerk when the patella tendon is struck).

B. How classical conditioning was discovered: Ivan Pavlov studied digestion in dogs, for which he won the Nobel Prize in Medicine in 1904. His discovery of classical conditioning was actually accidental. Here's how he discovered it:

    1. He put food powder in a dog's mouth and, through a tubelike device, he measured the amount of saliva the dog produced. After several occasions of putting the food powder in the dog's mouth, Pavlov noticed that the dog began salivating *before* the meat powder was even given to it!

    2. The dog salivating before the meat powder was presented perplexed Pavlov. After careful thought, he deduced that the sight and sounds of the laboratory technician and the food delivery apparatus became *associated* with the delivery of the food powder. That is, these stimuli (sight of technician and sound of food apparatus) always *predicted* the delivery of food powder in the dog's mouth.

V. How Classical Conditioning Works

A. Pavlov's Experiment. To test his hypothesis, Pavlov arranged the following experiment:

    1. He presented a *neutral* stimulus (the sound of a bell) to which the dog oriented. Next, he put food powder in the dog's mouth that caused the dog to salivate. In this case, the food powder is termed the *unconditioned stimulus (UCS)* and the

resulting salivation is termed the *unconditioned response (UCR)*. It is *unconditioned* because salivating to food powder requires no learning, as it is a reflex that occurs naturally.

2. The conditioning phase consisted of repeatedly (across several trials) sounding the bell right before putting food powder in the dog's mouth. (BELL + FOOD POWDER over and over again.) Each time he measured and recorded how much the dog salivated.

3. Finally, Pavlov presented the bell alone (i.e., not followed by food powder) and the dog salivated. In this case, the bell is termed the *conditioned stimulus (CS)* and the resulting salivation is termed the *conditioned response (CR)*. They are *conditioned* because learning had to occur for the dog to be able to salivate to the bell. Thus, Pavlov had correctly hypothesized that the dog *learned an association* between the sound of the bell and the presentation of food, which is why it salivated when it heard the bell. Remember, the bell (formally a neutral stimulus) became a conditioned stimulus, because it always predicted food delivery in the mouth.

    B. Phenomenon Relevant to Classical Conditioning

        1. *Stimulus generalization* defined: the association between the UCS and the CS is extended to include a broad array of similar stimuli.

        2. *Stimulus discrimination* defined: the CR occurs only to the exact CS to which it was conditioned.

        3. *Extinction* defined: the weakening and disappearance of a CR.

        4. *Spontaneous recovery* defined: the sudden reappearance of an extinguished response.

VI. The Conditioning of Little Albert by John Watson the "Father of Behaviorism" (p. 117)

    A. Watson conditioned a fear response in a baby known as Little Albert.

        1. Little Albert sat on the floor while Watson presented different stimuli. Once, when he presented a white rat to Little Albert his assistant made a loud noise by hitting a hammer against a steel bar right behind Albert's head. The loud sound (UCS) startled (UCR) Little Albert. This pairing was repeated several times after which the sight of the rat alone (CS) upset (CR) Little Albert.

        2. There are several ethical considerations regarding Watson's experiment, including the need to safeguard the rights of individuals who cannot give informed consent to participate in research.

VII. Operant Conditioning

    A. Edward Thorndike and the Law of Effect

        1. Edward Thorndike (1905) studied cats in puzzle boxes. He had a variety of boxes with doors that could be opened by manipulating several different devices (e.g., pulling a wire loop hanging from the ceiling, pushing a lever, or in some cases, the cat had to manipulate more than one device such as pressing a treadle and then push a screw to the side to open the door to escape).

2. After moving around in the box for a while the cat would eventually, via random movements, move the device that opened the door and the cat escaped (The first time this happened it was by chance.)

3. The *consequence* of opening the door (i.e., the escape) was a *reward* and Thorndike termed this principle, in which the consequences of a behavior increased (or decreased) the likelihood that the behavior would occur again, the *Law of Effect*.

4. Law of effect defined: the principle that the consequences of a behavior increase (or decrease) the likelihood that the behavior will be repeated).

B. Operant Conditioning and B. F. Skinner

1. Although John Watson is considered the "Father of Behaviorism," B. F. Skinner is, historically, the most famous behaviorist and the "Father of Operant Conditioning. He coined the term *operant* to refer to behavior that *operates* or acts on the environment to produce specific consequences (1938, 1953).

2. *Operant conditioning* defined: the process of changing behavior by manipulating the consequences of that behavior.

3. Operant conditioning requires action from an organism for learning to occur; that is, the organism must behave and the consequences of that behavior determine whether or not the behavior will occur again under similar circumstances in the future.

4. Operant conditioning differs from classical conditioning in that classical conditioning modifies a passive behavior (i.e., a reflex, such as salivation or an eye blink) and operant conditioning modifies an active behavior (i.e., an action, such as typing or playing the electric guitar).

VIII. Reinforcement and Punishment

A. *Reinforcer* defined: any environmental stimulus that increases the frequency of a response. That is, when delivered *contingent upon a response*, a reinforcer increases the likelihood of that response occurring in the future under similar circumstances. For example, your arm itches and you scratch it (which results in relief from the itching) and the next time you have an itch you scratch it, we can say that scratching is a reinforcer. That is, the consequence of scratching (removal of itch) increased the future frequency of scratching under similar circumstances (when you itch).

1. *Primary* reinforcers are innate, unlearned reinforcers that satisfy biological needs (such as food, water, or sex.)

2. *Secondary* (or *conditioned*) reinforcers are those that are learned by association, usually via classical conditioning. Examples of conditioned reinforces are money, grades, or concert tickets.

3. Conditioned reinforcers become effective because they are paired, or associated, with primary reinforcers (which are inherently reinforcing). This association usually occurs via classical conditioning.

B. *Reinforcement* is the process whereby a behavior is strengthened or increases in frequency by the contingent delivery of a reinforcer after that behavior has occurred. That is, the likelihood of a behavior occurring in the future depends on the consequence of that behavior.

    1. *Positive reinforcement* occurs when a stimulus is *added* to the environment, whereas *negative reinforcement* occurs when a stimulus is *removed* from the environment. It is important to note that BOTH positive and negative reinforcement *increase* behavior; they just do so differently.

    2. Some behavioral psychologists have argued that the distinction between positive and negative reinforcement is unnecessary and sometimes difficult to make. The text demonstrates this with an example of drinking coffee to stay awake. In this case, is the coffee adding wakefulness or decreasing tiredness? Regardless of whether you term drinking coffee positive or negative reinforcement, the outcome is the same: You continue to drink coffee.

C. *Punishment* is the process whereby a behavior decreases in strength or frequency by the contingent delivery of a *punisher* after that behavior has occurred. For example, if you put your hand on a hot stove (the behavior) and you experience a painful burn (the consequence) you will be less likely to put your hand on a hot stove in the future.

    1. The same distinctions for reinforcement are made for punishment. That is, positive punishment occurs when a stimulus, or punisher, is added to the environment, whereas negative punishment occurs when a stimulus is removed from the environment. Again, it is important to note that BOTH positive and negative punishment *decrease* behavior; they just do so differently.

    2. Skinner was against the use of punishment and advocated that behavior be changed via the use positive reinforcement.

IX. How Operant Conditioning Works

A. As discussed in detail above, in operant conditioning, organisms learn from the consequences their behaviors produce. Skinner studied, in detail, the consequences of behavior using a chamber he built, termed a *Skinner Box*, and lab rats.

    1. A Skinner Box is a chamber used for operant conditioning of small animals; it includes a food dispenser and has levers to press (for rats) or keys to peck (for pigeons). Using these chambers, psychologists can control many environmental conditions and study behavior in great detail.

    2. Skinner assumed that the principles of learning applied to all organisms and that what he learned with the rat would generalize to other organisms, including humans.

    3. To get the rat to press the lever, Skinner used a technique termed *shaping*. Shaping is the reinforcement of successive approximations of a desired behavior.

X. Schedules of Reinforcement

A. A reinforcer may be presented every time a behavior occurs or only occasionally. Psychologists have developed schedules of reinforcement to engender different patterns of behavior and these schedules can be useful tools in the laboratory. Note that not all schedules of reinforcement can clearly be generalized to human behavior in our daily lives as our behavior is often controlled by several variables at any one time. Nonetheless, they can be important in predicting which behaviors are going to be strong or difficult to extinguish. Skinner noted several such schedules:

1. *Continuous reinforcement*: a reinforcer is presented, or follows, each occurrence of the behavior.

2. *Intermittent reinforcement*: a reinforcer is not presented after each occurrence of the behavior, only occasionally or intermittently. Skinner discovered four types of intermittent schedules (see below).

3. *Fixed-ratio (FR) schedule*: a reinforcer is delivered after a fixed number of responses. For example, under a FR 5 schedule, a rat would receive a food pellet after every fifth response (e.g., at 5, 10, 15, 20, 15, and 30 responses). The pattern of responding for this schedule is usually stepwise, with a short pause after the reinforcer is delivered (i.e., a postreinforcement pause) and then an increase in responding.

4. *Variable-ratio (VR) schedule*: a reinforcer is delivered after a variable number of responses occur; that is, the response requirement to produce a reinforcer varies. For example, under a VR 5 schedule, a rat might earn a reinforcer after 3, then 7, then 10, then 2 responses. The average number of lever presses needed to earn a food pellet is 5, but the actual number of times the lever needs to be pressed varies. This schedule engenders very steady rates of responding; behavior is robust under this schedule.

5. *Fixed-interval (FI) schedule*: a reinforcer is delivered by a response only after a fixed time has elapsed. For example, under an FI 5, the rat would earn a food pellet for the first response that occurred after 5 seconds had elapsed (if he pressed the lever after 3 seconds he would not earn a pellet). This schedule results in a low rate of behavior immediately after reinforcer delivery, followed by an increase in response rates as the time to reinforcement nears.

6. *Variable-interval (VI) schedule*: reinforcer is delivered by a response only after an average time has elapsed. Thus, under a VI 5, the first response after a variable time elapsed would earn a food pellet (e.g., 2, 9, 4, 5, 10, 3 seconds, but the average time elapsed is 5 seconds).

Psychology in The Real World: Treating Autism With Applied Behavior Analysis (p. 310)

A. Autism is a debilitating developmental disorder that appears in the first few years of life. It is characterized by drastic deficits in communication and language, social interaction with others, emotional expression and experience, and imaginative play (Kanner, 1943).

B. Ivar Lovaas (1987) conducted a study using the principles of applied behavior analysis (ABA) in a program that involved at least 2 years of treatment for 35-40 hours each week.

1. The program used reinforcement to increase desirable behaviors, and in some cases, punishment to decrease undesirable (or maladaptive) behaviors. Undesirable behaviors such as hand flapping, twirling, or licking objects, as well as aggressive behaviors were ignored. Desired behaviors such as contact

with others, simple speech, appropriate play, and interactions with others were reinforced.

2. Of the 39 children with autism who participated in the original study, almost half who started treatment at 30 months of age went on to perform normally in the first grade; whereas only 2% of the control group children did so. Furthermore, IQ scores for the experimental group were significantly higher by age 7 than were those in the control group. These gains endured at age 13.

3. ABA continues to be the most effective treatment for autism, especially in terms of school performance and life skills (Beadle-Brown, Murphy, & Wing, 2006).

XI. Biological Constraints on Learning

A. Biology limits our (and other organisms) behavioral options in order to make the adaptive ones more likely. The *biological constraint model of learning* is a view on learning which proposes that some behaviors are inherently more likely to be learned than others.

1. *Instinctive drift*, identified by Keller and Marian Breland (1961), is learned behavior that shifts toward instinctive, unlearned behavior tendencies. Thus, it appears that there are biological limitations, or constraints, on learning.

2. *Latent learning* is learning that occurs in the absence of reinforcement and is not demonstrated until later, when reinforcement occurs.

Breaking New Ground: Conditioned Taste Aversion (p. 315)

A. *Conditioned taste aversion* is the learned avoidance of a particular taste or food if nausea occurs at the same time or shortly after exposure to the food. Whether or not the food is the actual cause of the sickness, it is experienced that way in future encounters.

1. Traditional learning theory would explain conditioned taste aversion as a kind of classical conditioning. That is, there is a learned association between the stimulus that precedes the sickness (the example of the chocolate doughnut and nausea provided in your text). However, classical conditioning requires repeated pairings of the CS and UCS.

2. Unlike Pavlov and his dogs, conditioned taste aversion can occur after a *single pairing, or trial*. Single session learning of long-lasting taste aversion is known as the *Garcia effect* (1955).

3. Garcia's research on taste aversion undermined to key assumptions of classical conditioning: (a) that conditioning could happen only if an organism was exposed repeatedly within a brief time span to the UCS and CS together, and (b) that organisms can learn to associate any two stimuli.

XII. Social Learning Theory (p. 318)

A. Albert Bandura proposed that we learn not only from our own, direct consequences of our behavior, but also from watching those around us. Indeed, he advocated that we learn both from doing and from watching.

1. Bandura called learning from doing *enactive learning* and learning by watching the behaviors (and consequences) of others *observational learning*.
2. Bandura's *social learning theory* goes beyond traditional conditioning approaches and includes observation and modeling as major components in learning.
3. *Modeling* is the process of observing and imitating behaviors performed by others.

B. Bandura and colleagues, in the 1960s, performed a series of experiments demonstrating the effects of observational learning. These experiments were some of the first to show that aggression could be learned through observational learning and modeling.
1. In one of Bandura's experiments half of the children observed adults playing politely with an inflatable clown doll, called Bobo. The other half saw the adults playing aggressively with the doll; they were punching it, hitting it with a rubber mallet, and even tackling it. Next, both groups had the opportunity to play with the Bobo doll. As Bandura had hypothesized, the children in each group modeled the behavior that they had seen the adults engage in. That is, the children who saw the adults play aggressively with Bobo engaged in the same behaviors when they had the opportunity to play with Bobo. In contrast, those who saw the adults play politely with Bobo did the same. Thus, the children had *learned by observation* and *modeled* the behavior they had witnessed.

XIII. The Interaction of Nature and Nurture in Learning (p. 322)

A. Learning is more than just environmental processes. Instead, learning is the result of a complex interplay between the environment and the brain. There are four processes that illustrate this dynamic interaction: imprinting, imitation, synaptic change, and brain growth with enrichment.

B. *Imprinting* is the rapid and innate learning of the characteristics of a caregiver within a very short period of time after birth (Lorenz, 1935, 1937).
1. Konrad Lorenz studied imprinting and learned that, when hatched, ducklings and goslings learned to follow whatever object they first saw. It didn't matter if that was the mother duck or even a human. Indeed, Lorenz demonstrated that ducklings would imprint to him if he were the first thing they saw!

C. *Imitation*, Mirror Neurons, and Learning
1. Humans imitate each other and this is fundamental to how we learn. In fact, it turns out that imitation by infants may be a result of mirror neurons in the brain (Lepage & Théoret, 2007). Studies have shown that babies as young as 7 hours old can imitate simple facial expressions (Meltzoff & Moore, 1977, 1983)

D. *Synaptic Change* During Learning
1. As discussed in the previous chapter (memory) we learned that the brain changes, structurally, as a function of learning and memory. "Neurons that fire

together wire together" and "use it or lose it" arose from Hebb's work on learning and memory.

2. The old saying, "practice makes perfect" is a great example of how our experiences can grow and strengthen synapses. Thus, practicing the scales on your electric guitar strengthens the neuronal connections for those behaviors and it becomes easier and easier for you to play without making errors.

3. These same connections can be weakened if they are not used regularly.

E. Experience, *Enrichment*, and *Brain Growth*

1. In a series of studies, Rosenzweig, Bennet, and Diamond (1972) randomly assigned rats to different environments: (a) impoverished, (b) standard care, and (c) enriched environment. Rats in the enriched environment had greater weight of the cerebral cortex, a thicker cortex, and more activity of the enzyme acetylcholinesterase.

2. Subsequent research has shown that a variety of enriched environments produce important changes in the brain structure and activity. Such enrichment can affect neuronal growth in other species including birds, primates, and humans.

Making Connections: Why Do People Smoke? (p. 327)

A. Any given behavior may be acquired an maintained by different types of learning, such as classical, operant, and/or social. Cigarette smoking is a good example. Why people first begin to smoke may be best explained by social learning theory (observation and modeling).

B. Once smoking is established, it is maintained by operant conditioning. There are several reinforcers associated with smoking such as arousal of the sympathetic nervous system, mild relaxation of muscles, and sometimes peer acceptance. Also, smoking can reduce stress and appetite. Importantly, the potential punishers from smoking (increased risk of lung cancer and heart disease) are far in the future for most (especially teens) so these factors are often ignored.

C. However, smoking, like other complex human behaviors is also influenced by factors other than conditioning such as sex, personality, and sociocultural characteristics.

D. Behavior modification techniques, which apply principles of operant conditioning to changing behavior, have been very effective in helping people quit smoking, especially when combined with nicotine replacement therapy.

GLOSSARY TERMS
learning: enduring changes in behavior that occur with experience.
association: process by which two pieces of information from the environment are repeatedly linked so that we begin to connect them in our minds.
conditioning: a form of associative learning in which behaviors are triggered by associations with events in the environment.

classical conditioning: form of associate learning in which a neutral stimulus becomes associated with a stimulus to which one has an automatic, inborn response.

unconditioned response (UCR): the automatic, inborn response to a stimulus.

unconditioned stimulus (UCS): the environmental input that always produces the same unlearned response.

conditioned stimulus (CS): a previously neutral input that an organism learns to associate with the UCS.

conditioned response (CR): a behavior that an organism learns to perform when presented with the CS.

stimulus generalization: extension of the association UCS and CS to include a broad array of similar stimuli.

stimulus discrimination: restriction of a CR (such as salivation) to the exact CS to which it was conditioned.

extinction: the weakening and disappearance of a conditioned response, which occurs when the UCS is no longer paired with the CS.

spontaneous recovery: the sudden reappearance of an extinguished response.

law of effect: principle that the consequences of a behavior increase (or decrease) the likelihood that the behavior would be repeated.

operant conditioning: the process of changing behavior by manipulating the consequences of that behavior.

reinforcer: environmental stimulus that increases the frequency of a behavior.

primary reinforcers: innate, unlearned reinforcers that satisfy biological needs (such as food, water, or sex).

secondary (or conditioned) reinforcers: reinforcers that are learned by association, usually via classical conditioning.

positive reinforcement: the presentation or addition of a stimulus after a behavior occurs that increases how often that behavior will occur.

negative reinforcement: removal of a stimulus after a behavior to increase the frequency of that behavior. An example is buckling your seat belt to stop the buzzer in the car.

punishment: stimulus, presented after a behavior, which decreases the frequency of the behavior.

positive punishment: the addition of a stimulus that may decrease behavior.

negative punishment: the removal of a stimulus to decrease behavior.

Skinner box: simple chamber used for operant conditioning of small animals; includes a food dispenser and a response lever to trigger food delivery.

shaping: the reinforcement of successive approximations of a desired behavior.

continuous reinforcement: reinforcement of a behavior every time it occurs.

intermittent reinforcement: reinforcement of a behavior—but not after every response.

schedules of reinforcement: patterns of reinforcement distinguished by whether reinforcement occurs after a set number of responses or after a certain amount of time has passed since the last reinforcement.

fixed ratio (FR) schedule: pattern of intermittent reinforcement in which reinforcement follows a set number of responses.

variable ratio (VR) schedule: a pattern of intermittent reinforcement in which the number of responses needed for reinforcement changes.

fixed interval (FI) schedule: a pattern of intermittent reinforcement in which responses are always reinforced after a set period of time has passed.

variable interval (VI) schedule: a pattern of intermittent reinforcement in which responses are reinforced after time periods of different duration have passed.

instinctive drift: learned behavior that shifts towards instinctive, unlearned behavior tendencies.

biological constraint model: view on learning proposing that some behaviors are inherently more likely to be learned than others.

latent learning: learning that occurs in the absence of reinforcement and is not demonstrated until later, when reinforcement occurs.

conditioned taste aversion: the learned avoidance of a particular taste or food.

enactive learning: learning by doing.

observational learning: learning by watching the behavior of others.

social learning theory: a description of the kind of learning that occurs when we model or imitate the behavior of another.

modeling: the imitation of behaviors performed by others.

imprinting: the rapid and innate learning of the characteristics of a caregiver very soon after birth.

ethology: the scientific study of animal behavior.

behavior modification : the application of operant conditioning principles to change behavior.

PRACTICE STUDY QUESTIONS

Multiple Choice

1. A rat presses a lever, resulting in food delivery. The rat then presses the lever more frequently. This is an example of:
    a. punishment.
    b. higher-order conditioning.
    c. reinforcement.
    d. extinction.

2. Which of the following behaviors is most likely to have been acquired through the process of classical conditioning?
    a. nausea from drinking too much alcohol
    b. pulling your hand away from a hot stove
    c. reading
    d. nausea from seeing a hospital in which you have received chemotherapy

3. _____schedules are useful for maintaining high, steady rates of behavior
    a. Fixed Interval
    b. Fixed Ratio
    c. Variable Interval

    d. Consecutive Choice

4. _____involves the control of behavior by its consequences:
    a. Respondent conditioning

b. Physical dependence
c. Operant conditioning
d. Tolerance

5. All of the following are likely to be conditioned reinforcers, EXCEPT:
    a. a chuckle from a friend when you make a joke.
    b. a $20 bill slipped to you by your dad.
    c. a plate of spaghetti when you are starving.
    d. a trophy for winning a miniature golf tournament.

6. Which of the following behaviors is most likely to have been acquired through the process of classical conditioning?
    a. blinking when a puff of air hits your eyes
    b. sneezing when an irritant enters your nasal cavity
    c. falling off your bicycle
    d. feelings of fear when you hear the dentist's drill

7. Reflex responses, which are central to classical conditioning, are:
    a. naturally occurring relationships between behaviors and consequences.
    b. learned responses to specific stimuli.
    c. conditioned behaviors.
    d. naturally elicited, unlearned responses to stimuli.

8. In a typical classical conditioning experiment, a neutral stimulus is:
    a. repeatedly paired with the UCR.
    b. not paired with any other stimulus.
    c. repeatedly paired with the CS.
    d. repeatedly paired with the UCS.

9. The process of ___ increases the range of stimuli to which a CR will be made, whereas ___ decreases or narrows the range of stimuli to which a CR will be made.
    a. stimulus generalization; stimulus discrimination
    b. extinction; spontaneous recovery
    c. stimulus discrimination; stimulus generalization
    d. spontaneous recovery; extinction

10. Thorndike's law of effect emphasized the relationship between behavior and its consequences.
    a. true
    b. false

11. B. F. Skinner is most closely associated with:
    a. Gestalt models of perception.
    b. observational learning.
    c. cognitive maps.
    d. operant conditioning.

12. Which of the following behaviors is NOT an instance of an operant?
   a. Jim's knee jerks forward when the doctor taps it with a mallet.
   b. A pigeon pecks a key to receive access to food
   c. Baby Tommy coos in order to be picked up by mom.
   d. Terri removes her tight-fitting shoes to reduce the pain in her feet

13. __ reinforcers have their effect as a result of evolutionary history; __ reinforcers have their effects as a result of a learning history
   a. Conditioned; unconditioned
   b. Unconditioned; conditioned
   c. Learned; unlearned
   d. Both a and c

14. __schedules of reinforcement require an organism to make a set number of responses per reinforcer
   a. Fixed interval
   b. Fixed ratio
   c. Variable ratio
   d. Variable interval

15. __ schedules of reinforcement require an organism to make a different number of responses for each reinforcer
   a. Fixed interval
   b. Fixed ratio
   c. Variable ratio
   d. Variable interval

17. Many complex human behaviors, such as smoking, result from a combination of different types of learning, such as classical, operant, and/or social.
   a. true
   b. false

Matching

Put the correct letter next to the correct item (i.e., match accomplishments or terms with the correct person). You may use each letter multiple times whenever applicable.

a. B. F. Skinner
b. Edward Thorndike
c. John Watson
d. Ivan Pavlov
e. Albert Bandura
Correct matching letter

1. Studied imitation and modeling. _____

2. Discovered classical conditioning. _____
3. Studied cats in puzzle boxes. _____
4. Studied rats in boxes. _____
5. Studied conditioned fear in humans. _____
6. Is the "Father of Behaviorism" _____
7. Is the most famous behaviorist. _____
8. Studied digestion in dogs. _____
9. Discovered schedules of reinforcement. _____
10. Won the Nobel Prize in Medicine. _____
11. Discovered the Law of Effect. _____

Answer key Chapter 8

Multiple Choice
1. c
2. d
3. b
4. c
5. c
6. d
7. d
8. d
9. a
10. a
11. d
12. a
13. b
14. b
15. c

Matching answers:
1. e
2. d
3. b
4. a
5. c
6. b
7. a
8. d
9. a
10. d
11. b

Chapter 9
LANGUAGE AND THOUGHT

KEY TERMS

Human language
Syntax
Grammar
Protolanguage
Cooing
Babbling
One-word utterances
Two-word utterances
Sentence phase
Child-directed speech
Nativist view of language
Language acquisition device (LAD)
Linguistic determinism hypothesis
Cognition
Cognitive psychology
Mental representation
Visual imagery

Mental rotation
Concept
Concept hierarchy
Category
Prototypes
Reasoning
Deductive reasoning
Inductive reasoning
Causal inferences
Confirmation bias
Critical thinking
Scientific thinking
Metacognitive thinking
Heuristics
Representativeness heuristic
Availability heuristic
Idioms

OUTLINE

I. Language (p. 335)

    A. The Nature of Language
        1. *Human language* is defined as an open and symbolic communication system that has rules of grammar and allows its users to express abstract and distant ideas (Bickerton, 1995). Words are put together in ways that follow rules of syntax and grammar.
            a. *Syntax* refers to the rules of arranging words and symbols in a particular language.
            b. *Grammar* comprises the entire set of rules for combining symbols and sounds to speak and write a particular language.

    B. The Evolution of Language in Humans
        1. Earlier species of humans (e.g., *Homo erectus* and *Homo neanderthalensis*) had a rudimentary language termed *protolanguage* or pre-language (Givon & Malle, 2002).
            a. Language is less than 150,000 to 200,000 years old.
            b. As the human brain, and especially the frontal lobes, grew larger people became capable of thinking and communicating in more complex and abstract thoughts.

C. Language Development in Individuals

    1. As children begin to develop their understanding of language they learn that the sounds coming from other's mouths are meaningful units that form words.

    2. Children gain the ability to understand words before their ability to produce words.

D. Stages of Language Development

    1. Most infants begin uttering repeated vowel sounds (e.g., aah, aah, aah) termed *cooing* during the first 6 months.

        a. Cooing sounds are universal. They vary little from hearing to deaf babies or among babies from the world over.

        b. *Babbling* refers to the infant's experimentation with a complex range of sounds, called phonemes, which include consonants and vowels.

        c. The next stage in language development is *one-word utterances* which occurs at around 12 months old.

        d. Around 18 months of age children begin making *two-word utterances*.

        e. Between 2½ to 3 years of age the third stage of language development, *sentence phase* emerges in which children begin speaking in fully grammatical sentences.

    2. The Critical Period

        a. An important principle in language development is that if children are not exposed to any human language before a certain age their language abilities never fully develop (Lennenberg, 1967; Newport, 2003, Uylings, 2006).

        b. The critical period for language acquisition begins in the 1st year of life and ends around age 12.

E. Theories of Language Acquisition

    1. Unless humans suffer from some type of disease or deficit, all humans learn to speak, including those born deaf. This suggests that humans have an innate, genetically based structures in the brain that enable us to learn language.

    2. Sociocultural Theories

        a. Much of what we learn comes from imitating family members, including imitating sounds. Adults encourage imitation and do by speaking in a higher pitch, raising and lowering the volume of their voice, and using emotion to communicate their messages (Fernald & Moridawa, 1993; Rice, 1989). This is referred to as *child-directed speech.*

    3. Conditioning and Learning Theory

        a. B. F. Skinner (1957) believed that language is like any other behavior; that is, it exists because it is reinforced and shaped.

        b. Skinner said that children learn to speak a particular language because when they say something that resembles a word they are highly praised and celebrated by the parents.

        c. Skinner also explained language progression across different stages by reinforcing successive approximations of complex verbal behavior.

    4. The Nativist Theory

a. This view suggests that the brain is structured or "wired" for language learning.

b. Noam Chomsky (1972, 1986) argues that humans are born with a *language acquisition device (LAD)* which is an innate, biologically based capacity to acquire language

      i. Chomsky believes that there is a single universal grammar underlying all human languages and that each individual language is simply a specific expression of this universal language.

5. Nature, Nurture, and Language Learning

      a. Most scholars of language agree that acquiring language involves   natural abilities that are modified by the language learner's environment   (Hoff, 2006; Lidz & Gleitman, 2004; MacWhinney, 1999).

F. Can Animals Learn Human Language?

1. Chimps are physically incapable of speaking and making the range of sounds that humans do because they lack the vocal apparatus needed to do so.

2. A number of captive apes have learned American Sign Language (ALS) to different degrees and have been able to communicate with humans.

      a. Kanzi is the most linguistically gifted ape. She has learned to comprehend as many as 3,000 English words (Raffaele, 2006).

      b. Sometimes chimps have used sign language to talk to each other. One chimp spontaneously began teaching her adopted son, Loulis, how to sign. After only 8 weeks, the chimp would regularly sign with humans and after 18 months he had learned 20 signs from his adopted mother, Washoe.

3. Given the success and limits of language acquisition by apes, the scientific community is divided on the question of whether apes really can us language to communicate with humans.

G. Language, Culture, and Thought

1. The *Whorf-Sapir hypothesis* suggests that language creates thought as much as thought creates language (Whorf, 1956).

      a. The *linguistic determinism hypothesis* states that our language determines our way of thinking and our perceptions of the world. Therefore, this view states that if there are no words for certain objects or concepts in one's language, it is not possible to think about those objects or concepts.

      b. The view that language determines our thinking is almost certainly overstated.

2. The position that language influences (rather than *determines*) our thinking is known as *linguistic relativism.*

II. Thinking, Reasoning, and Decision Making (p. 350)

A. *Cognitive psychology* is the science of how people think, learn, remember, and perceive (Sternberg, 2006). Humans are unique in their ability to represent ideas and think abstract and symbolic thoughts.

B. How Do Represent Thoughts in Our Minds?

    1. Cognitive psychologists propose that we represent ideas, knowledge, or memories as *mental representations.*

        a. A *mental representation* is a structure in our mind, such as an idea or image, which stands for something else, such as the eternal object or thing (Thagard, 1995).

        b. Mental representations allow us to think about and remember things in the past or imagine things in the future.

    2. Visual Representation

        a. Every animal with eyes perceives visual images, but only those animal with more cortex are better able to keep and store those visual sensations in mind after the sensory stimulation stops.

        b. *Visual imagery* involves visual representations created by the brain after the original stimulus is no longer present (Kosslyn, 2005).

        c. If you first form a mental image of an ideal performance you will actually perform that activity better (Hale, Seiser, & McGuire, 2005).

        d. The brain is activated in much the same way while imagining a task as it is while performing that task (Bonet, Decety, Jeannerod, & Requin, 1997).

        e. *Mental rotation* is the process of imagining an object rotating in three-dimensional space.

            i. Studies have shown sex differences in mental rotation ability with boys and men doing better than girls and women (Halpern, 2004; Hyde, 1990).

            ii. Cross-cultural studies have demonstrated this same effect in Ecuador, Ireland, and Japan (Flaherty, 2005).

    3. Verbal Representation

        a. A major function of thought is to organize and classify our into categories. One way humans organize their environment is by naming things and giving them labels.

        b. The most basic unit of knowledge is a *concept* which is a mental grouping of objects, events, or people.

            i. Concepts help us organize our perceptions of the world.

        c. A *concept hierarchs* lets us know that certain concepts are related in a particular way, with some being general and others specific.

            i. A particular dog, Jake, is a "Golden Retriever," which is a "dog," which is an "animal," which is a "living thing."

        d. A more complex model of how we store and organize knowledge in our brain in *parallel distributive processing (PDP),* which proposes that associations between concepts activate many networks or nodes at the same time (McClelland & Rogers, 2003; McClelland & Rumelhart, 1985).

        e. A *category* is a concept that organizes other concepts around what they all share in common.

            i. *Prototypes* are best-fitting examples of a category (Rosch, 1973).

C. How Do We Reason About Evidence?
      1. *Reasoning* is the process of drawing inferences or conclusions from principles and evidence (Sternberg, 2006).
      2. Cognitive psychologists distinguish between tow kinds of reasoning drawn from formal logic: deductive and inductive.
            a. *Deductive reasoning* occurs when we reason from general statements about what is known to specific conclusions.
            b. *Inductive reasoning* is defined as drawing general conclusions from specific evidence.
                  i. When we use inductive reasoning we often use *causal inferences,* which are how we make judgments about whether on thing causes another thing (Koslowski, 1996).
            c. *Confirmation bias* is the tendency to selectively attend to information that supports one's general beliefs while ignoring information or evidence that contradicts one's beliefs.

D. Critical Thinking
      1. *Critical thinking* is "the ability to analyze facts, generate and organize ideas, defend opinions, make comparisons, draw inferences, evaluate arguments, and solve problems" (Chance, 1986, p. 6).
            a. The qualities of critical thinking most agreed upon by experts are:
            Analyze
            Interpret
            Evaluate
            Explain
            Make Inferences
            Self-Regulate
      2. *Scientific thinking* involves the cognitive skills required to generate, test, and revise theories (Zimmerman, 2007).
      3. Critical and scientific reasoning involves the ability to think *metacognitively,* which is the ability first to think and then to reflect on one's own thinking (Feist, 2006; Kuhn & Pearsall, 2000).

Psychology in the Real World: Applying Critical Thinking beyond the Classroom (p. 358)

A. Critical thinking is a necessary skill for almost every walk of life and we can apply it to any domain in which we form beliefs or opinions.
      1. Many people, including adults, sometimes are lacking in critical and scientific reasoning.
B. Developing critical thinking has impacts beyond the classroom and even beyond studies in psychology.
      1. Facione (1990, p. 2) states that "the ideal critical thinker is habitually inquisitive, well-informed, trustful or reason, open-minded, flexible, fair- minded in evaluation, honest in facing personal biases, prudent in making judgments, willing to reconsider, clear about issues, orderly in assessing complex matters, diligent in seeking

relevant information, reasonable in the selection of criteria, focused in inquiry, and persistent in seeking results that are a precise as the subject and the circumstances of inquiry permit."

C. How Do We Make Judgments?
    1. Most people use *heuristics,* which are methods for making complex and uncertain decisions and judgments, when making decisions.
        a. Heuristics allow us to come to quick and efficient decisions.
    2. The Representative Heuristic
        a. We use the *representative heuristic* when we estimate the probability of one event based on how typical or representative it is of another event (Tversky & Kahneman, 1974).
    3. The Availability Heuristic
        a. The *availability heuristic* is a strategy we use when we make decisions based on the case with which estimates come to mind or how available they are to our awareness (Tversky & Kahnemann, 1974).

Breaking New Ground: Nonrational Decision Making (p. 362)

A. Rational Choice Theory
    1. For much of the 20th century, cognitive psychologists and economists who study human decision making believed that people generally make rational decisions. It was thought that when given a choice between two or more options, humans will choose the one that is most likely to help them achieve their particular goals. Economists called the *rational choice theory* (Scott, 2000).

B. Evidence Against Rational Choice Theory
    1. Through much research, Kahneman and Tversky found that people sometimes ignore base rates, sometimes are biased by stereotypes, and sometimes use shortcuts to arrive, quickly, but not completely rationally, at their decisions and conclusions.
        a. Kahneman and Tversky demonstrated that people bypass fully rational decision making and make use of automatic shortcuts in their reasoning and judgments.

C. How These Findings Changed People's Minds
    1. As a sign of how revolutionary their work was, in 2002 Kahneman won the Nobel Prize in Economics (Tverky had died in 1996).
    2. Kahneman discovered how human judgment may take heuristic that systematically depart from basic principles of probability.
        a. His work inspired a new generation of researchers in economics and finance to enrich theory using insights from cognitive psychology into intrinsic human motivation (The Prize, 2002).

Making Connections in Language and Thought: Learning a Second Language (p. 365)

A. Critical Periods and Second Language Acquisition

1. Children learn second languages more quickly than do adults, and they speak them more fluently (Birdsong, 2006; Kim et al., 1997; Sakai, 2005; Uylings, 2006).

2. As time for learning to speak a second language without an accent, childhood is better than adolescence and adolescence is better than adulthood.

B. Second Language Learning and the Brain

1. People who are fluent in two languages are apparently capable of more efficient cognitive processing compared to people who only speak one language.

   a. Psychologists found that people who spoke two languages performed better on cognitive tasks, and continued to do so later in life, than people who spoke one language (Bialystok, Craik, & Ryan, 2006).

2. Bilingual speakers have a greater density of neurons in the language centers of the brain (Mechelli et al., 2004) and the neural density is proportional to the age at which the person learned the second language.

   a. The earlier the second language is learned, the greater the neural density.

C. Complex Formation and Translation into Foreign Languages

1. Linguists have demonstrated that the more prototypical an idea is, the more easily it can be translated from one language to another (Gass, 1984; Kellerman, 1979).

D. Reasoning in a Second Language

1. In a study examining SAT questions that require deductive reasoning, such as analogies, it was found that students' deductive reasoning in their native language was better performed that their deductive reasoning in their second language (D'Anglejan, 1979).

E. Second Language Acquisition and Metacognition

1. Some linguists and psychologists have proposed that bilingual children should be better at knowing what they know and monitoring their thinking than monolingual children (Jimenez, Garcia, & Pearson, 1994; Ruan, 2004).

   a. A meta-analysis found that 20 out of 24 studies found that bilingual students scored higher on creativity tasks than did monolingual students (Ricciadelli, 1997).

   b. Flexible and creative thinking are closely aligned with metacognitive thinking (Sternberg, 2004).

GLOSSARY TERMS

human language: a communication system specific to *Homo* Sapiens; it is open and symbolic, has rules of grammar, and allows its users to express abstract and distant ideas.

syntax: the rules for arranging words and symbols to form sentences of parts of sentences in a particular language.

grammar: the entire set of rules for combining symbols and sounds to speak and write a particular language.

protolanguage: very rudimentary language, also known as pre-language.

cooing: the first sounds humans make other than crying, consisting almost exclusively of vowels; occurs during first 6 months of life

babbling: sounds made as a result of infant's experimentation with a complex range of phonemes, which including consonants as well as vowels; starts around 5-6 months.

one-word utterances: single words, such as "mama," "dada," "more," or "no!"; occurs around 12 months of age.

two-word utterances: phrases children put together, starting around 18 months, such as "my ball," "mo wawa", or "go way" [go away].

sentence phase: stage when children begin speaking in fully grammatical sentences; usually age 2 ½ to 3.

child-directed speech: changes in adult speech patterns—apparently universal—when speaking to young children or infants; characterized by higher pitch, changes in voice volume, use of simpler sentences, emphasis of the here and now, and use of emotion to communicate their messages.

nativist view of language: the idea that we discover language rather than learn it, that language development is inborn.

language acquisition device (LAD): an innate, biologically based capacity to acquire language, proposed by Noam Chomsky as part of his nativist view of language.

linguistic determinism hypothesis: the proposition that our language determines our way of thinking and our perceptions of the world; the view taken by Sapir and Whorf.

cognition: mental processes involved in acquiring, processing, and storing knowledge.

cognitive psychology: the science of how people think, learn, remember, and perceive.

mental representation: a structure in our mind—such as an idea or image—that stands for something else, such as the external object or thing sense in the past or future, not the present.

visual imagery: visual representations created by the brain after the original stimulus is no longer present.

mental rotation: process of imagining an object turning in three-dimensional space.

concept: a mental grouping of objects, events, or people.

concept hierarchy: arrangement of related concepts in a particular way, with some being general and others specific.

category: a concept that organizes other concepts around what they all share in common.

prototypes: the best-fitting examples of a category.

reasoning: the process of drawing inferences or conclusions from principles and evidence.

deductive reasoning: reasoning from general statements of what is known to specific conclusions.

inductive reasoning: reasoning to general conclusions from specific evidence.

casual inferences: judgments about causation of one thing by another.

confirmation bias: the tendency to selectively attend to information that supports one's general beliefs while ignoring information or evidence that contradicts one's beliefs.

critical thinking: process by which on analyzes, evaluates, and forms ideas.

scientific thinking: process using the cognitive skills required to generate, test, and revise theories.

metacognitive thinking: process that includes the ability to think and then to reflect on one's own thinking.

heuristics: mental shortcuts; methods for making complex and uncertain decisions and judgments.

representativeness heuristic: a strategy we use to estimate the probability of one event based on how typical it is of another event.

availability heuristic: a device we use to make decisions based on the ease with which estimates come to mind or how available they are to our awareness.

idioms: expressions unique to a particular language; usually their meaning cannot be determined by decoding the individual meanings of the words.

PRACTICE STUDY QUESTIONS

1. _____ refers to the rules for arranging words and symbols in a particular; whereas _____ comprises the entire set of rules for combining symbols and sounds to speak and write a particular language.
   a. Grammar; syntax
   b. Prototypes; concepts
   c. Syntax, grammar
   d. Concepts; prototypes

2. _____ occurs before _____ in language development.
   a. Babbling; cooing
   b. Cooing; babbling
   c. Two-word utterances; one-word utterances
   d. None of the above are correct

3. _____ believed that language exists because it is reinforced and shaped, just like any other behavior.
   a. Rogers
   b. Skinner
   c. Chomsky
   d. Watson

4. There is no evidence that apes or chimps can acquire language and communicate with each other and with humans.
   a. true
   b. false

5. The _____ hypothesis suggests that language creates thought as much as thought creates language.
   a. Chomksy language acquisition device
   b. Skinner verbal behavior
   c. Whorf-Sapir

d. Nativist neuronal

6. The term _____ means "to know" and refers to mental processes involved in acquiring, processing, and storing knowledge.
    a. reason
    b. active argument
    c. inquire
    d. cognition

7. Research suggests that men and boys are _____ at mental rotation that are women and girls.
    a. better
    b. worse
    c. the same

8. A _____ is a basic unit of knowledge in which people mentally group objects, events, or people.
    a. prototype
    b. syntax
    c. category
    d. concept

9. A concept that organizes other concepts around what they all share in common is termed a:
    a. prototype.
    b. syntax.
    c. category.
    d. network.

10. _____ reasoning occurs when we reason from general statements of what is known to specific conclusions.
    a. Inductive
    b. Deductive
    c. Informational
    d. Heuristic

11. _____ is the tendency to selectively attend to information that supports one's general beliefs while ignoring information or evidence that contradicts one's beliefs.
    a. Heuristic bias
    b. Stereotype threat
    c. Confirmation bias
    d. Ignorance bias

12. _____ involves the cognitive skills required to generate, test, and revise theories.
    a. Scientific thinking
    b. Heuristic thinking

c. Common thinking
d. Confirmational thinking

13. The ability to first think and then to reflect on one's own thinking is termed:
    a. heuristic thinking.
    b. scientific thinking.
    c. metacognitive thinking.
    d. deductive thinking.

14. _____ are methods for making complex and uncertain decisions and judgments.
    a. Concepts
    b. Prototypes
    c. Heuristics
    d. None of the above are correct

15. Humans sometimes bypass fully rational decision-making and make use of automatic shortcuts in their reasoning and judgments.
    a. true
    b. false

ANSWERS TO PRACTICE STUDY QUESTIONS

1. c
2. b
3. c
4. b
5. c
6. d
7. a
8. d
9. c
10. b
11. c
12. a
13. c
14. c
15. a

Chapter 10
INTELLIGENCE, PROBLEM-SOLVING, AND CREATIVITY

KEY TERMS

Intelligence
g-factor theory
Multiple-factor theory of intelligence
Fluid intelligence
Crystallized intelligence
General intelligence
Broad intelligence
Narrow intelligence
Successful intelligence
Triarchic theory of intelligence
Mental age
Reliability
Validity
Construct validity
Predictive validity
Cultural test bias hypothesis
Test bias
Test fairness
Mental retardation

Adaptive behavior
Down syndrome
Prodigy
Savant syndrome
Reaction range
Convergent thinking problems
Divergent thinking problems
Algorithms
Mental set
Eureka insight or insight solutions
Thinking outside the box
Fixation
Functional fixedness
Creativity
Genius
Ideational fluency
Flexibility of thought
Originality

OUTLINE

I. Intelligence: Is a set of cognitive skills that include abstract thinking, reasoning, problem solving, and the ability to acquire knowledge. Other less agreed-upon qualities of intelligence include mathematical ability, general knowledge, and creativity (p. 373).

    A. Theories of Intelligence
        1. Intelligence as a Single General Ability
            a. Charles Spearman (1904, 1923) developed the first theory of intelligence in which he proposed that human intelligence is best thought of as a single general capacity or ability.
                i. Spearman's theory is known as the general factor or *g-factor theory* of intelligence because it describes intelligence as a single factor made up of specific components.
        2. Intelligence as Multiple Abilities
            a. The *multiple-factor theory of intelligence* holds that the different aspects of intelligence are distinct enough that multiple abilities must be considered, not just one.
                i. The key difference between g-factor and multiple-factor theorists is whether they believe that a single IQ score accurately reflects a

person's overall intelligence: G-factor theorists say "yes" and multiple-factor theorists say "no."

ii. Raymond Cattell (1943; Horn & Cattell, 1966) was the first to "break intelligence in two" with the notion of fluid and crystallized intelligence.

b. *Fluid intelligence* involves raw mental ability, pattern recognition, abstract reasoning and is applied to a problem that a person has never confronted before.

i. Problems that require finding relationships, understanding implications, and drawing conclusions all require fluid intelligence. Neither culture nor vocabulary influence fluid intelligence.

c. *Crystallized intelligence* is knowledge that we have gained from experience and learning, education, and practice.

i. This form of intelligence is influenced by the size of your vocabulary and knowledge of your culture.

d. John Carroll (1993) suggested that intelligence consists of three levels arranged in a hierarchy: general intelligence at the top, broad intelligence at the middle, followed by narrow intelligence.

i. *General intelligence* is similar to Spearman's concept of "g."

ii. *Broad intelligence* consists of abilities such as crystallized and fluid intelligence, as well as memory, learning, and processing speed.

iii. *Narrow intelligence* consists of nearly 70 distinct abilities such as speed of reasoning and general sequential reasoning for fluid intelligence and reading, spelling, and language comprehension for crystallized intelligence.

e. Sternberg argues for a broader view of intelligence and suggests to not simply focus on intelligence, but rather *successful intelligence.*

i. Sternberg's three-part theory is known as the *triarchic theory of intelligence* which states that three interrelated but distinct abilities make up successful intelligence: analytic, creative, and

f. Gardner (1983, 1993) argues that intelligence comprises at least eight distinct capacities: linguistic, mathematical-logical, musical, bodily-kinesthetic, spatial, intrapersonal, interpersonal, and naturalist.

i. There have been little direct empirical tests on Gardner's theory and some argue his ideas are more theory than science.

Psychology in the Real World: Bringing Multiple Intelligences to School (p. 380)

A. The main reason for bringing multiple intelligences (MI) to school setting is to avoid some of the limitations of traditional testing and teaching. An educational principle based on MI theory is that children should have some freedom to choose activities of their own.

1. Entire schools have been designed to put into practice the development of all of Gardner's forms of intelligences.

i. There are over 40 such schools in the United States (Kornhaber et al. 2004).

ii. The Key Learning Community in Indiana opened in 1987 and assessment takes place at the end of the year when students present a project based on any or all intelligences that they focused on during the year.

iii. Presentations are videotaped and serve as a record of the student's cognitive and emotional development. However, the students must still take the local school district's standardized tests; the students do at least as well as students from other schools (Key Learning Community, n.d.; Kornhaber et al., 2004).

B. Measures of Intelligence

1. Alfred Binet deserves the most credit for developing the first true test of intelligence. He was hired by Paris education authorities to develop a test that would identify students that would benefit from special instruction techniques.

a. He and a colleague, Theodore Simon, developed a test containing problems of increasing difficulty; thinking that the ability to solve increasingly difficult items depends on age.

i. This idea became widely influential and is known now as *mental age* which is the equivalent chronological age a child has reached based on his or her performance on an IQ test.

2. William Stern, a German psychologist, developed the concept of the now-famous *intelligence ratio* in which mental age (MA) is divided by chronological age (CA) (times 100) to determine an IQ score.

a. MA/CA x 100 = IQ

i. This ratio was very useful in the early years of IQ testing, but it is no longer used.

ii. Today, IQ scores are calculated based on how well a child does on test relative to norms established by testing children of the same age.

3. An American psychologist, Lewis Terman, translated Binet's test for American students; because Terman taught at Stanford University in California, he named the test the *Stanford-Binet.*

4. In the 1930s, David Weschler created new intelligence tests in response for the need for a test that measured adult intelligence which became known as the *Weschler Adult Intelligence Scales (WAIS).*

Breaking New Ground: Changing Tests of Intelligence (p. 381)

A. Intelligence as a Single Quality

1. For the first 50 years that intelligence tests were used, they were based on the assumption that intelligence was a single quality.

a. Many developers of intelligence tests ignored new theories, including those of Jean Piaget who argued that cognitive development occurred in leaps and bounds as opposed to a gradual increase over time.

i. Many developers also ignored the advance in neuropsychology which showed such differences as how the hemispheres of the brain process information differently, with the right hemisphere processing information more globally and holistically and the left hemisphere processing it more analytically (Kaufman, 1979).

2. Modern Intelligence Tests Based on Psychological Theory

a. Two major shifts in the in the field of intelligence testing occurred in the 1980s.

i. The "Kaufman shift" resulted from Kaufman's book *Intelligent Testing with the WISC-R* which was a call to bring more intelligent methods and procedures to intelligence testing.

ii. Kaufman and his wife, Nadeen, developed the Kaufman-Assessment Battery for Children (K-ABC) which was built around the current state of knowledge which was informed by theories in psychology and neuroscience about how the brain worked and developed (the CHC was developed).

iii. The other shift away from intelligence as a single quality came when John Carroll applied the Cattell-Horn theory to the IQ test that Richard Woodcock had developed. Upon hearing this, some test developers know how they would create an intelligence test that matched evidence that intelligence was more than one general ability.

3. The Aftermath of the Shift in Intelligence Tests

a. Tests may still produce an overall IQ score, but they also include in up to seven domains of intelligence.

i. Influenced by the CHC, the newest version of the WAIS-III and the WISC-IV include scores on four factors: verbal comprehension, perceptual reasoning, working memory, and processing speed (Hogan, 2007).

b. Reliability and Validity of IQ tests

i. *Reliability* refers to how consistent results are; if a test is reliable, a person who takes the test on two different occasions would produce similar scores.

ii. *Validity* requires demonstrating: (a) that the tests really measure intelligence and not something else, and (b) that IQ scores can predict real-world outcomes.

iii. *Construct validity* is what a test measures the term or construct it claims to measure; whereas *predictive validity* refers to whether the test can predict real-world outcomes.

iv. IQ test do predict real-world outcomes such as academic performance, grades, school performance, and class rank in high school.

c. Are IQ Tests Biased?

i. Scientists refer to *test bias* in an IQ test when determining whether a test predicts outcomes equally well for different groups. Researchers have found very little evidence for the existence of this kind of bias in IQ tests (Brown, Reynolds, & Whitaker, 1999; Hunter & Schmidt, 2000; Reynolds, 2000).

ii. *Test fairness* reflects values, philosophical differences, and the ways in which test results are applied (Gregory, 2007). Test fairness concerns the *application of the test results* rather than the test itself. That is, an unbiased test result could be applied unfairly.

B. Extremes of Intelligence

1. When IQ scores are plotted on a graph we see a *bell curve* termed such because it is shaped like a bell; that is, most people fall in the middle and few people on the low and high ends of the curve. The bell curve represents a normal distribution of scores.

a. We find "extremes of intelligence" at the two ends of the curve; that is, mental retardation and giftedness.

2. Mental Retardation

a. The criteria for mental retardation is that the individual must show significant limitations in intellectual functioning as well as everyday adaptive behaviors and this must occur before the age of 18 (AAMR, 2002, APA, 2000).

b. *Adaptive behavior* is defined as how well a person adjusts to and copes with everyday life (Hogan, 2007). This criteria is now used in conjunction with overall IQ scores in the diagnosis of mental retardation.

i. The most current diagnosis emphasizes adaptive functioning over IQ scores; they measure a person's overall daily ability more than academic performance.

c. *Down syndrome* is a disorder that results from a condition known as Trisomy-21, in which a person has three rather than two number 21 chromosomes.

3. Giftedness

a. A *prodigy* is a young person who is extremely gifted and precocious in one area, such as math, music, art, or chess, and it a least average in intelligence (Feldman, 2004).

i. Wolfgang Amadeus Mozart is probably the world's most famous child prodigy, who was playing keyboard by age 3 and composing symphonies by age 8.

b. *Savants* or *savant syndrome* is a very rare condition characterized by serious mental handicaps and isolated areas of ability or remarkable giftedness (Treffert, 2006).

C. Nature and Nurture of Human Intelligence

1. Most people realize that intelligence results from a combination of "being born that way" and "being brought up that way" by our families and teachers. There is great complexity in the interaction of these two forces.

a. *Range reaction* is the genetically determined range within which a give trait, such as intelligence, mail fall; that trait's exact value, however, depends on the quality of the individual's environment (Scarr, 1981; Weinberg, 1989).

    i. Genes do not determine behavior; they establish the range of possible behaviors.

    ii. Only part of the environmental influence comes from being in the same household and sharing experiences; the other part comes from the individual's unique environmental experiences (one experience is the prenatal environment).

D. Group Differences in Intelligence Scores

    1. Research on this topic has necessary political and social implications: If there are differences in intelligence between racial or gender groups, what should we do as a society to compensate for those differences – to level the playing field? Can that even be done? Scientists who have studied the topic have been harassed or threatened.

    2. Race and Intelligence

        a. Herrnstein and Murray (1994) wrote *The Bell Curve: Intelligence and Class Structure in American Life* which ignited an academic, political, and culture firestorm over intelligence.

            i. They concluded that racial groups differed on IQ scores and that a large contributor to this was education and income (Gottfredson, 1997).

            ii. Some experts argue that racial differences in IQ result from biases in IQ tests that favor people from certain cultural backgrounds over others (Reynolds, 2000). Others have argued that a finding of race-based differences in IQ scores is meaningless because race is more of a social construction with little scientific and biological foundation (Sternberg, Brigorenki, & Kidd, 2005).

    3. Gender and Intelligence

        a. A review of six nationally representative data sets of cognitive ability scores (IQ scores) that ranged in size from 12,000 to 73,000 found that there were relatively few real differences between the sexes in cognitive ability. That is, men and women are equally intelligent.

            i. The one consistent difference is not ability but variability; that is, men are more variable in intelligence than are women.

E. Non-Western Views of Intelligence

    1. Western views emphasize verbal and cognitive skills first, whereas many African cultures see social skills, such as being socially responsible, cooperative, and active in family and social life, to be crucial aspects of intelligence (Ruzgis & Grigorenko, 1994; Kerpell, 1983).

    2. Asian cultures have traditionally emphasized humility, awareness, doing the right thing, and mindfulness as important qualities of intelligence (Sternberg, 2000).

II. Problem Solving (p. 395)

A. Types of Problems
   1. *Convergent thinking problems* have known solutions, which can be reached by narrowing down a set of possible answers.
      a. College entrance exams and intelligence tests include convergent problems.
   2. *Divergent thinking problems* refer to problems that have many possible solutions, some of which work better than others.
      a. To solve these we must break away from our normal problem solving strategies and make unusual associations to arrive a novel ways of thinking about the problem.

B. Solution Strategies
   1. Psychologists describe three kinds of strategies that people use to solve different kinds of problems: *algorithms, insight,* and *thinking outside the box.*
      a. *Algorithms* are formulas that guarantee correct solutions to a particular problem.
         i. Algorithms help one create a *mental set* which is a tendency to continue to use problem solving strategies that have worked in the past, even if better solutions are available (Luchins & Luchins, 1970).
      b. *Eureka insights* or *insight solutions* is when sudden solutions come to mind in a flash.
      c. *Thinking outside the box* requires one to break free of self-imposed conceptual constraints and think about a problem differently in order to solve it.

C. Obstacles to Solutions
   1. *Fixation* is one of the biggest blocks to solving problems and it refers to the inability to break out of a particular mindset in order to think about a problem from a fresh perspective.
   2. *Functional fixedness* refers to our tendency to be blind to unusual uses of common everyday things or procedure.

III. Creativity (p. 400)

A. *Creativity* is thought or behavior that is both novel-original and useful-adaptive (Amabile, 1996; Feist, 1999; MacKinnon, 1970; Simonton, 1999).

B. Stages of Creative Problem Solving
   1. State 1 is *preparation* or discovering and defining the problem and then attempting to solve it.
   2. Stage 2 is *incubation* or putting the problem aside for a while and working on something else.
   3. Stage 3 is *insight* which is the Eureka moment in which the solution comes immediately to mind.

4. The last stage, Stage 4, is *verification-elaboration* in which the solution needs to be confirmed, even if it has the feel of certainty.

C. Genius, Intelligence, and Creativity
    1. A *genius* is one with high intelligence combined with creative accomplishments that have a tremendous impact on a given field (Simonton, 1999).
        a. Having an IQ in the top 1% does not guarantee producing creative works of lasting influence.
        b. Considerable research that has focused on the relationship between intelligence and creativity has found that IQ and creativity are not strongly related (Albert & Runco, 1989; Sternbert & O'Hara, 1999).

D. Creativity and the Brain
    1. Research has shown that: (a) insights occur in the right hemisphere, and (b) creative people solving creative problems show more balanced activity between their right and left frontal lobes.
    2. Creative Insight and the Right Hemisphere
        a. Taking brain images using fMRI and EEG when people were solving insight problems revealed that sudden insights consistently activated the right hemisphere more than the left (Bowden et al., 2005).
            i. Patients with damage to the frontal region of their right hemisphere are less able to solve problems requiring insight than people without such damage (Miller & Rippett, 1996).
    3. Creativity and Balanced Activity between the Hemispheres
        a. Creative people have more balanced brain activity between hemispheres than less creative people.
            i. While solving problems, creative people show equally active areas in their right and left frontal lobes, which translates into a widening rather than a narrowing of attention and greater flexibility in moving from one way of thinking to another (Carlsson, Windt, & Risberg, 2000; Goel & Wartanian, 2005).

E. Cognitive Processes in Creative Thinking
    1. Psychologists who study the cognitive aspects of creative thought have focused on *visual thinking, fluency, flexibility,* and *originality.*
        a. *Visual imagery* occurs when we see a solution with our "mind's eye."
        b. *Ideational fluency* is the ability to produce many ideas and is central to creative thought (Guilford, 1967).
        c. *Flexibility of thought* is the ability to come up with many different categories of ideas and to think of other responses besides the obvious one (Guilford, 1967).
        d. *Originality* means thinking of unusual or novel ideas.

F. The Creative Personality
    1. Feist (1998) conducted a meta-analysis and found that creative artists and scientists do share some common personality traits.

Making Connections in Intelligence, Problem Solving, and Creativity: Whiz Kids in Science

    A. The Intel Science Talent Search (STS) competition attracts 1,500 to 1,700 high school student annually and only the top 2% (~40) become finalists.
        1. Six finalists have gone on to win Nobel Prizes, and many others have had illustrious careers in science, math, and medicine (Kaye, 2001).
        2. Becoming a finalist requires both fluid and crystallized intelligence.
        3. It takes more than a high level of intelligence to become a finalist; it requires an aptitude for solving difficult problems creatively.

GLOSSARY TERMS

intelligence: a set of cognitive skills that include abstract thinking, reasoning, problem solving, and the ability to acquire knowledge.

g-factor theory: Charles Spearman's theory that intelligence is a single general (g) factor made up of specific components.

multiple-factor theory of intelligence: idea that the different aspects of intelligence are distinct enough that it should not considered a single factor.

fluid intelligence: raw mental ability, pattern recognition, abstract reasoning that can be applied to a problem one has never confronted before.

crystallized intelligence: the kind of knowledge that one gains from experience and learning, education, and practice

general intelligence: one of Carroll's three levels of intelligence; very similar to Spearman's concept of "g,"

broad intelligence: one of Carroll's three levels of intelligence; includes abilities such as crystallized and fluid intelligence, as well as memory, learning, and processing speed.

narrow intelligence: one of Carroll's three levels of intelligence; includes nearly 70 distinct abilities.

successful intelligence: according to Robert Sternberg, the "use of an integrated set of abilities needed to attain success in life, however an individual defines it, within his or her sociocultural context"

triarchic theory of intelligence: Robert Sternberg's theory that three interrelated but distinct abilities make up successful intelligence: analytic, creative, and practical skill.

mental age: the equivalent chronological age a child has reached based on his or her performance on an IQ test.

reliability: consistency of a measurement, such as an intelligence test.

validity: the degree to which a test accurately measures what it purports to measure, such as intelligence, and not something-else; and the degree to which it predicts real-world outcomes.

construct validity: the degree to which a test measures the concept it claims to measure, such as intelligence.

predictive validity: the degree to which intelligence test scores are positively related to real-world outcomes, such as school achievement or job success, and thus have predictive value.

cultural test bias hypothesis: the notion that group differences in IQ scores are caused by different cultural and educational backgrounds, not by real differences in intelligence.

test bias: characteristic of a test that determines whether it predicts outcomes equally well for different groups.

test fairness: characteristic of a test that reflects values, philosophical differences, and the ways in which test results are applied to different groups

mental retardation: significant limitations in intellectual functioning as well as in everyday adaptive behavior, which start before age 18.

adaptive behavior: adjustment to and coping with everyday life.

Down syndrome a disorder that results from a condition known as trisomy-21, in which a person three rather than two number 21 chromosomes. Like retardation in general, it may be characterized by a degree of disability ranging from mild to profound.

Prodigy: a young person who is extremely gifted and precocious in one area and at least average in intelligence.

savant syndrome: a very rare condition in which people with serious mental handicaps show isolated areas of ability or brilliance.

reaction range: the genetically determined range within which a given trait may fall; its exact value depends on the quality of the individual's environment.

convergent thinking problems: problems that have known solutions and require analytic thinking and the use of learned strategies and knowledge to come up with the correct answer.

divergent thinking problems: problems that have no known solutions and that require thinking of new approaches (thinking about the box) to solve them.

algorithms: formulas that guarantee correct solutions to particular problems.

mental set: a tendency to continue to use problem-solving strategies that have worked in the past, even if better solutions are available.

Eureka insight or **insight solutions:** sudden solutions that come to mind in a flash.

thinking outside the box: approach to problem solving that requires one to break free of self-imposed conceptual constraints and think about a problem differently in order to solve it.

Fixation: the inability to break out of a particular mind-set in order to think about a problem from a fresh perspective.

functional fixedness: mind-set in which one is blind to unusual uses of common everyday things or procedures.

creativity: characteristic of a person whose thought and/or behavior is both novel-original and useful-adaptive.

Genius: high intelligence combined with creative accomplishments that have a tremendous impact on a given field.

ideational fluency: characteristic of creative thought that involves the ability to produce many ideas.

flexibility of thought: characteristic of creativity: ability to come up with many different categories of ideas and think of other responses besides the obvious one.

originality: characteristic of creative thought: ability to come up with unusual and novel ideas.

PRACTICE STUDY QUESTIONS

1. _____ developed the first theory of intelligence.
   a. Cattell
   b. Spearman
   c. Binet
   d. Sternberg

2. The _____ theory of intelligence describes intelligence as a single general factor made up of specific components.
    a. fluid intelligence
    b. crystallized intelligence
    c. g-factor
    d. multiple-factor

3. _____ intelligence involves raw mental ability, pattern recognition, abstract reasoning and is applied to a problem that a person has never confronted before.
    a. Innate
    b. Crystallized
    c. Creative
    d. Fluid

4. _____ intelligence is knowledge that we have gained from experience and learning, education, and practice.
    a. Innate
    b. Crystallized
    c. Creative
    d. Fluid

5. Sternberg's theory of intelligence is comprised of analytic, creative, and _____ intelligence.
    a. practical
    b. mathematical
    c. social
    d. scientific

6. _____ was commissioned by the French government to develop a test that would determine who could benefit from specialized instruction techniques.
    a. Binet
    b. Carroll
    c. Terman
    d. Spearman

7. The intelligence ratio, or IQ, is calculated as:
    a. CA/MA x 1000.
    b. MA/CA x 1000.
    c. MA/CA x 100.
    d. CA/MA x 100.

8. An IQ test is _____ if it measures what it purports to measure and not something else.
    a. reliable
    b. valid
    c. fluid
    d. crystallized

9. Mental retardation is diagnosed by IQ score second, but first by:
    a. adaptive behavior.
    b. emotional maturity.
    c. genetic testing.
    d. chromosome deficiency.

10. A(n) _____ is a young person who is extremely gifted and precocious in one area and is at least average in intelligence.
    a. genius
    b. savant
    c. prodigy
    d. super star

11. Research consistently shows that women are far more intelligent than men.
    a. true
    b. false

12. _____ problems have known solutions which can be reached by narrowing down a set of possible answers.
    a. Divergent thinking
    b. Algorithm thinking
    c. Cognitive thinking
    d. Convergent thinking

13. _____ is an obstacle to solutions that involved the inability to break out of a particular mind-set in order to think about a problem from a fresh perspective.
    a. Thinking inside the box
    b. Visual imagery
    c. Fixation
    d. Mental block

14. The four stages of creative problem solving are preparation, _____, insight, and verification-elaboration.
    a. reasoning
    b. incubation
    c. mental rotation
    d. logic

15. _____ is high intelligence combined with creative accomplishments that have tremendous impact on a given field.
    a. Prodigy
    b. Savant
    c. Genius
    d. Creativity

ANSWERS TO PRACTICE STUDY QUESTIONS
1. b
2. c
3. d
4. b
5. a
6. a
7. c
8. b
9. a
10. c
11. b
12. d
13. c
14. b
15. c

Chapter 11
MOTIVATION AND EMOTION

Key Terms

Motivation
Needs
Drives
Incentives
Homeostasis
Set-point
Yerkes-Dodson law
Self-actualization
Glucose
Sexual behavior
Sexual orientation
Achievement motivation
Emotions
Moods
Affective traits
Basic emotions
Self-conscious emotions
Broaden and build model

Antecedent event
Appraisal
Emotion regulation
Reappraisal
Expressive-suppression
Emotional response
Action tendencies
Facial action coding system (FACS)
Duchenne smile
Subjective experience of emotion
James-Lange theory of emotion
Culturally relative
Universal
Neuro-cultural theory of emotion
Display rules
Life-satisfaction
Subjective well-being

OUTLINE

I. Motivation: describes the urge to move toward one's goals, whatever they may be. (p. 415)

Three important terms associated with motivation are needs, drives, and incentive.
　　1. *Needs* are states of cellular or bodily deficiency that compel drives.
　　2. *Drives* are the perceived states of tension that occur when our bodies are deficient in some need.
　　3. An *incentive* is any external object or event that motivates behavior.

　A. Models of Motivation
　　1. The Evolutionary Model
　　　a. This theory looks at internal drives to explain why people do what they do.
　　　　i. The processes of natural and sexual selection have shaped motivation over time to make all animals, including humans, want those things that help them survive and reproduce (Buss, 2003).
　　　　ii. Our bodies *know* they want food, water, oxygen, and after adolescence, sex.
　　2. The Drive-Reduction Model

a. This model suggests that what drives our motivation is the perceived internal state of tension that arises when our bodies are lacking in some basic physiological capacity.

    i. Central to drive reduction is the idea of maintaining physiological balance, or *homeostasis.*

    ii. Researchers suggest that all organisms are motivated to maintain physiological equilibrium around an optimal *set point* which is defined as the ideal fixed setting of a particular physiological system.

3. The Optimal Arousal Model

a. This model proposes that we seek out stimulation and function best at an "optimal level of arousal."

    i. The *Yerkes-Dodson law* (see Figure 11.3 in your text) is a result of the common finding that low arousal and high arousal lead to poor performance, whereas moderate levels of arousal lead to optimal performance (Yerkes & Dodson, 1908).

    ii. Studies on sensory deprivation support this model of motivation.

4. The Hierarchical Model

a. This model of motivation is based on Abraham Maslow's hierarchy of needs (Maslow, 1970) which states that needs range from the most basic physiological necessities to the highest, most psychological need for growth and fulfillment (see Figure 11.4 in your text).

    i. From the lowest to the highest, Maslow's needs are: *physiological, safety, love and belongingness, need for esteem, need for self-actualization.*

    ii. *Self-actualization* defined: the full realization of one's potentials and abilities in life.

B. Hunger: Survival of the Individual

1. The Biology of When We Eat: Internal signals from the body control when we have the desire to eat or stop eating.

a. Cellular glucose found in our blood plays an important role in hunger. *Glucose* is a simple sugar in the blood that provided energy for cells throughout the body, including the brain.

b. The *hypothalamus* regulates all basic physiological needs, including hunger.

c. Hormones and neurochemicals also play a role in hunger.

    i. Four hormones suppress appetite: *insulin, leptin, peptide YY (PYY), and cholecystokinin* (Williams et al., 2004).

2. The Psychology of What We Eat: What we eat is influenced by different factors, many of which are either learned or part of our culture, or both.

a. Different cultures expose children to different flavors; however, exposure does not automatically lead to preference (Pliner, 1982; Rozin, 1996). It may take several exposures for children (sometimes 8–10) before a child comes to like a food he or she originally did not like (Birch & Fischer, 1996; Birch & Marlin, 1982).

3. The Motive to Be Thin and the Tendency Toward Obesity
   a. Fat provides a store of energy for future use and in our evolutionary past, this was important because of the uncertainty of available food.
   b. In today's modern industrialized societies where there is an abundance of food, fat has become a liability.
      i. Our ideas of beauty have changed and thinness has come to define attractiveness and there appears to be a cultural obsession with becoming and remaining thin.
   c. Genes control the number of fat cells a person has and recent research has shown that the number of fat cells a person has is set by childhood and adolescence, and does not change after that (Spalding et al., 2008).
      i. The stable number of adult fat cells may help explain why losing weight, and more importantly, *keeping off the weight* is so difficult.

C. Sex: Survival of the Species: Without sex our species would die.
   1. Human Sexual Response: *Sexual behavior* is defined as actions and arousal involving stimulation of the genitals, which may or may not involve orgasm.
      a. Masters and Johnson (1966) described four phases of sexual arousal that men and women go through, although they do so somewhat differently. Those phases are: *excitement, plateau, orgasm,* and *resolution.*
   2. The Biology of Sexual Behavior
      a. The hypothalamus plays an important role in sexual behavior.
      b. One study examined brain images of women while they were having an orgasm or faking an orgasm. The researchers found that achieving a real orgasm always involved deactivation of brain regions involved with fear and anxiety in the amygdala and hippocampus as well as parts of the cortex involved in consciousness (Georgiadis et al., 2007).
         i. *Testosterone,* the major male sex hormone, controls sex drive in both men and women (Morris, Udry, Khandawood, & Dawood, 1987; Persky et al., 1978).
      c. As women approach ovulation, the frequency and intensity of their fantasies involving sex with men other than their partner increase (Bullivant et al., 2004). This makes sense from an evolutionary perspective because it is at ovulation when a woman is most likely to get pregnant.
   3. Culture and Sexual Behavior: Accepted sexual behavior varies from culture to culture.
      a. Ford and Beach (1951) studied attitudes toward sex before and after marriage in 190 different cultures. They identified three kinds of societies in terms of sexual attitudes:
         i. *Restrictive societies* that restrict sex before and outside of marriage.
         ii. *Semirestrictive societies* in which there are formal prohibitions on pre- and extramarital sex that are not strictly enforced.
         iii. *Permissive societies* that place few restrictions on sex.

4. Gender and the Drive for Casual Sex: Studies consistently show that men are more willing and interested in casual sex than are women (e.g., Buss, 2003; Clark & Hatfield, 1989).

   a. *Parental investment theory* offers an explanation for gender difference in attitude toward casual sex. That is, if pregnancy results, the cost of having sex is very different for men and for women (Trivers, 1972).

      i. For women, a single sexual encounter could have consequences that endure a lifetime—from the initial nine months of pregnancy to the 18 years of caring for the child and beyond.

5. Sexual Orientation: is our disposition to be attracted to either the opposite sex (heterosexual) or the same sex (homosexual), or to both sexes (bisexual).

   a. Sexual orientation depends upon both biological and environmental (social) factors. The amount of testosterone one is exposed in the womb can influence sexual orientation.

   b. The *hypothalamus* also plays a role in sexual orientation. LeVay (1991) examined this structure in the brain of gay and straight men and found that the region was substantially smaller in gay men than in straight men. The gay men had a size that was similar to that of women.

   c. Social-environmental theories work best in cooperation with biological theories. Some social-environmental theories have argued that child play, early peer-relations, differences in how parents treat boys and girls, and gender identity are important factors in the development of sexual orientation.

D. The Needs Belong and to Excel

   1. The Need to Belong: Affiliation: Our need to belong with others and to be accepted by others is one of the strongest of all human needs (Adler, 1956; Baumeister & Leary, 1955; Murray, 1938/1962).

      a. Rejection hurts, both psychologically and physically. Evolution has made use of our existing physical pain system to help signal when we have been hurt or rejected by others (Eisenberger, Lieberman, & Williams, 2003; Mac Donald, Kingsbury, & Shaw, 2005; Macdonald & Leary, 2005).

         i. Psychologists argue that the reason it hurts to be left out is that our social connections are as important to us as our physical safety.

   2. The Need to Excel: Achievement

      a. Although some individuals are extremely motivated to excel, almost all people strive to overcome their shortcomings and imperfections (Adler, 1956).

         i. *Achievement motivation* is a desire to do things well and to overcome difficulties and obstacles (McClelland, 1985).

      b. Atkinson (1964) argued that the tendency to achieve success is a function of three things:

         i. *Motivation to succeed* is the extent to which you really want to be successful.

ii. *Expectation of success* is an individual's evaluation of the likelihood of succeeding at a task.

iii. *The incentive value of the success* stems from: (a) success at the task has to be important to you, and (b) the more difficult the task the lower the odds of succeeding at it, and thus, the more it will mean to you if you do succeed.

II. Emotion (p. 431)

A. Defining Emotion: Emotions emerge from our interactions with the world around us. They are brief, acute changes to experience and physiology that result from a response to a meaningful situation in the person's environment.

1. *Moods* are transient changes in affect that fluctuate throughout the day or over several days.

2. *Affective traits* are enduring aspects of our personalities, which set the threshold for the occurrence of particular emotional states (Ekman, 1984; Lazarus, 1991; Rosenberg, 1998).

3. Emotion, Basic Emotions, and the Dimensions of Affect

a. There are set of emotions that appear to be common to all humans and are a product of our evolutionary past (Ekman, 1992).

i. These *basic emotions* are: anger, fear, disgust, happiness, sadness, and surprise (see Figure 11.8 of your text).

4. *Self-Conscious Emotions* are emotions that occur as a function of how well we live up to our expectations, the expectations of others, or the rules set by society (Tracy, Robins, & Tangney, 2007; Tangney, Stuewig, & Mashek, 2007).

a. Self-conscious emotions include: shame, guilt, humiliation, embarrassment, and pride.

5. Emotions as Evolutionary Adaptations: From an evolutionary perspective, emotions are adaptations that have evolved because they helped solve a particular problem in our ancestral past and, by doing so, contributed to our survival and reproductive success (Tooby & Cosmoides, 1990).

a. The *broaden and build model* suggests that positive emotions (e.g., contentment, happiness, love, and amusement) broaden our cognitive perspective, making our thinking more expansive and enabling the acquisition of new skills (Fredrickson, 1998, 2001).

B. Emotion as a Process: Today, researchers view emotion as a process, which can best be understood by examining how various aspects of emotion unfold (Lazarus, 1991; Levenson, 1994).

1. Appraisal in the Emotion Process: Whether an event or situation leads to an emotion depends on how the person appraises it.

a. *Appraisal* is the evaluation of a situation with respect to how relevant it is to one's own welfare (Lazarus, 1991).

i. Appraisal drives the process by which emotions are elicited (Roseman, 1984; Scherer, Dan, & Flykt, in press) and it does not have to be a conscious, deliberate thought process.

143

ii. The type of appraisal that occurs determines the type of the emotion generated.

2. Regulation of Emotion: The term *emotional regulation* refers to the cognitive and behavioral efforts people use to modify their emotions.

   a. *Reappraisal* occurs when people reevaluate their views of an event so that a different emotion results and is an example of emotion regulation that occurs early in the emotion process.

   b. *Expressive-suppression* is the deliberate attempt to inhibit the outward manifestation of an emotion (Gross et al., 2006). This type of strategy is used when we want to make unpleasant feelings go away.

Psychology in the Real World: Social and Emotional Learning in Schools (p. 436)

A. Today, psychologists and educators argue that the development of skills for recognizing and regulating emotion are important skill-sets that need be taught because they are just as important as academic achievement. Social-emotional learning (SEL) programs have been developed to teach such skills.

   1. The *Providing Alternative Thinking Strategies (PATHS)* program (Greenberg & Kusche, 1998; Kusche & Greenberg, 1994) is one SEL that provides teachers with a detailed curriculum for improving children's emotional awareness and regulation skills and enhancing their social competence.

   2. Research has demonstrated that PATHS leads to improvements in social and emotional skills in high-risk children, reduction of aggressive behaviors in both normal and special-needs children, fewer depressive symptoms in special-needs children, and improvements in classroom functioning (Conduct Problems Prevention Research Group, 1999a, 1999b; Kam, Greenberg, & Kusche, 2004).

      a. A large-scale meta-analysis of more than 300 studies shows that SEL programs significantly improve children's academic performance (Weissberg & Durlak, 2005).

   3. The Emotional Response: includes physiological, behavioral/expressive, and subjective changes.

      a. *Physiological Changes* for the emotional response occur via the autonomic nervous system (ANS). Once elicited, emotions engage the ANS almost immediately.

      b. *Behavioral-Expressive Changes* can include facial expressions, change in vocal intonation and volume, and behavioral tendencies toward particular types of action (Frijda, 1986).

         i. The facial action coding system (FACS) is a widely used method by which coders score all observable muscular movements that are possible in the human face (Ekman & Friesen, 1978).

         ii. Using this method, researchers have found that many different facial expressions that are recognized across cultures (e.g., anger, disgust, fear, happiness, sadness, and surprise) are also shown when people spontaneously experience emotions (Ekman & Rosenberg, 2005).

c. *Subjective Changes in Emotion* is the quality of our conscious experience during an emotional response. When people talk about how an emotion *feels* they are referring to subjective experience.

    i. The *James-Lange theory of emotion* says that it is our perception of the physiological changes that accompany emotions that creates the subjective experience.

Breaking New Ground: The Universality of Facial Expressions of Emotion (p. 440)

A. Emotion Expression: Culturally Determined or Universal?

    1. In the 1960s, many social scientists believed that behavior was strongly determined by the environment. Some anthropologists believed that facial expressions of emotion were *culturally relative* meaning that expressions varied across cultures and could only be understood with the social laws, rules, or norms of the culture in which they occurred.

    2. Paul Ekman and his colleague Wallace Friesen examined this by showing photographs of European Americans to people in the United States, Japan, Argentina, and Chile and found a high degree of consensus with regard to the emotions people reported they saw in the pictures.

        a. Other scientists began to obtain similar findings leading to the idea that the facial expressions of certain "basic" emotions were *universal.*

        b. One argument against this idea was that, for example, people in the United States and Japan might report similar expressions due to the media to which they have both been exposed (e.g., actors in movies).

B. Evidence of Universality of Emotion Expression

    1. Ekman sought to investigate the universality of expression by examining an isolated, preliterate group from Papua New Guinea called the Fore tribe. Because they did not speak his language, he had them look at the pictures and tell a story to explain the emotion in the face of the picture. The Fore people found it difficult to make up stories and Ekman was left with a small sample size that, although he was able to publish the material in *Science,* he did not have a high degree of consensus.

    2. Using a new methodology, Ekman found success. He went back to the tribe and showed children three different pictures of facial expressions and presented a story about an emotional situation (e.g., he is angry and about to fight; she is looking at something that smells bad). The children (and later, adults) then had to choose which picture displayed the correct emotion for the story. This method yielded a greater degree of consensus as the participants correctly noted the proper expression.

C. Emotion Research After the Findings on Universality

    1. The study of emotion became one of the most widely studied areas in psychology by the late 1980s and throughout the 1990s (Rosenberg, 2005).

    2. Ekman (1972) proposed the *neuro-cultural theory of emotion,* which suggests that certain aspects of emotion, such as facial expressions and physiological

changes of basic emotions, are in all humans, whereas other aspects, such as how people appraise situations and regulate their emotional expressions in front of others vary from culture to culture.

D. How Culture Impacts Emotion Expression
1. Ekman and Friesen proposed the concept of *display rules,* which are learned norms or rules, often taught very early, about (a) when it is appropriate to show certain expressions of emotion and (b) to whom one should show them. This concept addressed the dilemma of the universality of facial expressions and the fact that there are cultural differences in emotions.

E. Emotion and the Brain
1. *Affective neuroscience* is a field of psychology devoted to answering which structures and systems of the brain are involved in the emotion process.
2. The *amygdala* appears to play a very important role in appraisal of the emotional significance of stimuli, with a specialized function for noticing fear-relevant information (Ohman, 2002; Phelps & LeDoux, 2005).
3. The *prefrontal cortex* is one of the most active regions of the brain in the experience and appraisal of emotion. In addition, due to its involvement in planning, impulse control, and working memory, the prefrontal cortex plays a role in the appraisal and reappraisal of emotion (Miller & Cummings, 1999; Miyake et al., 2000).
4. Other brain regions in emotion include the anterior cingulate cortex (ACC) which is active when people either recall or imagine emotional experiences and the insula is involved in *interoception* or the perception of sensations arising within the body.

F. Gender and Emotion
1. The sexes differ most in how they describe their emotional experiences in words and in frequency of smiling (women smile more). In addition, women talk more about emotions than do men.
   a. Studies of facial behavior during emotional experiences find no consistent differences between men and women (Gross & John, 1998).
   b. Exposure to pictures of animal or human attacks provokes greater amygdala activation in men than in women, which may indicate a possibility of greater tendency to aggression in men (Schienle et al., 2008).

Making Connections in Motivation and Emotion: Living a Satisfied Life (p. 449)

A. The word *happiness* often refers to a brief emotion, but it can also be used to mean a long-term sense of satisfaction with life.
1. *Life-satisfaction* is the overall evaluation we have for our lives (Diener et al., 1999) and psychologists consider life-satisfaction as a subset of *subjective well-being,* which includes satisfaction in different domains such as career and social networks.

B. Motivation and Happiness: Maslow's hierarchical model of motivation offers a useful way to illustrate the basic needs and the higher-level needs for life-satisfaction.

    1. Basic Needs and Happiness: Basic needs must be met for a person to be relatively satisfied with life. To illustrate, industrialized countries have a higher level of well-being than do nonindustrialized countries.

        a. Diet and weight also relate to overall happiness. For example, having a health diet is associated with high life-satisfaction (Due et al., 1991) whereas being overweight is associated with low life-satisfaction (e.g., Ball, Crawford, & Kenardy, 2004).

        b. Having a satisfying sex life can be a source of overall happiness and well-being, whereas having problems in your sex life can lead to problems with one's overall well-being.

    2. Higher Needs and Happiness

        a. Once a person or country crosses the $12,000/per person/year gross national product, close relationships and valuing family, friends, and people matter most for overall levels of happiness (Headey, 2008).

        b. The cognitive need to explore and understand the world is another higher level need. People who are curious and interested in exploring novel and challenging situations tend to be happier than people who would rather stick with what they know and not challenge themselves with new tasks and experiences (Diener et al., 1999; Gallagher & Lopez, 2007; Headey, 2008).

C. Emotions, Happiness and Meaning in Life

    1. The right balance of many different positive and negative emotions contribute to overall well-being and satisfaction in life.

        a. People who find meaning in their lives in general and even in negative and tragic experiences are likely to be happier in life that those who do not see meaning and purpose in life's difficult and unpleasant times (King et al., 2006).

GLOSSARY TERMS

motivation: the urge to move toward one's goals to accomplish tasks.

needs: inherently biological states of deficiency (cellular or bodily) that compel drives.

drives: the perceived states of tension that occur when our bodies are deficient in some need, creating an urge to relieve the tension.

incentive: any external object or event that motivates behavior; an environmental effect on motivation..

homeostasis: the process by which all organisms work to maintain physiological equilibrium or balance around an optimal set-point.

set-point: the ideal fixed setting of a particular physiological system, such as internal body temperature.

Yerkes-Dodson law: the principle that both low arousal and high arousal lead to poor performance, whereas moderate levels of arousal lead to optimal performance.

self-actualization: the full realization of one's potentials and abilities in life.

glucose: a simple sugar in the blood that provides energy for cells throughout the body, including the brain.

sexual behavior: actions and arousal involving stimulation of the genitals, which may or may not involve orgasm.

sexual orientation: the disposition to be attracted to either the opposite sex (heterosexual), the same sex (homosexual) or both sexes (bisexual).

achievement motivation: a desire to do things well and overcome difficulties and obstacles.

emotions: brief, acute, multi-faceted changes to experience and physiology that result from a response to a meaningful situation in the person's environment.

moods: affective states that operate in the background of consciousness, which tend to last longer than most emotions.

affective traits: stable predispositions toward certain types of emotional responses; they are enduring aspects of our personalities that make particular emotional states more or less likely to occur.

basic emotions: set of emotions that are common to all humans; includes anger, fear, disgust, happiness, sadness, and surprise.

self-conscious emotions: types of emotions that require a sense of self and the ability to reflect on actions; they occur as a function of meeting expectations (or not) and abiding (or not) by society's rules.

broaden and build model: Fredrickson's model for positive emotions, which posits that they widen our cognitive perspective and help us acquire useful life skills.

antecedent event: part of the emotion process; a situation that may lead to an emotional response.

appraisal: the evaluation of a situation with respect to how relevant it is to one's own welfare; it drives the process by which emotions are elicited.

emotion regulation: the cognitive and behavioral efforts people make to modify their emotions; includes appraisal and expressive-suppression.

reappraisal: an antecedent-focused emotion regulation strategy in which one re-evaluates an event so that a different emotion results.

expressive-suppression: a response-focused strategy for regulating emotion that involves the deliberate attempt to inhibit the outward manifestation of an emotion.

emotional response: the physiological, behavioral/expressive, and subjective changes that occur when emotions are generated.

action tendencies particular behavioral impulses that accompany certain emotions.

Facial action coding system (FACS): a widely used method for measuring all observable muscular movements that are possible and observable in the human face.

Duchenne smile: a smile that expresses true enjoyment, involving both the muscles that pull up the lip corners diagonally and those that contract the band of muscles encircling the eye to create crow's feet and raise the cheeks.

subjective experience of emotion: the changes in the quality of our conscious experience that occur during emotional responses.

James-Lange theory of emotion: idea that the subjective emotional experience is grounded in our perception of the physiological changes that accompany emotions.

culturally relative: term describing the idea that behavior varies across cultures and can only be understood within the social laws, rules, or norms of the culture in which they occur.

universal: term referring to something that is common to all human beings and can be seen in cultures all over the world.

neuro-cultural theory of emotion: Ekman's theory explaining why certain aspects of emotions, such as the facial expressions and physiological changes, are similar in all humans, whereas others, such as how people appraise situations and regulate their emotional expressions in front of others, vary from one culture to another.

display rules: learned norms or rules, often taught very early, about when it is appropriate to show certain expressions of emotion and to whom one should show them.

life-satisfaction: the overall evaluation we make of our lives; an aspect of subjective well-being.

subjective well-being: state that consists of life satisfaction, domain satisfactions, and positive and negative affect.

PRACTICE STUDY QUESTIONS

1. _____ are states of cellular or bodily deficiency that compel drives.
   a. Incentives
   b. Emotions
   c. Needs
   d. Homeostasis

2. The lowest level of Maslow's hierarchy of needs are _____ needs.
   a. love and belongingness
   b. safety
   c. self-actualization
   d. physiological

3. The most important source of energy for the body is cellular:
   a. glucose.
   b. homeostasis.
   c. neuropeptide y.
   d. endocannabinoids.

4. Women smile more than do men.
   a. true
   b. false

5. _____ is the major male sex hormone and it controls sex drive in both men and women.
   a. Estrogen
   b. Testosterone
   c. Progesterone
   d. None of the above

6. Our disposition to be attracted to either the opposite sex (heterosexual) or the same sex (homosexual) or both sexes (bisexual) is referred to as:
   a. gender identity disorder.
   b. gender identity orientation.

c. sexual orientation.

d. sexual orientation disorder.

7. _____ are brief, acute changes to experience and physiology that result from a response to a meaningful situation in the person's environment.

   a. Needs

   b. Beliefs

   c. Emotions

   d. Affective traits

8. Anger, fear, disgust, happiness, sadness, and surprise are examples of _____ emotions.

   a. basic

   b. advanced

   c. difficult

   d. isolated

9. Children exposed to social-emotional learning programs have been demonstrated to have improved classroom attendance, less disruptive class behavior, like school more, and have higher GPAs.

   a. true

   b. false

10. The emotional response includes _____, behavioral/expressive, and subjective changes.

   a. physiological

   b. hostile

   c. genetic

   d. maladaptive

11. The most recognized facial expression of emotion is the smile of happiness.

   a. true

   b. false

12. The _____ theory of emotion states that it is our perception of the physiological changes that accompany emotions that creates the subjective emotional experience.

   a. Skinner-Pavlov

   b. Rogers-Callahan

   c. Hypothalamus-Amygadala

   d. James-Lange

13. _____ studied the Fore tribe in New Guinea to examine his idea of the universality of facial expressions of emotions.

   a. Ekman

   b. Skinner

   c. Freud

   d. None of the above

14. The _____ plays a very important role in appraisal of the emotional significance of stimuli, with a specialized function for noticing fear-relevant information.
    a. hypothalamus
    b. amygdala
    c. medulla
    d. occipital cortex

15. Having a healthy diet is associated with high life satisfaction, whereas being overweight is associated with low life satisfaction.
    a. true
    b. false

ANSWERS TO PRACTICE STUDY QUESTIONS

1. c
2. d
3. a
4. a
5. b
6. c
7. c
8. a
9. a
10. a
11. a
12. d
13. a
14. b
15. a

Chapter 12
STRESS AND COPING

KEY TERMS

Stress
Stressors
Primary appraisal
Secondary appraisal
Neuroendocrine system
Glucocorticoids
Catecholamines
Adrenal-medullary system
Norepinephrine
Hypothamamic-pituitary-adrenal (HPA) axis
Cortisol
General adaptation syndrome (GAS)
Alarm stage
Resistance stage
Exhaustion threat
Allostasis
Coping
Problem-focused coping

Emotion-focused coping
Emotional disclosure
Psychomatic theory
Health psychology
Physiological reactivity model
Health behavior approach
Cardiovascular system
Psychoneuroimmunology (PNI)
Natural immunity
Inflammation
Acquired immunity
Cellular immunity
Immunosuppression
Type A behavior pattern
Cardiovascular reactivity (CVR)
Anorexia nervosa
Bulimia nervosa

OUTLINE

I. What Is Stress? (p. 457)

    A. *Stress* is part of a dynamic interplay between people's interpretations of events in their lives and their reactions to those events. Stress occurs when an emotionally evocative situation overwhelms a person's perceived ability to meet the demands of that situation.

    B. Stress as a Stimulus or Response
        1. *Stressors* defined: events that push us to the limit or exceed our ability to manage the situation at hand.
        2. *Stimulus view of stress* focuses on the situation that causes the stress.
        3. *Response view of stress* focuses on the physiological changes that occur when someone encounters an excessively challenging situation.
        4. *Relational view of stress* views stress as a particular relationship between people and the situations in which they find themselves.

    C. Stress as a Stimulus
        1. Psychologists can measure stress as a stimulus by administering scales that have been developed to assess stress. There are some potential drawbacks for using these scales, including the fact that people view situations differently.

D. Relation between Person and Situation: Larazus and Folkman (1984) discuss two kinds of appraisal; that is, how we appraise a situation we encounter.

1. *Primary appraisal* is an assessment of what a situation means to us. The outcome of this appraisal determines whether an emotional response might occur.

2. *Secondary appraisal* is when we assess the resources available to cope with stress (Lazarus & Folkman, 1984). When we find ourselves in a stressful situation, we try to figure out what to do about the situation to relieve the stress and the accompanying negative emotions or unpleasant feelings.

E. The Physiology of Stress: When stressful situations lead to negative emotions, physiological changes occur in the autonomic nervous system (ANS), the endocrine system, and the brain.

1. The ANS consists of all the neurons that serve the organs and the glands and it plays a critical role in the responses of stress and emotion.

2. The endocrine system is the second major system involved in stress.

   a. The *neuroendocrine system* refers to the hormonal systems involved in emotion and stress.

3. The key structures involved in the neuroendocrine regulation of stress responses are the hypothalamus, the pituitary gland, and the adrenal glands.

   a. The *hypothalamus* releases chemicals that stimulate the release of hormones from the pituitary gland.

      i. The pituitary gland releases hormones that play a key role in the stress response.

   b. The *adrenal gland* releases *catecholamines,* which control ANS activation, and *glucocorticoids,* which are responsible for maintaining the activation of physiological systems during emergencies.

   c. The *adrenal-medullary system* refers to when the hypothalamus sends instructions to the brain stem to activate sympathetic neurons. Next, the sympathetic neurons tell the adrenal gland to release *norepinephrine* which activates the sympathetic response (increased heart rate, rate of respiration, and blood pressure).

   d. The *hypothalamic-pituitary-adrenal (HPA) axis* is the other major neuroendocrine pathway that is relevant to the stress response (see Figure 12.2 of your textbook).

F. The General Adaptation Syndrome (GAS): Proposed by Hans Selye the GAS "is the sum of all the nonspecific, systemic reactions of the body which ensue upon long continued exposure to stress" (1946, p. 119). GAS consists of three stages:

1. The *alarm state* occurs when one is exposed to a stressor and it is the body's emergency response to an environmental threat (i.e., the stressor).

2. Organisms can only persist in the alarm stage for a limited time. When they find ways to cope (as opposed to death) they enter the *resistance stage* in which the organism maintains efforts to fight off or manage the threat.

3. The *exhaustion stage* occurs with repeated or continuous exposure to a stressor. At this stage, the organism's resources for fighting off threats have been depleted and illness becomes much more likely.

G. How We Adapt to Stress: Rather than operating at a state of balance (i.e., homeostasis), our normal state is one of actively responding to the world around us.

    1. *Allostasis* means that the body achieves stability through change (Schulkin, 2005; Sterning & Eyer, 1998); it is an alternative explanation of how the body is usually operating.

H. Stress and the Brain: Stress-related cortisol release can cause dendrites to wither and shrink which can interfere with several types of memory.

    1. Stress reduces neurogenesis in the hippocampus and it may inhibit the synaptic plasticity in the hippocampus and neocortex, impacting learning and memory function (Artola, 2008; Wang et al., 2008).

II. Coping (p. 466)

A. *Coping* refers to anything people do to deal with or mange stress or emotions. Larazus and Folkman (1984) distinguish between two types of coping:

    1. *Problem-focused coping* defined: involves strategies that aim to change the situation that is creating stress.

    2. *Emotion-focused coping* defined: involves strategies aimed at regulating the experience of distress. There are several forms of emotion-focused coping: *reappraisal, distancing, escape-avoidance, seeking social support, self-control,* and *accepting responsibility.*

        a. *Reappraisal* is the emotional regulation strategy of reevaluation of a situation in light of new information or additional thought.

        b. *Distancing* is attempting to separate oneself from an emotional experience.

        c. *Escape-avoidance* is wishful thinking or doing something to get one's mind off the situation.

        d. *Seeing social support* is talking with friends or family for purposes of emotional support.

        e. *Self-control* is trying to regulate one's feelings or actions regarding the problem.

        f. *Accepting responsibility* is acknowledging one's role in the stress-eliciting situation.

B. Traumatic Disclosure

    1. *Emotional disclosure* refers to the notion of "letting it all out" as a means of coping. An emotional disclosure task it is a technique in which people write down recent emotional experiences as a means of improving health outcomes related to stress.

C. Social Support: a coping strategy that combines problem- and emotion-focused coping.

    1. Social support is one of the most frequently used ways of coping and it can have positive benefits for physical health.

a. *Direct effects hypothesis* states that social support is beneficial to mental and physical health whether or not the person is under stress.

b. *Buffering hypothesis* states that social support works as a buffer only under certain conditions, such as a highly stressful life.

2. A *social network* is a cluster of related people such as family members, spouses, friends, or neighbors. Whether social resources are beneficial to health depends upon whether a person is integrated into a social network.

a. Social networks can also be harmful to health. For example, one study showed that the risk of obesity spread among people who were socially connected.

D. The Positive Psychology of Coping: Relates to the various ways in which positive psychological states have been studied in relation to stress and coping.

1. *Optimists* tend to emphasize the positive, see the glass has "half full" rather than "half empty" and believe that things will turn out well (Scheier, Weintraub, & Carver, 1989).

a. Optimism may have health benefits.

2. *Pessimists* emphasize the negative; for them the glass is always half empty and the future uncertain.

E. Finding Meaning: Research suggests that positive psychological traits and states play a big role in whether people are able to find meaning in stressful and tragic events (e.g., Folkman, 1997; Folkman & Moskowitz, 2000).

Psychology in the Real World: Effects of Chronic Stress on Aging (p. 472)

A. As discussed by Selye, the physiological effects of long-term stress is a wearing out or wearing down of the body, which makes the person more vulnerable to illness. It follows, then, that psychologists would inquire whether stress makes one age quicker.

1. Epel and her colleagues examined indicators of cellular aging in healthy women who were biological mothers of either normal or chronically ill children. The mothers reported the amount of stress they perceived and the researchers also collected blood samples.

a. The researchers found that the more stress a woman perceived in her life, the women's cells were "the equivalent to 9-17 additional years" older than the women who perceived less stress (Epel et al., 2004, p. 17314).

III. How Stress and Coping Affect Health (p. 472)

A. *Psychosomatics* deals with how emotional factors can increase the likelihood of certain disorders occurring or worsening. The field of *health psychology* grew out of psychosomatic medicine.

B. *Health psychology* is the study of psychological factors related to health and illness. It includes disease onset, prevention, treatment, and rehabilitation, and involves clinical practice as well as research.

1. The *physiological reactivity model* examines how the sustained physiological activation associated with the stress response can affect body systems in such a way as to increase the likelihood that illness or disease occurs.

2. The *health behavior approach* focuses on the behaviors in which people engage, such as diet, exercise, or substance abuse, which may make them more susceptible to illness or may enhance health.

   a. The *cardiovascular system,* which consists of the heart and all the blood vessels of the body, may be at risk for heart disease if exposed to repeated, sustained physiological activation. Frequent blood pressure elevations can damage arteries by reducing their elasticity and increasing the likelihood of fatty buildup.

   b. Sustained stress might increase susceptibility to disease by its effects of sustained stress on the immune system; immunosuppression as a potential indicator of diseases as lead to the development of a new field of study termed *psychoneuroimmunology (PNI).*

Breaking New Ground: Psychological Processes and the Immune System (p. 475)

A. The job of the immune system is to defend the body against foreign substances. Before the 1970s, people thought the immune system operated independently from the CNS, as such it would not be susceptible to the effects of thoughts, feelings, and stress. Most physicians did not think that psychological conditions could affect the immune system.

B. Psychologist Robert Ader was studying conditioned taste aversion (see Chapter 8 for a review) and paired a chemical that induced nausea with saccharine water to create taste aversion to the saccharine water. He found that some of the rats that had been exposed to a lot of saccharine water and had learned to associate the water with nausea were dying. The chemical, in addition to causing nausea, was also an immunosuppressant. Ader and his colleagues conducted a series of experiments to test whether immunosuppression could be classically conditioned in rats (Ader & Cohen, 1975). They found that rats with conditioned immunosuppression were less able to defend themselves against a foreign substance (injected sheep blood cells in this case).

C. By demonstrating that one could classically condition the suppression of an antibody response to an antigen, Ader and colleagues demonstrated that there was a connection between the CNS and the immune system.

   1. Scientists later discovered that the ANS is linked to the immune system structures such as the thymus gland, and that immune cells have receptors for and can produce certain stress hormones (Smith & Blalock, 1998).

      a. There is now solid behavioral and biological evidence that psychological processes and immune processes interact.

D. Stress and Immune Function: Today the field of psychoneuroimmunology examines the relationships among the brain, thought, feeling, endocrine changes, and immune system functioning.

1. Overview of the immune system: The human immune system defends the body against invasion by disease-causing agents (i.e., pathogens), inspects the body for cells that may take on dangerous mutations, and performs basic housekeeping functions such as cleaning up cellular debris after injury. There are two basic lines of defense: *natural immunity* and *acquired immunity*.

> a. *Natural immunity* consists of a number on inborn processes that help remove foreign substances from the body. Two form of natural immunity include: *phagocytosis* and *inflammation.*
>> i. *Phagocytosis* is a process in which a white blood cell engulfs a substance (usually an antigen or another cell) and digests it or moves it to a place where it will be destroyed.
>> ii. *Inflammation* is a process in which tissues are restored following injury.
> b. *Acquired immunity* involves a number of endocrine and cellular processes that recognize specific antigens and then reproduce specialized cells or circulating proteins to fight that antigen.

E. Research on Stress, Immune Function, and Health

> 1. Theorists have suggested that *immunosuppression* increases susceptibility to disease by reducing the body's ability to fight invading bacteria or viruses or its ability to fight off potentially cancerous cells, or both.

F. Psychological Risk Factors for Heart Disease: Type A and Anger

> 1. *Type A Behavior Pattern* refers to psychological characteristics that psychologists believed could be risk factors for heart disease. Such characteristics include: impatience, competitiveness, hostility, and time urgency.
>> a. Subsequent studies have found that *hostility* better predicts heart disease than does Type A personality.
>> b. The *cardiovascular reactivity (CVR)* model suggests that hostility can increase the likelihood of heart disease through two different causal routes: *hostility* or *hostile disposition* and *depression*.

G. Depression

> 1. Depression is a mood disorder associated with sadness and lethargy. It is also associated with an increased severity of symptoms and increased risk of death from coronary heart disease (Geerlings et al., 2002)

H. Research on Health-Relevant Behavior

> 1. Smoking cigarettes reduces life expectancy by an average of 10 years, increases one's risk for lung cancer more than 10-fold, and triples the risk of death from heart disease in both men and women (CDC, 2001; Doll et al., 2004)
> 2. Alcohol consumption can cause liver damage and heavy alcohol consumption can increase the likelihood of liver cancers and cancers of the digestive tract. However, moderate alcohol consumption may reduce the risk of coronary heart disease.

3. Diet and eating: eating well promotes health. However, sometimes a person's relationship with food can become maladaptive leading to *eating disorders.*

    a. *Anorexia nervosa* occurs when people cannot maintain 85% of their ideal body weight for their height, have an intense fear of eating, and a distorted body image (American Psychiatric Association, 2000).

    b. *Bulimia nervosa* is when a person is prone to binge eating and feeling a lack of control during the eating session.

4. Exercise: Besides not smoking, regular exercise is the best thing you can do for your health.

5. Mindfulness and meditation have shown positive effects for overall health.

Making Connections in Stress and Health: The Health Psychology of HIV and AIDS (p. 488)

A. Living with HIV is a serious challenge involving enormous stressors such as managing the symptoms of a chronic illness, dealing with the threat of death, and carrying out a complex treatment regimen.

    1. Both the person with HIV and those caring for him or her endure extreme stress.

    2. Even in the presence of highly effective medications, psychosocial factors influence immune variables and disease progression in men and women.

        a. In a longitudinal study of psychological factors in men and women with HIV, baseline reports of stress, depression, hopelessness, and avoidant coping predicted significant reductions in the kinds of T-lymphocytes that are most dramatically targeted by HIV (Ironson et al., 2005). More stressful life events, more depressive symptoms, and less social support all correlated with a faster progression to AIDS in gay men infected with HIV (Lesserman et al., 1999).

Glossary Terms

stress: condition that occurs when a situation that elicits a strong emotional response overwhelms a person's perceived ability to meet the demands of that situation.

stressors: events related to the experience of stress—that push people to their limits of control and capability.

primary appraisal: assessment made upon first encountering a situation in the environment; an appraisal made—often very quickly—in terms of what the situation means for the individual.

secondary appraisal: assessment of the resources available to cope with stress.

neuroendocrine system: the hormonal systems involved in emotions and stress.

glucocorticoids: hormones responsible for maintaining the activation of physiological systems during emergencies.

catecholamines: hormones that control ANS activation.

adrenal-medullary system: one of the major neuroendocrine pathways stimulated when we experience a stressful event; the hypothalamus sends instructions to the brain stem to activate sympathetic neurons.

norepinephrine: a neurotransmitter that activates the sympathetic response to stress, increasing heart rate, rate of respiration, and blood pressure in support of rapid action.

hypothalamic-pituitary-adrenal (HPA) axis: a major neuroendocrine pathway relevant to the stress response and consisting of the hypothalamus, pituitary gland, and the adrenal cortex.

cortisol: the stress hormone; the primary glucocorticoid produced by the body; it ensures that the body gets enough fuel.

general adaptation syndrome (GAS): as defined by Hans Selye, a generalized, nonspecific set of changes in the body, composed of three stages: alarm, resistance, and exhaustion.

alarm stage: the part of the general adaptation syndrome that is the body's emergency response to a threat, when all of the body's resources respond.

resistance stage: the part of the general adaptation syndrome that is an extended effort by the body to deal with a threat.

exhaustion threat: the part of the general adaptation syndrome when all resources for fighting the threat have been depleted and illness is more likely.

allostasis: explanation for the body's dynamic way of responding to the world in which the body achieves stability through change.

coping: act of dealing with or managing stress or emotions, consciously or unconsciously.

problem-focused coping: way of dealing with stress that aims to change the situation that is creating stress.

emotion-focused coping: way of dealing with stress that aims to regulate the experience of distress.

emotional disclosure: way of coping with stress that involves unburdening, through writing or talking about the situation.

psychosomatic theory: the idea that emotional factors can lead to the occurrence or worsening of illness.

health psychology: the study of psychological factors related to health and illness.

psychological reactivity model: explanation for how the stress response leads to an increased likelihood of illness or disease.

health behavior approach: explanation for illness or health that focuses on the behaviors people engage in, such as diet, exercise, or substance abuse.

cardiovascular system: bodily system that consists of the heart and all the blood vessels of the body.

Psychoneuroimmunology (PNI): the science of how psychological factors lead to immune suppression that might make a person more susceptible to certain diseases.

natural immunity: form of immunity that is the first response to antigens and includes phagocytosis and inflammation.

inflammation: a process in which tissues are restored following injury.

acquired immunity: endocrine and cellular processes that recognize specific antigens and then reproduce specialized cells or circulating proteins to fight that antigen.

cellular immunity: the immune response that occurs when the T-lymphocytes (T cells) fight antigens by means of a variety of cellular processes instead of by releasing antibodies.

immunosuppression: condition in which susceptibility to disease is increased because the body's ability to fight invading pathogens or its ability to kill potentially cancerous cells, or both, is reduced.

Type A Behavior Pattern: a way of responding to challenge or stress, characterized by hostility, impatience, competitiveness, and time-urgency; predictive of heart disease and mortality.

cardiovascular reactivity (CVR) model: hypothesis that hostility can increase the likelihood of heart disease through at least two different causal routes.

anorexia nervosa: an eating disorder in which people cannot maintain 85% of their ideal body weight for their height, and have an intense fear of eating and a distorted body image.

bulimia nervosa: an eating disorder characterized by binge eating and feeling a lack of control during the eating session.

PRACTICE STUDY QUESTIONS

1. _____ occurs when an emotionally evocative situation overwhelms a person's perceived ability to meet the demands of that situation.
    a. Depression
    b. Stress
    c. Anorexia nervosa
    d. Bulimia nervosa

2. The _____ refers to the hormonal systems involved in emotions and stress.
    a. neuroendocrine
    b. adrenal-medullary system
    c. general adaptation syndrome
    d. hypothalamic-pituitary-adrenal axis

3. The general adaptation syndrome consists of three stages: alarm stage, resistance stage, and:
    a. primary appraisal stage.
    b. HPA stage.
    c. exhaustion stage.
    d. allostasis stage.

4. _____ coping involves strategies that aim to change the situation that is creating stress; whereas _____ involves strategies aimed at regulating the experience of distress.
    a. Emotion-focused; problem-focused
    b. Problem-focused; emotion-focused
    c. Emotional disclosure; buffering hypothesis
    d. Buffering hypothesis; emotional disclosure

5. _____ tend to see the glass has "half full" rather than "half empty" and emphasize the positive.
    a. Pessimists
    b. Type A personalities
    c. Optimists
    d. Resilient personalities

6. Health psychology is the study of psychological factors related to health and illness.
    a. true
    b. false

7. In a study presented in the text, rats with conditioned imunosuppression were less able to defend themselves against a foreign substance (i.e., injected sheep blood cells)
    a. true
    b. false

8. _____ consists of a number of inborn processes that help remove foreign substances from the body.
    a. Natural immunity
    b. PNI
    c. Cellular immunity
    d. Acquired immunity

9. Studies examining whether Type A behavior patterns found that the characteristic _____ was most likelihood to be correlated with heart disease.
    a. hostility
    b. jealousy
    c. diet
    d. joy

10. Besides not smoking, regular exercise is the best thing one can do for health.
    a. true
    b. false

11. Drinking excessive amounts of alcohol is correlated with negative health outcomes, however, moderate intake of alcohol has positive effects on health.
    a. true
    b. false

12. People with this eating disorder cannot maintain 85% of their ideal body weight.
    a. Bulimia nervosa
    b. Anorexia nervosa
    c. Obesity nervosa
    d. physically; psychologically

ANSWERS TO PRACTICE STUDY QUESTIONS

1. b
2. a
3. c
4. b
5. c
6. a
7. a
8. a
9. a
10. a
11. a
12. b

Chapter 13
PERSONALITY: THE UNIQUENESS OF THE INDIVIDUAL

KEY TERMS

Personality
Trait
Behavioral thresholds
Quantitative trait loci (QTL) approach
Unconscious
Id
Ego
Superego
Defense mechanisms
Repression
Reaction formation
Projection
Sublimation
Psychosexual stage theory
Oral stage
Anal stage
Phallic stage
Latency stage
Genital stage
Fixation

Striving for superiority
Inferiority complex
Personal unconscious
Collective unconscious
Archetypes
Anima
Animus
Self-actualization
Unconditional positive regard
Big Five or five-factor model
Basic tendencies
Cortical arousal
Inter-rater reliability
Projective tests
Rorschach Inkblot Test
Thematic Apperception Test
Questionnaires
Likert scales
Rational (face valid) method
Empirical method

OUTLINE

I. Defining Personality (p. 495)

A. *Personality* refers to the unique and relatively enduring set of behaviors, feelings, thoughts, and motives that characterize an individual (Feist & Feist, 2006; Roberts & Mroczek, 2008).
> 1. Personality is what distinguishes us and makes us unique from one another. It is also relatively enduring or consistent.
>> a. *Consistency across situations* refers to the notion that people behave in the same way in different situations and carry who they are into almost every situation.
>> b. *Consistency over time* in the extent to which people behave the same way over time.
> 2. A personality *trait* is a disposition to behave consistently in a particular way.
>> a. An important principle of traits is they are directly connected to behavior. They lower *behavioral thresholds,* or the point at which you move from not behaving to behaving (Allport, 1937; Feist & Barron, 2003; Rosenbert, 1998).

164

b. A low threshold means you are very likely to behave in a particular way, whereas a high threshold means you are not.

II. The Nature and Nurture of Personality (p. 497)

    A. The Evolution of Personality Traits
        1. Human personality traits evolved as adaptive behavioral responses to fundamental problems of survival and reproduction.

    B. Genetics and Personality
        1. *Behavioral geneticists* study the relationship between genes and personality.
            a. The *quantitative trait loci (QTL)* approach to studying the relationship between genes and personality looks for "genetic markers" of behavior. The QTL method uncovers the location on particular genes that are associated with high or low levels of a trait.
            b. The QTL research points to genetic markers for several basic personality traits, such as novelty- or thrill-seeking, impulsivity, and neuroticism (Benjamin et al., 1996; Hamer & Copeland, 1998; Lesch et al., 1996; Plomin & Caspi, 1999; Rutter, 2006).
            c. A second approach to studying the effects of genetics and personality is the study of twins, both identical and fraternal, who have been raised together or apart.
                i. Studying twins allows researchers to obtain estimates of how heritable personality traits are.
                ii. If a trait is genetically influenced, identical twins should be more similar on that trait than fraternal twins.

    C. Temperament and the Fetal Environmental
        1. Some aspects of personality are present at birth and evidence suggests that temperament and personality differences are evident even *before* birth.
            a. Fetal activity and heart rate can reveal something about temperament differences over the first year of life.
            b. The prenatal environment may play an important role in shaping personality.
                i. Infants born to mothers who have experienced an unusual amount of stress during pregnancy tend to have impaired stress function, higher baseline levels of glucocorticoids, and a faster, stronger, and more pronounced stress response, all of which persist into childhood (Barbazanges, Piazza, La Moal, & Maccari, 1996).

    E. Personality and Culture: Universality and Differences
        1. If personality dispositions are part of our biology then we would expect the same personality dimensions or traits to appear in cultures all over the world.
        2. Research confirms that the personality traits of extraversion, neuroticism, agreeableness, openness to experience, conscientiousness, and psychoticism have appeared not only in Western cultures (e.g., the United States, the United

Kingdom, Germany, Australia, Iceland, Spain, Portugal), but also Asian (China, Japan, South Korea), African (Zimbabwe), Middle Eastern (Iran, Israel), and Pacific Rim cultures (Malaysia and the Philippines) (McCrae, 2002; McCrae & Allik, 2002; McCrae & Costa, 1997).

    a. Differences do exist in personality based on culture as well. For example, Asian cultures tend be more concerned about the impact of their behavior on their family, friends, and social groups which is termed *collectivism*. People in Western cultures, however, tend to be more concerned with how their behavior will affect their personal goals which is termed *individualism* (Cross & Markus, 1999; Hofsteder, 2001).

III. How Do Theorists Explain Personality? (p. 502)

    A. *Psychoanalytic theories* are based on are on variation of Freud's seminal ideas. Freud proposed an overarching theory of personality and psychotherapy and also founded the movement known as psychoanalysis.

        1. Freud described three layers of consciousness: *unconscious, preconscious,* and *conscious.*

            a. The *unconscious* contains all the drives, urges, or instincts that are outside awareness but still motivates most of our speech, thoughts, feelings, or actions.

        2. Freud also described three distinct "provinces" or regions that involve control and regulation of impulses.

            a. The *id* develops in infancy and is the area of impulse and desire. Its sole function is to seek pleasure and operates on the "do it" principle.

            b. The *ego* develops by the end of our first year of life and it is a sense of self that begins to emerge. It operates on the "reality principle."

            c. The *superego* develops around age 2 or 3 and is the part that monitors and controls behavior. It "stands over us" and evaluates actions in terms of right or wrong; it is our conscious.

        3. Freud developed the concept of *defense mechanisms* which share two qualities: (1) They operate unconsciously, and (2) they deny and distort reality in some way.

            a. *Repression* is the unconscious act of keeping threatening or disturbing thoughts, feelings, or impulses out of consciousness.

            b. *Reaction formation* occurs when an unpleasant idea, feeling, or impulse is turned into its opposite.

                i. Homophobia is an example of reaction formation in that hatred and aggression toward homosexuals might me a reaction against one's fears of one's own latent homosexual impulses.

            c. *Projection* is when we deny and repress particular ideas, feelings, or impulses but project them onto others.

d. *Sublimation* involved expressing a socially unacceptable impulse in a socially acceptable and even desirable way.

2. The *psychosexual stage theory* was one of Freud's most controversial ideas regarding personality development. He believed that sexual feelings were key to each stage of personality development, even infancy.

> a. The *oral stage* occurs during the first 12–18 months and the mouth is the center of pleasure. Infants suck, bit, and chew as a means of nourishment and exploring their environment.
>
> b. The *anal stage* takes place during the 2nd and 3rd years and involves pleasure gained from holding and releasing one's bladder and bowels.
>
> c. The *phallic stage* occurs from 3 to 6 years when the child discovers that the genitals are a source of pleasure.
>
>> i. During this stage desire for the opposite-sex parent and hostility toward the same-sex parent occurs and is termed the *Oedipal complex.*
>
> d. The last stage is the *genital stage,* which starts with puberty and lasts for the rest of one's life. Here the source of pleasure is once again the genitals, but this time in a more mature, adult fashion.
>
>> i. This last stage occurs after a *latency period* where no region of the body is erogenous and the sense of sexuality goes beneath the surface.
>
> e. *Fixation* was Freud's notion of a defense mechanism whereby a person continues to be concerned and even preoccupied with an earlier stage of development.

3. It is important to note that although Freud's theory of psychosexual stages has been very influential, there is actually little empirical research to support his ideas.

4. Alfred Adler (1870–1937) viewed himself as a colleague of Freud's but disagreed with him on the major motives underlying behavior.

> a. Adler assumed that humans naturally strive to overcome their inherent inferiorities or deficiencies, both physical and psychological. This *striving for superiority,* as opposed to sex or aggression, is the major drive behind all behavior (Adler, 1956).
>
> b. According to Adler, people who over compensate for their feelings of weakness or inferiority may develop an unhealthy need to dominate or upstage others as a way of compensating for those feelings of inferiority which he termed *inferiority complex.*
>
>> i. Adler also emphasized the importance of birth order in influencing personality.

5. Carl Jung (1875–1961) proposed that the unconscious had two distinct forms: personal and collective (Jung, 1918, 1964).

> a. The *personal unconscious* consists of all our repressed and hidden thoughts, feelings, and motives.
>
> b. The *collective unconscious* belongs not to the individual but to the species; it consists of shared experiences from our ancestors—God,

mother, life, death, water, earth, aggression, survival—that have been transmitted from generation to generation.

    i. Jung thought that there must be some kind of collective unconscious that would explain the many instances in which dreams, religions, legends, and myths share the same content even though the people who created them have never directly or indirectly communicated with one another.

    ii. The collective unconsciousness is made up of *archetypes,* which are ancient or archaic images that result from common ancestral experiences.

    iii. The *anima* is the female part of the male personality, and the *animus* is the male part of the female personality.

6. Karen Horney (1885–1952) was one of the first major female voices in the psychoanalytic movement. She focused more on the social and cultural forces behind neurosis and neurotic personality. Her approach is termed the *psychoanalytic social theory.*

B. Humanistic Approach

1. The humanistic approach is optimistic about human nature and believes that humans are naturally interested in realizing their full potential.

2. Abraham Maslow (1908–1970) developed the hierarchy of needs with regard to human motivation.

    a. *Self-actualization* refers to people's inherent drive to realize their full potential (Maslow, 1970). Only a few people attain this highest level.

3. Carl Rogers (1902–1987) developed a unique form of psychotherapy based on the assumption that people naturally strive toward growth and fulfillment and need unconditional positive regard for that to happen (Rogers, 1980).

    a. *Unconditional positive regard* is the ability to respect and appreciate another person unconditionally—that is, regardless of their behavior.

    b. Rogers believed that we have two ways of seeing ourselves: the *real self* and the *ideal self.*

C. Social-Cognitive Learning Theories

1. Walter Mischel believes that people are not consistent across situations because it would be pathological not to change one's behavior when the situation changes (Mischel & Shoda, 1995, 1999).

D. Trait Theories

1. Gordon Allport (1897–1967) attempted to identify how many personality traits existed (Allport & Odbert, 1936). Based on his findings he argued that most individuals could typically be described about 10 central traits.

2. The *Big Five* or *five-factor model* states that there are five universal and widely agreed-upon dimensions of personality:

    Openness to experience

    Conscientiousness

Extraversion
Agreeableness
Neuroticism
A mnemonic device for this is O-C-E-A-N or C-A-N-O-E
3. The Big Five personality dimensions, along with out talents, aptitudes, and cognitive abilities are referred to as our *basic tendencies.*

E. Biological Theories
1. The biological approach assumes that differences in personality are partly based in differences in structures and systems in the central nervous system, such as genetics, hormones, and neurotransmitters.
2. Hans Eysenck (1916–1997) argued for the fundamental importance of biology in shaping our personality and he proposed that there are three, rather than five, dimensions of personality:
Neuroticism
Extraversion
Psychoticism
A mnemonic device for this is P-E-N
a. Psychoticism consists of traits such as aggressiveness, coldness, impulsivity, egocentricity, nonconformity, and creativity (see Figure 13.8 of your text).

Breaking New Ground: Animal Personality (p. 516)

A. Only Humans Have Personality
1. Until the 1990s, most psychologists would have argued that the term *personality* could only be applied to humans.
a. Samuel Gosling, attempting to argue that animals could not have personalities, found that he could not accept his own assumption.

B. Evidence for Personality in Other Animals
1. Gosling and John (1999) conducted a review of the literature and found 19 studies across 12 nonhuman species. The researchers provided evidence for at least 14 major nonhuman species in which personality traits existed (see Figure 13.9 for a summary).
a. Primates and other mammals tend to share the largest number of personality traits with humans.
b. Only chimpanzees have a distinct "conscientiousness" dimension as they possess more highly developed brain regions that are capable of controlling impulse and organizing and planning their activities in advance.
c. Domestic dogs and cats have a "competence" or "learning" dimension that is a mixture of openness and conscientiousness.
d. There even appears to be human-like personality traits in wild birds, fish, and octopus.

A. How these Studies Changed People's Minds
    1. Although at first some dismissed the ideas of personalities in other animals, today top research journals are publishing research on animal personality.
        a. Research on genetics, health, and the biological and evolutionary basis of personality all benefit from an understanding of how animals differ in their personalities.

IV. How is Personality Measured? (p. 519)

    A. Behavioral Observation
        1. Observing behavior directly is the most objective method for obtaining personality data. One can count specific behaviors associated with personality traits, such as aggression or friendliness.
            a. If two or more raters are to accurately rate and agree upon their ratings there must be *inter-rater reliability.*
            b. Behavioral observations are costly and time-consuming.

    B. Interviewing
        1. Interviewing is an ideal method for obtaining important information about a person's life.
            a. Interviewing allows for open-ended answers and is more personable than filling out a questionnaire. However, a drawback to this method is that it may be difficult to objectively determine what a person means.
                i. It may be difficult to objectively score the answers provided.

    C. Projective Tests
        1. *Projective tests* present an ambiguous stimulus or situation to participants and ask them to give their interpretation of or tell a story about what they see.
        2. The *Rorschach Inkblot Test* is a series of ambiguous inkblots that are presented to the client one at a time and the client tells the therapist what he or she sees in each one.
            a. This test is used to measure unconscious motives.
        3. The *Thematic Apperception Test* consists of a series of hand-drawn cards depicting simple scenes that are ambiguous and the client is asked to make up a story about what she or he things in happening in the scene.

    D. Questionnaires
        1. The expense and time involved with the methods of personality assessment presented thus far has lead to less costly and easier to score methods, such as *questionnaires* which are the most common way to measure personality.
        2. *Personality questionnaires* consist of individual statements that respondents indicate the extent to which they agree or disagree with a statement.
            a. Responses are often provided via a *Likert scale,* which is comprised of categories such as "strongly agree" and "neither agree nor disagree" and "strongly disagree."

b. The *rational* or *face valid method* involves using reason or theory to come up with a question for the personality measurement tool.

c. The *empirical method* disregards theory and face validity and focuses on simple whether a question distinguishes groups it is supposed to distinguish (Gough & Bradely, 1996).

Psychology in the Real World: Screening and Selecting Police Officers (p. 522)

A. Measures of personality have many real-world applications. Career guidance counselors use them to advise students on career choices (Costa, 1996; Mount, Barrick, Scullen, & Rounds, 2005). Therapists use them to help determine causes for marital fighting (Atkins et al., 2005). Finally, government and businesses use them to select the right people for particular jobs (Carless, 1999; De Fruyt & Murvielde, 1999).

1. Most major police departments routinely include personality assessments in their selection process. Such tests alter those making hiring decisions to candidates who might be better suited for one line of work rather than indicating which ones will perform best as police officers.

a. The California Psychological Inventory is used to reliable identify police officers who consistently used excessive force and provided drugs to inmates (Hargrave & Hiatt, 1989).

Making Connections in Personality: Does Personality Change Over Time? (p. 524)

A. Personality Consistency

1. Longitudinal studies have shown high levels of stability of personality.

a. One study found that children who were impulsive, aggressive, and tended to cry at age 3 were more likely to use drugs during adolescence (Block, Block, & Keyes, 1988).

2. Genetics contribute to the personality consistency we see from adolescence to adulthood, and environmental factors contribute to both the stability and change in personality traits (Takahashi et al., 2007).

B. Personality Change

1. Typical Personality Change Across the Life Span

a. A meta-analysis of 92 studies and 50,000 people measured on the Big Five dimensions found that people become steadily more agreeable and conscientious from adolescence to late adulthood. Also, people become more assertive or dominant and emotionally stable from adolescence to middle adulthood. Lastly, people become more social and open from adolescence to early adulthood, the level off, and then decline in these traits in late adulthood (Roberts, Walton, & Viechtbauer, 2006).

2. Personality Change after Changes in Life Circumstances

a. Experiencing drastic changes in our lives, such as being a parent, suffering brain injury, or developing Alzheimer's disease can lead to changes in personality.

i. Parenting and Personality Change: Parenthood affects the personalities of mothers and fathers differently

ii. Brain Injury and Personality Change: Injury to the brain, as happened with Phineas Gage, can result in profound personality changes.

iii. Alzheimer's Disease and Personality Change: Alzheimer's is a major degenerative brain disease that results in severe dementia and memory loss, and affects personality, eventually, it leads to death.

GLOSSARY TERMS

personality: the unique and relatively enduring set of behaviors, feelings, thoughts, and motives that characterize an individual.

trait: a disposition to behave consistently in a particular way.

behavioral thresholds: the point at which a person moves from not behaving to behaving.

quantitative trait loci (QTL) approach: a technique in behavioral genetics that looks for the location on genes that might be associated with particular behaviors.

unconscious: the level of consciousness containing all drives, urges, and instincts that are outside awareness but nonetheless motivate most behavior.

id: Freud's term for the seat of impulse and desire; the pleasure-seeking part of our personality.

ego: Freud's term for the sense of self; the part of the mind that operates on the "reality principle."

superego: Freud's term for the part of the mind that monitors behavior and evaluates it in terms of right and wrong; the conscience.

defense mechanisms: unconscious strategies used by the mind to protect itself from harmful, threatening, and anxiety-provoking thoughts, feelings, or impulses; they deny or distort reality in some way.

repression: defense mechanism for keeping unpleasant thoughts, feelings, or impulses out of consciousness.

reaction formation: a defense mechanism that turns an unpleasant idea, feeling, or impulse into its opposite.

projection: a defense mechanism in which people deny and repress particular ideas, feelings, or impulses but project them onto others.

sublimation: a defense mechanism in which a socially unacceptable impulse is expressed in a socially acceptable and even desirable way.

psychosexual stage theory: Freud's stages of personality development, in different stages a different region of the body is most erogenous.

oral stage: according to Freud, the psychosexual stages between birth and 12–18 months.

anal stage: according to Freud, the psychosexual stage between 18 and 36 months, when pleasure is gained from controlling elimination.

phallic stage: according to Freud, the psychosexual stage between ages 3 to 6 when the child discovers that the genitals are a source of pleasure.

latency stage: according to Freud, a developmental phase, lasting from age 6 until puberty, in which the sense of sexuality is dormant.

genital stage: according to Freud, the psychosexual stage that starts with puberty and lasts for the rest of one's life when the source of pleasure is once again the genitals, but this time in a mature adult fashion.

fixation: a defense mechanism whereby a person continues to be concerned and even preoccupied with earlier stages of development; occurs when stages are left unresolved.

striving for superiority: according to Adler, the major drive behind all behavior, whereby humans naturally strive to overcome their physical and psychological deficiencies.

inferiority complex: an unhealthy need to dominate or upstage others as a way of compensating for feelings of deficiency.

personal unconscious: according to Jung, all of our repressed and hidden thoughts, feelings, and motives.

collective unconscious: according to Jung, the shared experiences of our ancestors that have been passed down from generation to generation.

archetypes: ancient or archaic images that result from common ancestral experiences; often expressed in dreams, hallucinations, and myths.

anima: according to Jung, the female part of the male personality.

animus: according to Jung, the male part of the female personality.

self-actualization: people's inherent drive to realize their full potential.

unconditional positive regard: in Roger's approach to psychotherapy, the ability to respect and appreciate another person regardless of his or her behavior.

Big Five or **five-factor Model**: a categorization scheme for personality that includes five dimensions: openness to experience, conscientiousness, extraversion, agreeableness, and neuroticism (OCEAN).

basic tendencies: the essence of personality: the Big Five personality dimensions plus talents, aptitudes, cognitive abilities.

cortical arousal: how active the brain is at a resting state as well as how sensitive it is to stimulation.

inter-rater reliability: measure of how much agreement there is in ratings when using two or more raters or coders to rate personality or other behaviors.

projective tests: method of measuring personality traits by presenting an ambiguous stimulus or situation to participants and asking them to give their interpretation of or tell a story about what they see.

Rorschach Inkblot Test: a projective test involving a series of ambiguous inkblots presented one at a time; the participant is asked to say what he or she sees in each one.

Thematic Apperception Test (TAT): a projective test that consists of a series of hand-drawn cards depicting simple scenes that are ambiguous; the participant makes up a story about what he or she thinks is going on in the scene.

questionnaires: self-report instruments that consist of individual statements, or *items;* respondents indicate the extent to which they agree or disagree with each statement as it applies to their personality.

Likert scales: response categories on a questionnaire, in which answers are given on a numeric scale ranging from complete agreement on one end to complete disagreement on the other.

rational (face valid) method: a method for developing questionnaire items that involves using reason or theory to come up with a question.

empirical method: a method for developing questionnaire items that disregards theory and face validity and focuses instead on simply whether a question distinguishes groups it is supposed to distinguish.

PRACTICE STUDY QUESTIONS

1. The term _____ refers to the unique and relatively enduring set of behaviors, feelings, thoughts, and motives that characterize an individual.
   a. social complex
   b. traits
   c. personality
   d. individual differences

2. The evolution of personality traits demonstrates how our bodies, brain, and behavior can be shaped by environmental forces over long periods of time.
   a. true
   b. false

3. _____ is a method behavioral genetics uses to look for biological markers of behavior.
   a. Rorschach test
   b. Face validity
   c. Quantitative trait loci
   d. Thematic Apperception test

4. Infants born to mothers who have experienced an unusual amount of stress during pregnancy tend to have higher levels of:
   a. serotonin.
   b. dopamine.
   c. norepinephrine.
   d. glucocorticoids.

5. In general, people from Asian cultures tend to be _____; whereas people from Western cultures tend to be _____.
   a. individualistic; collectivistic
   b. aggressive; shy
   c. shy; aggressive
   d. collectivistic; individualistic

6. _____ refers to people who are more concerned about the impact of their behavior on family, friends, and social groups; whereas _____ refers to people who are more concerned with how their behavior will affect their personal goals.
   a. Shyness; aggressiveness
   b. Aggressiveness; shyness
   c. Collectivism; individualism
   d. Individualism; collectivism

7. _____ is the unconscious act of keeping threatening or disturbing thoughts, feelings, or impulses out of consciousness.
   a. Reaction formation
   b. Repression
   c. Projection
   d. Sublimation

8. _____ is when we deny and repress particular ideas, feelings, or impulses but project them onto others.
   a. Reaction formation
   b. Repression
   c. Projection
   d. Sublimation

9. _____ occurs when an unpleasant idea, feeling, or impulse is turned into its opposite.
   a. Reaction formation
   b. Repression
   c. Projection
   d. Sublimation

10. Most adults reach the self-actualization level of Maslow's hierarchy of needs.
    a. true
    b. false

11. _____ developed the psychosexual stage theory of personality development.
    a. Rogers
    b. Allport
    c. Freud
    d. Jung

12. _____ developed the idea of an individual striving for superiority and the inferiority complex.
    a. Rogers
    b. Adler
    c. Freud
    d. Jung

13. _____ believed that people had two distinct forms of the unconscious: the personal unconscious and the collective unconscious.
    a. Rogers
    b. Allport
    c. Freud
    d. Jung

14. _____ developed a unique form of psychotherapy which practiced unconditional positive regard for the client.

a. Rogers
b. Allport
c. Freud
d. Jung

15. The five dimensions of the Big Five refer to: openness to experience, conscientiousness, extraversion, _____, and neuroticism.
    a. aggressiveness
    b. ability
    c. agreeableness
    d. anger

16. Eysenck's model of personality included only three dimensions: _____, extraversion, and neuroticism.
    a. politeness
    b. psychoticism
    c. potential
    d. personality

17. There is no evidence that animals have personality traits.
    a. true
    b. false

18. The Rorschach Inkblot Test and the Thematic Apperception Test are examples of _____ personality tests.
a. objective
b. questionnaire
c. survey
d. projective

ANSWERS TO PRACTICE STUDY QUESTIONS

1. c
2. a
3. c
4. d
5. d
6. c
7. b
8. c
9. a
10. b
11. c
12. b
13. d
14. a
15. c
16. b
17. b
18. d

Chapter 14
SOCIAL BEHAVIOR

KEY TERMS

Social psychology
Social facilitation
Social loafing
Social norms
Conformity
Informational social influence
Normative social influence
Groupthink
Obedience
Attributions
Self-serving bias
Fundamental attribution error
Stereotypes
In-group/out-group bias
Out-group homogeneity
Prejudice

Discrimination
Attitude
Cognitive dissonance
Persuasion
Aggression
Prosocial behavior
Bystander effect
Altruism
Kin selection
Reciprocal altruism
Social exchange theory
Empathy
Empathy-altruism hypothesis
Sexual strategies theory
Triangular theory of love
Cult

OUTLINE

I. Group Living and Social Influence (p. 533)

    A. *Social Psychology* defined: The study of the effects of the real or imagined presence of others on people's thoughts, feelings, and actions.

        1. *Social facilitation* occurs when the presence of others improves our performance. The opposite effect, *social loafing,* occurs then the presence of others causes one to relax one's standards and slack off (Harkins, 1987).

    B. Conformity: occurs when people adjust their behaviors to what others are doing or adhere to the norms of their culture.
        1. Society imposes rules about acceptable behavior termed *social norms.*

        2. *Informational social influence* occurs when people conform to the behavior of others because they view them as a source of knowledge about what they are supposed to do.

        3. *Normative social influence* occurs when people go along with the behavior of others in order to be accepted by them.

            a. *Social impact theory* states that our likelihood of following either informational or normative influence depends on three different aspects

of the group (Latane, 1981; Latane & Wolf, 1981):
   i. *How important the group is to you*
   ii. *How close the group is to you in space and time*
   iii. *How many people are in the group*

C. Obedience: Is a kind of conformity in which people yield to the social pressure of an authority figure.

   1. Stanley Milgram conducted a famous experiment examining people's obedience to authority. Naïve participants thought they were in a learning experiment and were told to provide electric shock to other participants (confederates) for incorrect answers. Although no shock was actually delivered, the participant was unaware of this fact.

   2. Twenty-six of the original forty participants (65%) gave the maximum 450 volt shock. Participants displayed signs of anguish throughout the experiment which resulted in a great debate regarding the ethics of the experiment.

II. Social Perception: How we make sense of our social world (p. 542)

A. *Attributions* are the inferences we make about the causes of other people's behavior.

   1. Heider (1958) made an important distinction between two types of attributions:

      a. *Dispositional (internal) attributions* occur when one thinks that someone's behavior is caused by something within them, such as their personality, motive, or attitude.

      b. *Situational (external) attributions* occur when people think that something outside the person, such as the nature of the situation, cause her or his behavior.

   2. The tendency to make situational attributions for our failures but dispositional attributions for our successes is known as a *self-serving bias.*

   3. The *fundamental attribution error* (Ross, 1977) states that people tend to explain other people's behavior in terms of dispositional rather than situational.

      a. People living in Asian cultures are much less likely to make the fundamental attribution error than European-Americans (Choi, Nisbett, & Norenzayan, 1999).

B. Detecting Deception

   1. Most are poor at detecting lies. Ekman and O'Sullivan (1991) noted that most people perform no better than chance in detecting deception from people's

demeanor.

C. Stereotypes: Are schemas of how people are likely to behave based simply on the groups to which they belong.

    1. One reason people resort to stereotypes is because they are easy and fast; they allow us to form quick, but often inaccurate, impressions.

D. Exclusion and Inclusion

    1. When we show positive feelings toward people who belong to the same group as us, and negative feelings toward those in other groups we are displaying *in-group/out-group bias*.

        a. *Out-group homogeneity* is the tendency to see all members of an out-group as the same.

E. Prejudice and Discrimination

    1. *Prejudice* is a biased attitude toward a group of people or an individual member of a group based on unfair generalizations about what members of that group are like (Allport, 1954).

        a. Prejudices about race are termed *racism*.

        b. Prejudices about sex are termed *sexism*.

    2. *Discrimination* is preferential treatment of certain people that is usually driven by prejudicial attitudes.

Breaking New Ground: The Study of Implicit Bias (p. 546)

A. Traditional Approaches to the Study of Prejudice: Psychologists study prejudice by surveying people about the conscious attitudes toward individuals from different racial backgrounds.

    1. This approach had drawbacks, including not knowing whether people are giving honest responses or responses that they think the researchers want to hear. Social psychologists now differentiate between *implicit* and *explicit* prejudice.

        a. Explicit ideas are plainly stated, for example, the statement "I want to have sex with you" is explicit; whereas the statement "Would you like to come by and see my new hockey stick?" is implicit. Implicit knowledge or beliefs are more difficult to measure.

B. Innovations in Measuring Implicit Bias

    1. Greenwald and Banaji developed a test called the *Implicit Associations Test* (IAT) in which they took European-American and African-American names and paired them with both pleasant and unpleasant words. Both Greenwald and Banaji were shocked at their results: they had difficulty pairing African-Americans names with pleasant words.

C. Moving Research on Bias Forward: The findings from the IAT test were powerful and it became obvious that even those of us who are convinced that we are not biased may harbor some prejudice of which we are unaware.

III. Attitudes and Behavior (p. 549)

A. *Attitudes* are people's favorable or unfavorable beliefs, feelings, or actions toward an object, idea, or person (Olson, & Zanna, 1993). Attitudes can have three components:

    1. *Affective* components include the feelings or emotions associated with the belief.

    2. *Cognitive* components consist of the rational thoughts and beliefs that make up an attitude.

    3. *Behavioral* components include the motive to act in a particular way toward the person or object of the attitude.

B. The Nature and Nurture of Attitudes: Where do attitudes come from?

    1. Some theorists suggest that we have evolutionary pressures to form quick evaluations. Others propose that we acquire attitudes from experience.

        a. *Mere exposure* or direct experience with an object, idea, or person increases one's overall preference for it (Zajonc, 1968).

    2. Conditioning can also play a role in the formation of our attitudes.

C. Attitude Change: Two major ways of attitude change are *cognitive dissonance* and *persuasion.*

    1. *Cognitive dissonance* is the feeling of discomfort caused by information that is different from your conception of yourself as a reasonable and sensible person (Festinger, 1957).

        a. A person who smokes has to deal with the conflict between their notion of themselves as a rational an intelligent being and the fact the he smokes, which is not a smart thing to do. To reduce unpleasant feelings and dissonant thoughts and behaviors the person could behave in one of three ways:

    i. Change the behavior (quit smoking)
    ii. Justify the smoking by changing cognitions associated with it ("Smoking isn't that bad").
    iii. Change the cognitions so as to justify the smoking ("It makes me feel good and I deserve some pleasure, whatever the risks.")

2. *Persuasion* occurs then a person or group attempts to change our opinions, beliefs, or choices by explaining or arguing their position.

    a. The effectiveness of persuasion can depend upon: (a) how trustworthy, prestigious, and likeable the person; (b) the methods of persuasion used (e.g., fear); and (c) who the targeted audience is.

IV. Social Relations (p. 553)

A. The Nature and Nurture of Aggression: Aggression is a part of animal life and although many animals kill in order to survive, humans are unique in that they often engage in aggression and violent behavior when their survival is not at issue.

1. *Aggression* defined: the violent behaviors that are intended to cause psychological or physical harm, or both, to another being. It is intentional.

    a. When aggression stems from feelings of anger, it is termed *hostile aggression.*

    b. When aggression is a means to achieve some goal, it is termed *instrumental aggression.*

B. Social Influences on Aggression: Observing aggressive people and the consequences of their action can make us more aggressive.

1. Bandura's *social learning theory* is relevant here as he showed with his Bobo doll experiments that if children watched adults punching an inflatable Bobo doll, they would do the same thing; they would behave aggressively even more so if they saw the adult get rewarded for the aggressive behavior.

2. Longitudinal research with men and women has shown that the more people watch TV when they are children, the more violent behavior they exhibit as adults (Huesmann, Moise-Titus, & Podolski, 2003).

Psychology in the Real World: Violent Media, Violent World (p. 556)

A. Social learning theory provides convincing data on how observing aggressive behavior of others plays a role in the development of aggression.

    1. Bushman and Anderson (2001) conducted a meta-analysis to objectively assess the relationship between TV violence and aggression. They found numerous studies that showed a much stronger relationship between TV violence and aggression than what is portrayed by the media (see Figure 14.7).

B. Some psychologists suggest hat desensitization to violence can increase aggression by reducing the perceived seriousness of a situation individuals encounter and reducing the likelihood of helping behavior in emergencies (Carnagey et al., 2007).

A. Prosocial behavior: Refers to behavior that is beneficial to others.

    1. The Bystander Effect arose out of the murder of Kitty Genovese who was attacked with no less than 38 witnesses. No one came to help. Social psychologists Darley and Latane (1968) conducted experimental research in an attempt to determine why no one came to Kitty's aid.

        b. Darley and Latane found that as the number of people increase in the presence of an emergency, the less likely any one person is to help. This phenomenon is referred to at the *bystander effect.*

    2. One explanation for the bystander effect is *diffusion of responsibility* which means that when there are many other people around, the responsibility of each individual present seems lessened. That is, people may think, "somebody else must have called the police" when a crowd of people are present at an emergency when, in fact, nobody had called.

B. Altruism: Is the selfless concern for and helping others.

    1. Evolutionary theory offers two explanations for why people may engage in altruistic behaviors: *kin selection* and *reciprocal altruism.*

        a. *Kin selection* is the evolutionary favoring of genes that prompt individuals to help their relatives or kin (Hamilton, 1964).
        b. *Reciprocal altruism* is when you help others in the hope that they will help you in the future (Tirvers, 1971, 1985).

    2. *Social exchange theory* suggests that in our relations with others we try to maximize our gains and minimize our losses (Thibaut & Kelly, 1959).

E. Empathy: Sharing feeling and understanding about another person's situation.

F. Liking, Attraction, and Love: Psychologists study factors related to how and why we form close relationships with others.

1. Familiarity, Similarity, and Attraction all play an important role in determining whether we like someone.

    a. People tend to be attracted to and partner with people of a similar level of attractiveness to themselves; this is known as *assortative mating* (Buss, 2004).

2. Sexual Attraction and Mate Selection: *Sexual strategies theory* suggests that men and women face different problems when they seek out mates, and so they often approach relationships in very different ways (Buss & Schmitt, 1993).

3. Love is one of the most difficult to understand of all human behaviors. It takes many different forms and means different things to different people at different times in their lives.

    a. The *triangular theory of love* developed by Sternberg (1986) proposes three components that explain human forms of love:

        i. *Intimacy* refers to close, connected and bonded feelings in a loving relationship.

        ii. *Passion* refers to the drives that lead to romance, physical attraction, sexual consummation, and is accompanied by physiological changes and arousal.

        iii. *Commitment* refers to both the decision to love someone or not as well as the decision to commit to it long term.

    b. *Companionate love* exists when intimacy and commitment are high and passion is low.

    c. *Passionate love* exists when intimacy and passion are high and commitment is low.

    d. *Lust* exists when there is a lot of passion but not intimacy or commitment.

4. Love is also related to *attachment* which is a well-known psychological phenomenon.

Making Connections in Social Psychology: An Analysis of the Jonestown Cult (p. 565)

A. Over 900 members of the People's Temple in Jonestown, Guyana killed themselves and their children by drinking a poison-laced drink. The members went willingly to their deaths, but only after years of being led into total commitment into the

Jonestown cult. A *cult* is an extremist group led by a charismatic, totalitarian leader in which coercive methods are used to prevent members from leaving the group.

    B. Four concepts discussed in this chapter pertain to how this large number of people would kill themselves because the leader of their cult, Jones, had devised the plan.

        1. Persuasion

        2. Conformity

        3. Obedience

        4. Cognitive dissonance

GLOSSARY TERMS
social psychology: study of how living among others influences thought, feeling, and behavior.
social facilitation: phenomenon in which the presence of others improves our performance.
social loafing: phenomenon in which the presence of others causes one to relax one's standards and slack off.
social norms: rules about acceptable behavior imposed by the cultural context in which one lives.
conformity: tendency of people to adjust their behavior to what others are doing or to adhere to the norms of their culture.
informational social influence: conformity to the behavior of others because one views them as a source of knowledge about what one is supposed to do.
normative social influence: conformity to the behavior of others in order to be accepted by them.
groupthink: situation in which the thinking of the group takes over, so much so that group members forgo logic or critical analysis in the service of reaching a decision.
obedience: act of following the direct commands of another person.
attributions: inferences made about the causes of other people's behavior.
self-serving bias: the tendency to make situational attributions for our failures but dispositional attributions for our successes.
fundamental attribution error: the tendency to explain other's behavior in terms of dispositional attributions rather than situational ones.
stereotypes: schemas about people based on what they are likely to do or be like based simply on groups to which they belong .
in-group/out-group bias: tendency to show positive feelings toward people who belong to the same group as we do, and negative feelings toward those in other groups.
out-group homogeneity: the tendency to see all members of an out-group as the same.
prejudice: a biased attitude toward a group of people or an individual member of a group based on unfair generalizations about what members of that group are like.
discrimination: preferential treatment of certain people, usually driven by prejudicial attitudes.
attitude: an individual's favorable or unfavorable beliefs, feelings, or actions toward an object, idea, or person.

cognitive dissonance: the feeling of discomfort caused by information that is different from your conception of himself or herself as a reasonable and sensible person.

persuasion: act of attempting to change the opinions, beliefs, or choices of others by explaining or arguing a position.

aggression: the violent behaviors that are intended to cause psychological or physical harm, or both, to another being.

prosocial behavior: action that is beneficial to others.

bystander effect: phenomenon in which the greater the number of bystanders who witness an emergency, the less likely any one of them is to help.

altruism: selfless attitudes and behavior toward others.

kin selection: the evolutionary favoring of genes that prompt individuals to help their relatives or kin

reciprocal altruism: the act of helping others in the hope that they will help us in the future.

social exchange theory: the idea that we help others when we understand that the benefits to ourselves are likely to outweigh the costs.

empathy: the ability to share the feelings of others and understand their situation.

empathy-altruism hypothesis: the idea that people help others selflessly only when they feel empathy for them.

sexual strategies theory: the idea that men and women face different problems when they seek out mates, and so they often approach relationships in very different ways.

triangular theory of love: Robert Sternberg's idea that three components (intimacy, passion, and commitment), in various combinations, can explain all the forms of human love.

cult: an extremist group led by a charismatic, totalitarian leader in which coercive methods are used to prevent members from leaving the group.

PRACTICE STUDY QUESTIONS

1. _____ is the study of the effects of the real or imagined presence of others on people's thoughts, feelings, or actions.
   a. Evolutionary psychology
   b. Cognitive psychology
   c. Health psychology
   d. Social psychology

2. _____ occurs when the presence of others improves our performance; whereas _____ occurs when the presence of others causes one to relax one' standards and slacks off.
   a. Social loafing; social facilitation
   b. Social facilitation; social loafing
   c. Normative influence; conformity
   d. Conformity; normative influence

3. _____ occurs when people adjust their behavior to what others are doing or adhere to the norms of their culture.
   a. Conformity
   b. Obedience
   c. Normative social influence

d. Peer group pressure

4. _____ occur when one thinks that someone's behavior is caused by something within them, such as their personality, motive, or attitude.
    a. Situational attribution
    b. Social perception
    c. Dispositional attribution
    d. Fundamental attribution error

5. _____ are schemas of how people are likely to behave based simply on the groups to which they belong.
    a. Prejudices
    b. Confirmation biases
    c. Stereotypes
    d. Norm groups

6. Prejudice is a biased attitude toward a group of people or an individual member of a group based on unfair generalizations about what members of that group are like.
    a. true
    b. false

7. Social psychologist distinguish between two types of prejudice: explicit and implicit.
    a. true
    b. false

8. Attitudes can have affective, cognitive and _____ components.
    a. physical
    b. opposite
    c. mental
    d. behavioral

9. _____ is the feeling of discomfort caused by information that is different from your conception of yourself as a reasonable and sensible person.
    a. Hostility
    b. Cognitive dissonance
    c. Situational attribution
    d. Out-group bias

10. Swearing at someone who just cut you off on the highway is an example of _____ aggression.
    a. instrumental
    b. hostile
    c. physical
    d. psychological

11. Research has shown that the more TV one watches as a child the more aggressive that person is when he or she is older.
    a. true
    b. false

12. The more people present at an emergency, the less likely any one person is to offer help. This phenomena is known as the:
    a. instrumental aggression hypothesis
    b. buffer hypothesis
    c. bystander effect
    d. altruism fallacy

13. Two possible explanations for altruistic behavior are reciprocal altruism and:
    a. paired altruism.
    b. kin selection.
    c. anti-aggression altruism.
    d. sensitivity altruism.

14. People tend to be attracted to people of a similar level of attractiveness as themselves. This is termed:
    a. selection identity process.
    b. assortative mating.
    c. the law of liking.
    d. psychological absurdness.

15. The triangular theory of love consists of three components: intimacy, passion and:
    a. sex.
    b. commitment.
    c. high regard.
    d. love.

ANSWERS TO PRACTICE STUDY QUESTIONS

1. d
2. b
3. a
4. c
5. c
6. a
7. a
8. d
9. b
10. b
11. a
12. c
13. b
14. b
15. b

Chapter 15
PSYCHOLOGICAL DISORDERS

KEY TERMS

Deviant
Distressing
Dysfunctional
Axis I disorders
Syndromes
Axis II disorders
Cormorbidity
Generalized anxiety disorder (GAD)
Panic attacks
Panic disorder
Agoraphobia
Post-traumatic stress disorder (PTSD)
Phobia
Social anxiety disorder
Social phobia
Specific phobias
Obsessive-compulsive disorder (OCD)
Obsession
Compulsion
Impulse control disorder
Diathesis-stress model
Mood disorders
Major depressive disorder
Dysthymia
Bipolar disorder
Manic episodes
Psychotic disorders
Schizophrenia

Positive symptoms (of schizophrenia)
Hallucinations
Delusion
Negative symptoms (of schizophrenia)
Cognitive symptoms (of schizophrenia)
Word salad
Paranoid schizophrenia
Catatonic schizophrenia
Undifferentiated schizophrenia
Disorganized schizophrenia
Dissociative disorders
Dissociative identity disorder (DID)
Schizoid personality disorder
Personality disorders
Schizotypal personality disorder
Paranoid personality disorder
Histrionic personality disorder
Narcissistic personality disorder
Borderline personality disorder
Antisocial personality disorder
Avoidant personality disorder
Dependent personality disorder
Obsessive–compulsive personality disorder
Attention deficit hyperactivity disorder (ADHD)
Autistic syndrome disorder or autism
Asperger's syndrome

OUTLINE

I. Defining Psychological Disorders: Most psychologists agree on three criteria that distinguish disordered from normal or even different behavior. The behavior must be defiant, distressing, and dysfunctional (APA, 2000). (p. 573)

　　1. *Deviant* literally means "different from the norm" or different from what most people do. Behavior may be deviant in one culture but not in another.

　　2. *Distressing* means that the behavior leads to real discomfort or anguish, either in the person directly or in others. This is why we may says someone is "suffering."

3. *Dysfunctional* means that the behavior interferes with everyday functioning and occasionally may be a risk to oneself or others.

A. How do psychologists decide who is suffering from a psychological disorder?

    1. The *Diagnostic and Statistical Manual (DSM)* published by the American Psychiatric Association is a major tool for determining if one has a disorder. Now at its fourth edition (DSM-IV-TR) disorders are placed on one of two different branches of information or axes.

        a. *Axis I disorders* are the major clinical *syndromes* or clusters of related symptoms that cause significant impairment: anxiety, depression, bipolar, and schizophrenia. These disorders tend to develop after adolescence, can wax and wane, are not permanent.

        b. *Axis II disorders* are the more long-standing personality disorders as well as mental retardation

            i. Almost half of U.S. adults will suffer from at least some Axis I or Axis II disorder at some point in their life, and more than half of those will suffer from two or more disorders (Kessler et al., 2005).

            ii. *Comorbidity* is when a person has two or more disorders occurring at the same time.

            iii. The DSM-IV-TR lists over 250 Axis I disorders and more than 100 Axis II disorders.

II. Anxiety Disorders (p. 577)

A. Generalized Anxiety Disorder (GAD)

    1. GAD is a common disorder and it is characterized by a pervasive and excessive state of anxiety lasting at least six months (APA, 2000). People with GAD have often been anxious throughout their lives and cannot recall a specific time when they began to feel that way (Kessler et al., 2005).

        a. More women than men experience GAD (Kessler et al., 2005).

B. Panic Disorder with or without Agoraphobia

    1. *Panic attacks* are associated with perceptions of threat and can occur for a number of reasons: fear of danger, inability to escape, embarrassment, or specific objects.

a. Panic attacks last about 10 minutes but some may last over one hour. These attacks are characterized by an overwhelming sense of impending doom, accompanied by heart palpitations, trembling, dizziness, intense dread, and even fear of dying. Often people think they are "going crazy" or having a heart attack.

b. People with *panic disorder* get panic attacks and experience persistent worry, embarrassment, and concern about having more attacks (APA, 2000).

    i. Approximately 10% of the U.S. population has experienced a panic attack in the past 12 months; however, only about 2%-5% of the population has panic disorder (Grant et al., 2006).

2. *Agoraphobia* is an intense anxiety and panic about being in places from which escape might be difficult or in which help might not be available should a panic attack occur (APA, 2000).

a. The "fear" in agoraphobia is not really being out in public; it is the fear of being in an inescapable situation.

C. Post-Traumatic Stress Disorder (PTSD)

1. This disorder is triggered by exposure to a catastrophic or horrifying event that posed serious harm or threat to the person-such as experiences of war, attempted murder, rape, natural disasters, sudden death of a loved one, or physical or sexual abuse. Symptoms of PTSD are grouped into three categories:

a. Re-experiencing the trauma.

b. Avoiding of thoughts, feelings, and activities associated with the trauma; emotional numbing and distancing from loved ones.

c. Increased arousal, such as irritability, difficulty sleeping, or exaggerated startle response (Duke & Vasterling, 2005).

    i. War veterans are at increased risk for not only PTSD but also for depression, drug abuse, and suicide after returning home.

    ii. Approximately 20% of Iraq war veterans have developed PTSD.

D. Social Phobia (Social Anxiety Disorder)

a. A *phobia* is a persistent and unreasonable fear of a particular object, situation, or activity (APA, 2000).

b. *Social phobia,* or *social anxiety disorder* is a pronounced fear of humiliation in the presence of others, is marked by severe self-consciousness about appearance or behavior or both.

E. Specific Phobias: Results in undue anxiety about particular objects or situations. They are marked by an intense and immediate fear, even panic, when confronted with very particular situations or objects; even thinking about those situations or objects may result in a fear reaction.

a. *Arachnophobia* is the fear of spiders.

b. *Claustrophobia* is the fear of heights, flying, and/or enclosed spaces.

F. Obsessive-compulsive Disorder (OCD) is an anxiety disorder that is manifested in both thought and behavior.

1. An *obsession* is an unwanted thought, word, phrase, or image that persistently and repeatedly comes into a person's mind and causes distress. People with OCD have thoughts they cannot dismiss, especially negative thoughts that most people can disregard (APA, 2005).

2. A *compulsion* is a repetitive behavior performed in response to uncontrollable urges or according to a ritualistic set of rules.

a. Most often, OCD involves cleaning, checking, or counting behaviors that interfere with everyday functioning. For example, a person with OCD may wash her hands over a hundred times a day so as to avoid germs.

b. People who have OCD know their behaviors are excessive and their thoughts irrational, but they are unable to stop engaging in these activities.

3. *Impulsive control disorder* involves those behaviors that people cannot control and feel an intense, repetitive desire to perform them (APA, 2000). Moreover, these behaviors interfere with everyday functioning.

a. Some behaviors that develop into impulsive control disorder include gambling, shopping, hair pulling, and substance abuse.

Psychology in the Real World: Can Internet Behavior Become an Addiction? (p. 580)

A. There are some people who are online almost constantly and to such an extent that it interferes with their personal and professional lives.

193

1. Mental health professionals do not agree on whether Internet abuse is an addiction, compulsion, or impulse disorder. Most empirical support suggests that it is a problem of impulse control (Aboujaoude et al., 2006).

   a. A large-scale telephone survey found that 4-13% of 2500 adults in the U.S. answered at least one question that indicated problematic Internet use and approximately 1% met proposed diagnostic criteria for Internet-based impulsive disorder (Aboujaoude et al., 2006).

   b. Internet abuse in common in the workplace, which can impair worker productivity because people use the internet obsessively and impulsively. This results in a waste of company resources (Chen, Chen, & Yang, 2007; Stewart, 2000).

   c. One study of college students found that those who spent excessive amounts of time online were more likely to report depressive symptoms and engage in less fact-to-face social interactions (Forsten et al., 2007).

A. What Causes Anxiety Disorders? Nature and Nurture Explanations

   1. There is an interplay of biological and environmental factors that result in explanations of disorders, including anxiety disorders.

   2. The *diathesis-stress model* of disease was historically used by professionals to explain disorders and refers to the view that biological predispositions plus stress or abusive environments together result in psychological disorders.

      a. Research in *epigenetics* has found that genes do not just turn on at predetermined times in our lives, instead they can and do respond to experience.

      b. Three biological factors that make people vulnerable to anxiety disorders are: *deficiencies in the neurotransmitter GABA,* their *genetic heritage,* and their *personality.*

III. Mood Disorders are disturbances in emotional behavior that prevent people from functioning effectively in everyday life. (p. 583)

   A. Depression and its Causes

      1. *Major depressive disorder* is characterized by pervasive low mood, lack of motivation, low energy, and feelings of worthlessness and guilt that last for at least two consecutive weeks (APA, 2000)

         a. Approximately 10% of U.S. adults have clinical depression at some point in their lives.

  b. Sleep is often disturbed for those with depression which sometimes results in insomnia or sometimes in hypersomnia (excessive sleep).

  c. Although an environmental event can be the cause for some people's depression, for others it just seems to turn on (like turning on a light switch).

 2. *Dysthymia* is a milder form of depression in which the symptoms are the same as depression but less intense.

B. Bipolar Disorder and its Causes

 1. People with bipolar disorder experience substantial mood fluctuations, cycling between very low (depression) and very high (manic) episodes.

  a. *Manic episodes* typically involve increased energy, sleeplessness, euphoria, irritability, delusions of grandeur, increased sex drive, and "racing" thoughts.

  b. Your text provides the following mnemonic for remembering the symptoms of mania: D-I-G-F-A-S-T (Carlat, 1998).

   D = distractibility
   I = indiscretion
   G = grandiosity
   F = flight of ideas
   A = activity increased
   S = sleep (decreased need for)
   T = talkativeness

  c. Men and women are affected by bipolar about equally.

  d. *Cyclothymia* is a milder form of bipolar and is characterized by manic and depressive episodes that are less severe than found with bipolar disorder.

 2. The environment plays a role in shaping the brain in bipolar disorder, just as it does so with other disorders. For example, fetuses that are exposed to large amounts of alcohol suffer permanent effects such as increased risk for bipolar disorder, depression, schizophrenia, alcoholism, mental retardation, and drug abuse (Famy, Streissguth, & Unis, 1998; O'Conner & Paley, 2006).

 3. There is also a genetic component to bipolar disorder and although complex, researchers have identified several genes that may play a role in the disorder, but they do not know which of those genes are most critical (Comer, 2007;

Shastry, 2005).

    a. One study found that if one genetic twin develops bipolar disorder, there
       is a 40-70% chance that the other twin will also develop the disorder
       (Muller-Oerlinghausen et al., 2002; Shastry, 2005).

    b. Brain regions that consistently seem to malfunction in those with
       bipolar disorder are the prefrontal cortex, amyygdala, and basal ganglia
       (Muller-Oerlinghausen, Berghofer, & Bauer, 2002; Shastry, 2005).

    c. Serotonin and thyroid hormones also play a role in bipolar which
       demonstrates a neurochemistry component to the disorder.

IV. Schizophrenia (p. 590)

  A. *Psychotic disorders* are those of thought and perception and are characterized by an
     inability to distinguish real from imagined perceptions. *Schizophrenia* is a very serious
     psychotic disorder that involves profound changes in thought and emotions, and
     includes impairments in perceptions such as hallucinations.

    1. Approximately 1% of the U.S. population has this disorder (making it much
       less common than depression, for example).

    2. If a first-degree relative has the disorder, the odds of a related individual having
       the disorder rises to 10% (NIMH, 2007).

  B. Major Symptoms of Schizophrenia

    1. At least one of the following symptoms must persist for six months and at least
       two must be present sometime during those six months for an individual to be
       diagnosed with schizophrenia: *delusions, hallucinations, disorganized speech,
       grossly disorganized or catatonic behavior (immobile and unresponsive, though
       awake), negative symptoms (such as not speaking or being unable to experience
       emotion).*

    2. Symptoms of schizophrenia fall into three categories: positive, negative, and
       cognitive.

      a. *Positive symptoms* include the bizarre perceptual experiences including
         hallucinations, delusional thinking, and disorganized thought and
         speech.

      b. *Hallucinations* are convincing sensory experiences that occur in the
         absence of an external stimulus; that is, the brain receives faulty sensory
         input.

i. Auditory hallucinations are the most common form of hallucination and can result in hearing voices. Visual hallucinations are the next most frequent, followed by tactile hallucinations.

c. *Delusions* are false beliefs, often of an exaggerated claim, that the person holds despite evidence to the contrary (e.g., thinking one is Jesus Christ).

d. *Negative symptoms* include nonresponsiveness, being emotionally flat, immobility or striking strange poses (catatonia), reduced speaking, and inability to complete tasks. These symptoms have been harder to treat and to diagnose than positive symptoms.

e. *Cognitive symptoms* exhibited by people with schizophrenia include problems with working memory, attention, verbal and visual learning and memory, reasoning and problem solving, speed of processing, and disordered speech (Barch, 2005).

i. A person with schizophrenia's speech may follow grammatical rules, but the content may make little sense. This type of talk is often referred to as *word salad.* See your text for an example from a woman who speaks in this way.

3. Subtypes of Schizophrenia

a. *Paranoid schizophrenia* consists of persistent preoccupation with one or more delusions or frequent auditory hallucinations, but the person must be free of disorganized speech, catatonic behavior, and flat and inappropriate affect.

i. The most common side effect is feeling persecuted, followed, slandered, or discriminated against. There may also be delusions of grandeur.

b. *Catatonic schizophrenia* is when a person exhibits at least two of the following symptoms: extreme immobility, excessive activity, peculiar posturing, mutism or parroting what other people say.

c. *Undifferentiated schizophrenia* is diagnosed when the individual exhibits general symptoms (e.g., delusions, hallucinations) but otherwise do not fit into any of the specific subtypes.

d. *Disorganized schizophrenia* occurs when the patient shows no signs of catatonia but exhibits both disorganized speech and behavior and flat or inappropriate affect.

C. Nature and Nurture Explanations of Schizophrenia

    1. Genetics play an important role in the development of schizophrenia, however, given that heritability rates are 80-85%, the role of the environment cannot be overlooked as an important contributing factor. Research suggests that genes are turned on or off by environmental experiences during brain development to produce this disorder (Grossman et al., 2003; Moffitt et al., 2005; Petronis, 2004).

    2. Maternal Infections and Schizophrenia

        a. If a woman contracts an infection during pregnancy, the risk of the child developing schizophrenia later in life increases dramatically. Prenatal exposure to infections and diseases such as influenza, rubella, toxoplasmosis, and herpes has been linked to increased risk of schizophrenia (Brown, 2006).

    3. Brain Structures and Schizophrenia

        a. Abnormal brain development during gestation may be responsible for many of the brain dysfunctions that are characteristic of schizophrenia.

        b. One brain abnormality that occurs with schizophrenia is in the prefrontal cortex. There is evidence of both reduced and excessive activity in that area (Andreasen et al., 1997; Goldman-Rakic, 1999; Weinberger et al., 2001).

            i. When using working memory, people with schizophrenia process information less efficiently and less automatically than people without schizophrenia (Barch, 2005; Weinberger et al., 2001).

            ii. One of the oldest findings on the brain and schizophrenia is that those individuals with the disorder tend to have enlarged ventricles (the fluid-filled spaces in the brain (Lieberman et al., 2001). It is not known, however, whether this is a cause or an effect of schizophrenia.

    4. Neurochemistry of Schizophrenia

        a. There are also neurochemical differences in those with schizophrenia. One difference lead to the development of the *dopamine hypothesis* which states that people with schizophrenia have an excess of dopamine in certain areas of the brain (Javitt & Coyle, 2004). There are some problems with this hypothesis as only a minority of people receiving dopamine-specific medications find them effective for treating the positive symptoms.

   b. Newer research suggests that glutamate deficiencies rather than dopamine excesses may explain the symptoms of schizophrenia (Javitt & Coyle, 2001).

V. Dissociative Disorders (p. 595)

 A. Dissociative Identity Disorder (DID): occurs when people develop at least two distinct personalities, each of whom has a unique set of memories, behaviors, thoughts, and emotions.

  1. The disorder develops in childhood, but may not be diagnosed until adolescence (Comer, 2007). In addition, women are approximately three times more likely to have DID than are men (APA, 2000).

   i. In one study, over 90% of people with DID reported having been sexually or physically abused (Ellason, Ross, & Fuchs, 1996).

  2. Symptoms of DID include amnesia, self-destructive behaviors, and hearing voices.

  3. The diagnosis of DID is somewhat controversial and some psychiatrists claim the diagnosis is not real but instead is unintentionally produced by the therapists themselves (Putnam & McHugh, 2005).

 B. Dissociative Amnesia and Fugue

  1. When some people are exposed to truly painful or traumatic experiences they develop amnesia that is too complete to be explained by normal "forgetting." People with this disorder become somewhat detached from the experience.

  2. *Dissociative fugue* is related to dissociative amnesia but with more serious consequences. Here, the individual not only forgets her or his identity and past but also flees to a new location and may establish a new identity there.

 C. Causes of Dissociative Identity Disorder

  1. One common characteristic shared by those who have DID is that they experienced some highly traumatic event.

Breaking New Ground: Abuse, Disorders, and the Dynamic Brain (p. 597)

 A. Early Views on Sexual and Physical Abuse

199

1. Before the 1950s, medical and psychiatric professionals did not recognize the pervasiveness of childhood sexual and physical abuse. After studies on the abuse of orphans and battered children became known people acknowledged this problem.

2. Clinicians and researchers viewed the long-term consequences of abuse for mental health as products of learned behaviors and bad environments. They did not know that abuse could change the brain and interact with genetic variability that may increase the likelihood of certain psychological disorders

B. Abuse and Neglect Change the Brain

1. The Adverse Childhood Experiences (ACE) study began in the mid-to late 1990s with more then 17,000 participants who were interviewed about eight "adverse childhood experiences" including abuse, domestic violence, and serious household dynamics (i.e., someone in the household abused drugs, had a psychological disorder, or committed criminal acts).

   a. Fore every adverse childhood experience participants reported, psychological outcomes deteriorated.

   b. One example from this study showed that someone who reported four or more adverse childhood experiences was almost four times as likely to be depressed and 2.5 times as likely to suffer from anxiety disorder as someone who reported not adverse childhood experiences (Anda et al., 2006).

C. How ACE Researched Changed the Course of the Field

1. Before ACE research most therapists and researchers focused on social and environmental explanations of child abuse. They the effects on adult personality and behavior caused by childhood abuse were learned through modeling and shaping of behavior. Although this is true, it is also limited.

2. Due to ACE research, it is now widely recognized that the interaction of genetic factors with exposure to abusive or neglectful environments plays a major role in the development of psychological disorders.

VI. Personality Disorders: Are different from clinical disorders in that they generally start in childhood and are more stable than clinical disorders such as depression, schizophrenia, and bipolar disorder. There are three distinct personality disorders: *odd-eccentric, dramatic-emotional,* and *anxious-fearful.* (p. 599)

A. Odd-Eccentric Personality Disorders

1. *Schizoid personality disorder* refers to individuals who do not want close

relationships, are emotionally aloof, reclusive, humorless, and want to live a solitary life.

    2. Thos with *schizotypal personality disorder* are isolated and asocial, but in addition have very odd thoughts and beliefs.

    3. *Paranoid personality disorder* refers to individuals who are extremely suspicious and mistrustful of other people, in ways that are both unwarranted and not adaptive.

B. Dramatic-Emotional Personality Disorders

    1. *Histrionic personality disorder* refers to people who want very much to be the center of attention and often behave in very dramatic, seductive, flamboyant, and exaggerated ways. They can also be very emotional, intense, self-centered, and shallow in their emotions and relationships.

    2. *Borderline personality disorder* refers to individuals who have out-of-control emotions, are very afraid of being abandoned by others, and vacillate between idealizing and despising those who are close to them. They are likely to hurt themselves (like cutting) or have eating disorders.

    3. *Narcissistic personality disorder* refers to individuals who have an extremely positive and arrogant self-image, and most of their time and attention is self focused. In addition, they have an exaggerated sense of self-importance and are grandiose.

    4. *Antisocial personality disorder* is marked by extremely impulsive, deceptive, violent, ruthless, and callous behaviors. It is a serious and potentially dangerous disorder.

        i. About 3% of the population has the disorder, but between 45-75% of male prison inmates are diagnosed with the disorder (Fazel & Danesh, 2002, Hare, 1993).

C. Anxious or Fearful Personality Disorders

    1. *Avoidant personality disorder* refers to people who are so afraid of being criticized that they avoid interacting with others and become socially isolated.

    2. *Dependent personality disorder* refers to those who fear being rejected and have such a strong need to be cared for that they form clingy and dependent relationships with others.

        i. Although people with this disorder only feel safe in relationships with others, they often tend to drive others away because they are so demanding.

        3. *Obsessive-compulsive personality disorder* refers to people who are very rigid in their habits and extremely perfectionistic.

D. Nature and Nurture Explanation of Personality Disorders: Focus on Antisocial Personality Disorder

        1. Research on those who have committed murder has identified a cluster of traits possessed by most violent criminals: being male, coming from abusive and neglectful households, having at least one psychological disorder, and having suffered some kind of injury to the head or brain (Pincus, 1999, 2001; Stueber, Lueck, & Roth, 2006-2007).

            a. Being male is the single strongest predictor of violent behavior.

        2. As a result of head injury or living in a constant state of fear and abuse, or both, murderers almost always have moderate to severe problems of impulsive control, social intelligence, working memory, and attention (Stueber at al., 2006-2007).

VII. Childhood Disorders (p. 602)

A. Subtypes of Childhood Disorders

        1. *Conduct disorder* refers to children who may behave aggressively toward people and animals, destroy property, lie and steal, and seriously violate basic rules.

        2. *Attention-deficit/hyperactivity disorder* refers to children who have great difficulty focusing or paying attention; for example, they may only stay on task for a few minutes and may fidget, disrupt others, and blurt out responses in class.

        3. *Autistic syndrome disorder* or *autism* is characterized by rather severe language and social impairment combined with repetitive habits and inward-focused behaviors.

            a. Evidence suggests that those with autism have an oversensitivity to sensory stimulation or trouble integrating multiple sources of sensory information, such as sight, sound, and touch (Iarocci & McDonald, 2006; Reynolds & Lane, 2008).

            b. Autism is a range or spectrum of disorders, ranging from severe disability to high functioning. On the high functioning end is *Asperger's syndrome.*

i. Children with Asperger's syndrome have impaired social interest and skills and restricted interests, but are not at all delayed or deficient in language and often have above average intelligence (APA, 2000).

B. Causes of Childhood Disorders

1. Childhood disorders stem from genetic factors bust often remain latent unless triggered by some environmental condition (Larsson, Larsson, & Lichtenstein, 2004).

a. For ADHD and conduct disorder, one of the environmental factors is whether the mother smokes while pregnant.

b. In autism, the brain is smaller than normal at birth but grows much faster during the first few years of life than the brains of non-autistic children (Courchesne, Carper, & Akshoomoff, 2003). The brain of a 5 year old with autism is the same as that of a typical 13 year old (Blakeslee, 2005).

Making Connections in Psychological Disorders: Creativity and Mental Health (p. 605)

A. Evidence for a Relationship between Creativity and Psychological Disorders

1. Ludwig (1995) studied creativity and psychological disorders and found that lifetime rates for any psychiatric illness are remarkable high for people in the arts: 87% of poets, 77% of fiction writers, 74% of actors, 73% of visual arts, 72% of nonfiction writers, 68% of musical performers, and 60% of musical composers.

B. Which Disorders Affect Creative Arts?

1. Psychotic Symptoms and Creativity: Having unusual thoughts is common to both creative people and those with schizophrenia.

C. Depression and Creativity

1. Many highly creative people have suffered from major depression. Although highly creative artists and writers may suffer from depression more than most people, depressive episodes themselves do not generate much creative output.

D. Bipolar Disorder and Creativity

1. Many highly creative people, such as poets, actors, architects and

nonfiction writers have higher rates of bipolar disorder. Ludwig (1995) found that individuals such as these had 10 times the rate of bipolar compared to the general population.

   a. There is a positive relationship between bipolar disorder and creative thought.

   b. The manic phase is more likely to generate creative behavior that is the depressive phase (Andresaon & Glcik, 1988; Jamison et al., 1980).

E. Anxiety Disorders and Creativity

   1. There is some evidence that anxiety disorders are more common in creative people, the evidence for a link with creativity is not as compelling as it is for the other disorders.

F. Autism and Creativity

   1. Some, but not most, autistic savant prodigies do produce truly creative works of art, usually math analyses, musical compositions, drawings, or paintings (Fitzgerald, 2004).

GLOSSARY TERMS

deviant: characteristic of disordered behavior; refers to actions that are different from what most people do; different from what is accepted as normal.

distressing: characteristic of disordered behavior; leading to discomfort or anguish.

dysfunctional: characteristic of disordered behavior; interfering with everyday functioning and perhaps posing a risk to oneself or others.

Axis I disorders: in the *DSM-IV*, the major clinical syndromes that cause significant impairment, such as the anxiety disorders, depression, bipolar disorder, and the psychotic disorders.

syndromes clusters of related symptoms.

Axis II disorders: in the *DSM-IV,* the more long-standing personality disorders as well as mental retardation.

comorbidity: occurrence of two or more disorders at the same time.

generalized anxiety disorder (GAD): pervasive and excessive state of anxiety lasting at least six months.

panic attacks: an anxiety disorder associated with perceptions of threat and fear of danger, inability to escape, embarrassment, or specific objects, for example.

panic disorder: an anxiety disorder; involves panic attacks and persistent anxiety about having more attacks.

agoraphobia: an anxiety disorder; intense anxiety and panic about being in places from which escape might be difficult or in which help might not be available should a panic attack occur.

post-traumatic stress disorder (PTSD): a type of anxiety disorder triggered by exposure to a catastrophic or horrifying event that poses serious harm or threat.

phobia: an anxiety disorder; an ongoing and irrational fear of a particular object, situation, or activity.

social phobia (social anxiety disorder): fear of humiliation in the presence of others, characterized by intense self-consciousness about appearance or behavior or both.

specific phobias: anxiety disorders; fear about particular objects or situations, such as spiders, heights, or flying.

obsessive-compulsive disorder (OCD): an anxiety disorder in which compulsive thoughts lead to obsessive behavior.

obsession: an unwanted thought, word, phrase, or image that persistently and repeatedly comes into a person's mind and causes distress.

compulsion: a repetitive behavior performed in response to uncontrollable urges (including obsessions) or according to a ritualistic set of rules.

impulse control disorder: an anxiety disorder related to obsessive-compulsive disorders; uncontrollable behaviors that a person feels an intense, repetitive desire to perform.

diathesis-stress model: explanation for the original of psychological disorders; it holds that a combination of biological predispositions (diathesis) plus stress or abusive environments are usually needed to produce psychological disorders.

mood disorders: category of psychological disorder characterized by severe disturbances in emotional behavior.

major depressive disorder: mood disorder characterized by pervasive low mood, lack of motivation, low energy, and feelings of worthlessness and guilt that last for at least two consecutive weeks.

dysthymia: a milder form of depression.

bipolar disorder: mood disorder characterized by substantial mood fluctuations, a cycling between very low (depressive) and very high (manic) episodes.

manic episodes: one cycle in bipolar disorder, typically involving increased energy, sleeplessness, euphoria, irritability, delusions of grandeur, increased sex drive, and "racing" thoughts.

psychotic disorders: psychological disorders of thought and perception, characterized by the inability to distinguish between real and imagined perceptions.

schizophrenia: psychotic disorder characterized by significant changes in thought and emotion, specifically problems with perception, including hallucinations.

positive symptoms (of schizophrenia): the perceptual experiences associated with schizophrenia, including hallucinations, delusional thinking, and disorganized thought and speech.

hallucinations: convincing sensory experiences that occur in the absence of an external stimulus—in other words, the brain receives false sensory input.

delusion: one of the symptoms of schizophrenia: a false belief or exaggeration held despite evidence to the contrary; such as the idea that one is a famous person.

negative symptoms (of schizophrenia): symptoms that include nonresponsiveness, emotional flatness, immobility, catatonia, problems with speech, and inability to complete tasks.

cognitive symptoms (of schizophrenia): problems with working memory, attention, verbal and visual learning and memory, reasoning and problem solving, processing, and speech.

word salad: term used to describe the speech of people with schizophrenia, which may follow grammatical rules but be nonsensical in terms of content.

paranoid schizophrenia: subtype of schizophrenia characterized by preoccupation with delusions and auditory hallucinations.

catatonic schizophrenia: subtype of schizophrenia characterized by two of the following symptoms extreme immobility, excessive activity, peculiar posturing, mutism, or parroting what other people say.

undifferentiated schizophrenia: cases of schizophrenia characterized by the general symptoms of delusions, hallucinations, and disorganized speech.

disorganized schizophrenia: cases of schizophrenia characterized by disorganized speech and behavior and fl at or inappropriate affect but no catatonia.

dissociative disorders: psychological disorders characterized by extreme splits or gaps in memory, identity, or consciousness.

dissociative identity disorder (DID): dissociative disorder in which a person develops at least two distinct personalities, each with its own memories, thoughts, behaviors, and emotions.

schizoid personality disorder: odd–eccentric personality disorder characterized by a desire to avoid close relationships and to live a solitary life as well as by emotional aloofness, reclusivity, and a lack of humor.

personality disorders: maladaptive and inflexible patterns of cognition, emotion, and behavior that develop in late childhood or adolescence.

schizotypal personality disorder: odd–eccentric personality disorder characterized by a desire to live an isolated and asocial life, but also by the presence of odd thoughts and beliefs.

paranoid personality disorder: odd–eccentric personality disorder characterized by extreme suspicions and mistrust of others in unwarranted and maladaptive ways.

histrionic personality disorder: dramatic–emotional personality disorder characterized by the desire to be the center of attention and by dramatic, seductive, flamboyant and exaggerated behaviors.

narcissistic personality disorder: dramatic–emotional personality disorder characterized by having an extremely positive and arrogant self-image and being extraordinarily self-centered.

borderline personality disorder: dramatic–emotional personality disorder characterized by out-of-control emotions, fear of being abandoned by others, and a vacillation between idealizing and despising people who are close to the person with the disorder.

antisocial personality disorder: dramatic–emotional personality disorder characterized by extremely impulsive, deceptive, violent, ruthless, and callous behaviors; a serious and potentially dangerous disorder.

avoidant personality disorder: anxious–fearful personality disorder characterized by an extreme fear of being criticized as well as low self-esteem, with the result that interaction with others is avoided and social isolation results;.

dependent personality disorder: anxious–fearful personality disorder characterized by fear of being rejected and having a strong need to be cared for so that dependent relationships with others are formed.

obsessive–compulsive personality disorder: anxious–fearful personality disorder characterized by rigid habits and extreme perfectionism; more general than the clinical disorder with the same name (see obsessive–compulsive disorder).

attention deficit hyperactivity disorder (ADHD): childhood disorder characterized by inability to focus attention for more than a few minutes, to remain still and quiet, to do careful work.

autistic syndrome disorder or autism: childhood disorder characterized by severe language and social impairment along with repetitive habits and inward-focused behaviors.

Asperger's syndrome: a childhood disorder at the high-functioning end of the autistic spectrum; characterized by impaired social interest and skills and restricted interests.

PRACTICE STUDY QUESTIONS

1. Most psychologists agree that there are three criteria to distinguish disordered from normal behavior: deviant, distressing, and:
    a. genetic.
    b. scary.
    c. exaggerated.
    d. dysfunctional.

2. People with this disorder have a pervasive and excessive state of anxiety lasting at least six months.
    a. agoraphobia
    b. obsessive-compulsive behavior
    c. post-traumatic stress disorder
    d. generalized anxiety disorder

3. _____ are associated with perceptions of threat and can occur for reasons such as fear of danger, inability to escape, embarrassment, or specific objects. One may experience increased heart rate and feelings of impending doom.
    a. Panic attacks
    b. Hallucinations
    c. Perceptual disruptions
    d. Seizures

4. This disorder is triggered by exposure to a catastrophic or horrifying event that posed serious harm or threat to the person. It can result from exposure to war, rape, or natural disasters.
    a. agoraphobia
    b. obsessive-compulsive behavior
    c. post-traumatic stress disorder
    d. generalized anxiety disorder

5. People with this disorder may have a repetitive behavior performed in response to uncontrollable urges or according to a ritualistic set of rules. For example, they may wash their hands up to 100 times a day.
    a. agoraphobia
    b. obsessive-compulsive behavior
    c. post-traumatic stress disorder
    d. generalized anxiety disorder

6. People with schizophrenia have _____ ventricles.

a. enlarged
b. decreased
c. missing
d. additional

7. The _____ model states that biological predispositions plus stress or abusive environments together produce psychological disorders.
    a. Freud-Dopamine
    b. diathesis-stress
    c. glutamate reduction
    d. dopamine increasing

8. People who have a genetic predisposition to anxiety have low levels of which neurotransmitter?
    a. glutamate
    b. GABA
    c. serotonin
    d. dopamine

9. Depression is always produced by an external event; that is, it never just turns on.
    a. true
    b. false

10. People with this disorder experience substantial mood fluctuations, cycling between very low phases and very high phases. Which is it?
    a. major depression disorder
    b. generalized anxiety disorder
    c. schizophrenia
    d. bipolar disorder

11. Positive symptoms of schizophrenia include: disorganized thought and speech, delusional thinking, and:
    a. increased body temperature.
    b. hallucinations.
    c. seizures.
    d. catatonia.

12. People with _____ schizophrenia have a persistent preoccupation with one or more delusions or frequent auditory hallucinations, but they are free of disorganized speech, catatonic behavior, and flat and inappropriate affect.
    a. undifferentiated
    b. disorganized
    c. catatonic
    d. paranoid

13. Although many have thought that an increase in dopamine was a causal factor for the positive symptoms of schizophrenia, new evidence suggests that it is a deficiency in the neurotransmitter:
    a. GABA.
    b. glutamate.
    c. serotonin.
    d. None of the above

14. People with this personality disorder want very much to be the center of attention and often behave in very dramatic, seductive, flamboyant, and exaggerated ways. Which is it?
    a. Borderline personality disorder
    b. Narcissistic personality disorder
    c. Histrionic personality disorder
    d. Antisocial personality disorder

15. Being male is the single strongest predictor of violent behavior.
    a. true
    b. false

16. This childhood disorder is characterized by rather severe language and social impairment combined with repetitive habits and inward-focused behaviors. Which is it?
    a. conduct disorder
    b. autism
    c. attention-deficit/hyperactivity disorder
    d. None of the above are correct

17. There is no evidence for a link between creativity and mental health.
    a. true
    b. false

ANSWERS TO PRACTICE STUDY QUESTIONS
1. d
2. d
3. a
4. c
5. b
6. a
7. b
8. b
9. b
10. d
11. b
12. d
13. b
14. c
15. a
16. b
17. b

Chapter 16
TREATMENT OF PSYCHOLOGICAL DISORDERS

KEY TERMS

Monoamine oxidase (MAO) inhibitors
Tricyclic antidepressants
Selective serotonin reuptake inhibitors
(SSRIs)
Bupropione
Benzodiazepines
Barbiturates
Lithium
Phenothiazines
Traditional antipsychotic
Tardive dyskinesia
Atypical antipsychotics
Prefrontal lobotomy
Electroconvulsive therapy (ECT)
Repetitive transcranial magnetic stimulation
Psychotherapy
Psychodynamic psychotherapy
Free association

Transference
Defense mechanisms
Repression
Catharsis
Client-centered therapy
Unconditional positive regard
Behavior therapies
Token economies
Systematic desensitization
Flooding
Cognitive therapy
Cognitive-behavioral therapy
Group therapy
Support groups
Integrative therapy
Mindfulness-based cognitive therapy
(MBCT)
Dialectical behavior therapy (DBT)

OUTLINE

I. Biological Treatments (p. 613)

    A. *Drug Therapies:* There are a wide variety of pharmaceuticals that are used to treat psychological disorders.

        1. Drug Treatments for Mood and Anxiety Disorders

            a. *Monoamine oxidase (MAO) inhibitors* were some of the first medications to treat depression. These are used less often today because they can produce undesirable side effects and even death due to interaction with common foods and other over-the-counter medications.

            b. *Tricyclic antidepressants* remain popular for treating depression. They act by blocking the reuptake of serotonin and norepinephrine.

            c. *Selective serotonin reuptake inhibitors (SSRIs)* are among the most widely prescribed psychotherapeutic drugs in the United States. They act by blocking the reuptake of serotonin which results in more of that neurotransmitter in the synapse.

d. *Bupropione* is used to treat depression and also as a smoking cessation aid. It inhibits the reuptake of norepinephrine and dopamine.

e. Benzodiazepines and barbiturates are prescribed for anxiety. Barbiturates have a higher risk of overdoses.

f. *Lithium* is used the mania associated with bipolar disorder.

2. Drug Treatments of Schizophrenia

a. *Phenothiazines* help to reduce hallucinations, confusion, agitation, and paranoia in people with schizophrenia. They work by blocking dopamine receptors in the brain.

i. The phenothiazines and haloperidol are known as *traditional antipsychotics* because they were the first medicines used to manage psychotic symptoms.

ii. *Tardive dyskinesia* results from use of the traditional antipsychotics and includes repetitive, involuntary movements of jaw, tongue, face, and mouth, and body tremors.

b. *Atypical antipsychotics* are newer drugs that to do not have the side effects produced by traditional antipsychotics.

B. Psychosurgery

1. A *prefrontal lobotomy* consists of severing the connections between the prefrontal lobes and the lower portion of the brain. This procedure often left people with profound changes in personality, often resulting in them being listless or subject to seizures. In addition, some patients were reduced to vegetative states (Mashour, Walker, & Martuza, 2005).

C. Electric and Magnetic Therapies

1. *Electroconvulsive therapy (ECT)* involves passing an electrical current through a person's brain in order to induce a seizure and is used to treat severe depression.

2. In *repetitive transcranial magnetic stimulation,* physicians expose particular brain structures to bursts of high-intensity magnetic fields instead of electricity and is also used to treat severe depression.

Breaking New Ground: Deep Brain Stimulation for the Treatment of Severe Depression (p. 621)

    A. Helen Mayberg discovered how a brain region called Brodmann's Area 25 may control depression.

    B. Prevailing Thinking About Brain Circuitry in Depression

        1. Most theories on the brain mechanism of depression hypothesized the role of depletion of various neurotransmitters, such as serotonin, as the cause of depression.

    C. Mayberg's Breakthrough Research

        1. Using PET imaging of brain activation to study patients with both Parkinson's disease and depression, Mayberg found that the patients have reduced activity in both the frontal cortex thinking areas and the limbic emotional areas. To her surprise, she also found that Area 25 was hyperactive, or overactive.

            a. The same finding occurred in patients with depression and Alzheimer's, epilepsy, and Huntington's disease (Mayberg, 1997).

        2. Mayberg and colleagues performed PET scans of depressed people before and after a 15-20 week course of cognitive behavioral therapy and also of depressed people receiving an SSRI. Both groups of patients showed reduced activity in Area 25 that corresponded to clinical improvement of depressive symptoms (Goldapple et al., 2004; Kennedy et al., 2001).

            b. Area 25 may be a gateway between thinking and emotion; an overactive Area 25 may enable the type of negative thinking that feeds depressive states.

        3. Mayberg next used deep brain stimulation (delivering voltage from an external stimulator) to Area 25 with 12 patients whose severe depression had failed to respond to anything else. For 11 of the patients, the depression ceased almost immediately (Mayberg et al., 2005).

            a. Although most people who have had this procedure experience dramatic improvements or complete elimination of their depression, some do not. There is currently a large-scale clinical trail assessing this procedure in a larger population.

II. Psychological Treatments (p. 624)

    A. Psychodynamic Therapy

1. *Psychotherapy* is the use of psychological techniques to modify maladaptive behaviors or thought patterns, or both, and to help patients develop insight into their own behavior. It is carried out by a therapist and a client, either alone or in groups.

2. *Psychodynamic psychotherapy* aims to uncover unconscious motives that underlie psychological problems. The therapist's role is to help the client gain insight into the unconscious influences behind unwanted behavior.

    a. Freud had two major techniques for interpreting dreams in order to uncover their unconscious content: *free association* and *symbols*.

    b. In *transference* the client reacts to a person in a present relationship as though that person were someone from the client's past.

    c. *Defense mechanisms* operate unconsciously and involve defending against anxiety and threats to the ego.

        i. *Repression* is the most basic defense mechanism and it involves forcing threatening feelings, ideas, or motives into the unconscious.

        ii. Some, or all of these techniques may lead to *catharsis* which is the process of releasing intense, often unconscious, emotions in a therapeutic setting.

B. Humanistic Therapy

1. Humanistic therapies seek to help the client reach his or her greatest potential.

2. Carl Rogers developed *client-centered therapy* and he is the most prominent figure in humanistic therapy. This type of therapy centers around the idea that people are not well because there is a gap between who they are and who they would ideally like to be.

    a. During therapy, the therapist must show *unconditional positive regard* which is showing a genuine liking and empathy for the client, regardless of what she has said or done.

C. Behavioral Treatments

1. In *behavioral therapies,* therapists apply the principles of classical and operant conditioning to treat psychological disorders.

2. *Token economies* are a technique in which desirable behaviors are reinforced with tokens (such as poker chips) that can be exchanged for privileges or

desired items.

3. An especially effective treatment for treating simple phobia is *systematic desensitization.* In this procedure, relaxation is paired with a gradual exposure to a phobic object. People cannot be both relaxed and anxious at the same time and the pairing procedure works effectively to reduce the anxiousness associated with the phobia.

   a. *Flooding,* or implosion therapy, is an extreme form of in vivo exposure in which the client experiences extreme exposure to the phobic object (for example, asking a person who is arachnophobic to hold three hairy tarantulas at once).

D. Cognitive and Cognitive-Behavioral Treatments

1. *Cognitive therapy* is any type of psychotherapy that works to restructure irrational thought patterns. It is structured and problem-oriented, with the primary goal of fixing erroneous thought patterns.

2. *Cognitive-behavioral therapy (CBT)* is used to change both thoughts and behavior. CBT entails restructuring thoughts, loosening the client's belief in irrational thoughts that may perpetuate the disorder, and offering incentives for acquiring more adaptive thought and behavior patterns.

   a. CBT has been used successively to treat a variety of disorders including depression, phobias, PTSD, OCD, eating disorders, and substance abuse.

E. Group Therapies

1. In *group therapies* several people who share a common problem all meet regularly with a therapist to help themselves and one another; the therapist acts as a facilitator.

   a. *Support groups* are regular meetings of people who share a common situation (e.g., a disorder or disease) and offer a sense of community and a place to share feelings.

Psychology in the Real World: Preventing Depression (p. 632)

A. *Prevention* focuses on identifying risk factors for disorders, targeting at-risk populations, and offering training programs that decrease the likelihood of disorders occurring.

1. The majority of prevention efforts are for the prevention of depression which is the number one mental health concern in the U.S. (Kessler et al., 2005).

a. A large-scale study that examined risk factors for adolescent depression found that being female, of a nonwhite ethnicity, low-income status, poor health, and experiencing parental conflict were all risk factors for depressive episodes for teens (van Voorhees et al., (2008).

b. Some interventions programs for teens focus on helping them learn better skills for dealing with stress, including developing a more optimistic outlook.

2. The Penn Resiliency Program (PRP) is designed to prevent depression and other psychological disorders through cultivation of resilience and skills for coping with stress, problem solving (flexibility in the face of adverse or challenging circumstances), and cognitive restructuring (learning to change one's perspective of events).

a. A large-scale study of administering PRP to middle school children found that PRP significantly reduced depressive symptoms at follow-up compared with a control group and other intervention (not aimed at resiliency) in two of the three schools participating.

b. Outlooks ingrained early in life should help to offset a lifetime of depression.

III. Combined Approaches (p. 634)

A. Drugs and Psychotherapy

1. Combining these two approaches might work better than either one alone. The drugs can modify some of the debilitating symptoms associated with the disorder such that the client is well enough to learn new techniques that can help him or her acquire more adaptive behaviors.

B. Integrative Therapies

1. *Integrative therapies* result from a therapist drawing from many methods that seem the most appropriate given the situation; that is, they are not loyal to any particular orientation or treatment.

a. *Prolonged Exposure therapy* is used for people with PTSD. It combines CBT with methods of imagines exposure from systematic desensitization and relaxation.

C. Mindfulness Training Combined with Psychotherapy

1. Mindfulness meditation practices help people become aware of everything that

occurs in the mind for what it is: a thought, an emotion, or a sensation that will arise and dissipate. There are several combined approaches involving mindfulness:

    a. *Mindfulness-based cognitive therapy (MBCT)*

    b. *Dialectical behavior therapy (DBT)*

    c. *The Four Steps* (aimed at helping people with OCD to recognize intrusive thoughts as nothing but a symptom, not a defining characteristic of the individual) (Schwartz, 1997). The four steps are:

        i. Relabel
        ii. Reattribute
        iii. Refocus
        iv. Revalue

IV. Effectiveness of Treatments (p. 637)

A. Effectiveness of Biological Treatments

1. The SSRIs and tricyclics show comparable effectiveness in the treatment of depression (Kendrick et al., 2006).

2. Lithium is widely used to treat mania associated with bipolar, however, there is weak evidence for it's effectiveness in treating acute phases of mania.

3. The traditional and atypical antipsychotic drugs are effective for treating the positive symptoms of schizophrenia (i.e., hallucinations and delusions) but are not very effective for the negative symptoms (i.e., flattened affect and cognitive confusion) (Javitt & Coyle, 2004).

    a. Because of the unpleasant side effects, many patients have difficulty with medication compliance.

4. ECT is effective in many individuals with severe depression who have not found relief with other treatments; it is a last resort treatment.

B. Effectiveness of Psychological Treatments

1. Psychiatry is now focused on choosing treatments based on the empirical evidence for effectiveness; that is, they need to be *evidenced-based therapies.*

2. For those with schizophrenia, long-term group therapy appears to improve their basic life skills (Sigman & Hassan, 2006).

3. Systematic desensitization if effective for treating simple phobia.

4. Cognitive therapy (CT) and CBT are the most effective or any form of psychotherapy for treating various disorders, but especially effective for treating depression and anxiety.

C. Effectiveness of Integrative Approaches

1. Treating ADHD with a combination of medication and behavioral therapy is superior than using either one treatment option alone (Edwards, 2002).

2. MBCT has been shown to prevent relapse in individuals who have experienced at least three depressive episodes.

3. DBT is effective in reducing the symptoms of borderline personality disorder.

Making Connections in the Treatment of Disorders: Approaches to the Treatment of Anxiety Disorders (p. 640)

A. Drug Therapies: Play a major role in the management and treatment of anxiety disorders.

1. Antidepressants: Many doctors prescribe SSRIs for treating OCD, social phobia, PTSD, generalized anxiety disorder, and panic disorder.

a. These drugs help loosen the grip of anxious thinking and thus allow the patient to apply cognitive techniques to learn how to think differently.

b. Most of the tricyclics do not appear to work for the treatment of OCD, but they do work for other anxiety disorders.

i. One tricyclic, CMI, does reduce the symptoms of OCD.

2. Anti-Anxiety Medications: Are drugs that sooth the agitation of anxiety and are used to treat anxiety disorders, especially those suffering from panic attacks.

a. Beta-blockers work by blocking the action of norepinephrine which acts to calm the physiological symptoms of anxiety by bringing down heart rate, blood pressure, and rate of breathing.

b. The benzodiazepines are prescribed for anxiety disorders such as social phobia, panic disorder, and generalized anxiety. These drugs also calm the physiological arousal caused by anxiety.

i. There are withdrawal symptoms associated with the

benzodiazepines such as insomnia, tremor, increased anxiety, tachycardia, and sweating.

B. Psychotherapeutic Treatments

1. Both CBT and group CBT are effective in helping people with anxiety disorders identify irrational thoughts and undo thinking patterns that support fear. These therapies also help clients modify their responses to anxiety-providing situations.

2. Systematic desensitization if effective for treating specific phobias.

3. Often times, medication is used in conjunction with psychotherapies and the medicine is used short-term or is decreased slowly during the course of psychological treatment.

   a. There is some debate as to whether combined therapies are more effective than single therapies in the treatment of anxiety disorders.

C. Integrative Therapies and Anxiety

1. There is evidence that integrative psychotherapeutic approaches provide potential relief from a range of anxiety disorders (e.g., MBCT for treating generalized anxiety disorder and DBT for treating bipolar).

2. Due to ACE research, it is now widely recognized that the interaction of genetic factors with exposure to abusive or neglectful environments plays a major role in the development of psychological disorders.

GLOSSARY TERMS
monoamine oxidase (MAO) inhibitors: one of the first class of dugs used to treat depression; they reduce the action of the enzyme monoamine oxidase, which breaks down monoamine neurotransmitters (including norepinephrine, epinephrine, dopamine, and serotonin) in the brain.
tricyclic antidepressants: drugs used for treating depression, including imipramine and amitriptyline (trade names Elavil and Anafranil); also used in chronic pain management, treatment of ADHD, and as a treatment for bedwetting.
selective serotonin reuptake inhibitors (SSRIs): drugs used primarily for depression and for some anxiety disorders that work by making more serotonin available in the synapse; include Prozac (fluoxetine), Zoloft (sertraline), Paxil (paroxetine), and Celexa (citalopram).
bupropione: another widely used antidepressant (trade name Wellbutrin) chemically unrelated to the tricyclics, MAO inhibitors, and SSRIs; inhibits the reuptake of norepinephrine and dopamine.
benzodiazepines: a class of drugs (including Valium and Librium) prescribed for anxiety; produce calming effects and can be addictive, but less dangerous than the barbiturates.

barbiturates: a class of drug for anxiety; has sedative, calming effects; can be addictive and carry risk of overdose.

lithium: a salt that is prescribed for its ability to stabilize the mania associated with bipolar disorder.

phenothiazines: the first class of drugs used to treat schizophrenia; help diminish hallucinations, confusion, agitation, and paranoia; creates adverse side effects including tardive dyskinesia.

traditional antipsychotics: historically, the first medications used to manage psychotic symptoms.

tardive dyskinesia: a side effect from the extended use of traditional antipsychotics; consists of repetitive, involuntary movements of jaw, tongue, face, and mouth (such as grimacing and lip-smacking) and body tremors.

atypical antipsychotics: newer antipsychotic drugs, which do not create tardive dyskinesia; include Clozapine (Clozaril), olanzapine (Zyprexa), and risperidone (Risperdal).

prefrontal lobotomy: a form of psychosurgery, in which the connections between the prefrontal lobes and the lower portion of the brain are severed; no longer in use.

electroconvulsive therapy (ECT): involves passing an electrical current through a person's brain in order to induce a seizure; currently in limited use for treatment of severe depression.

repetitive transcranial magnetic stimulation: exposure of particular brain structures to bursts of high-intensity magnetic fields instead of electricity; usually reserved for people with severe depression.

psychotherapy: the use of psychological techniques to modify maladaptive behaviors or thought patterns, or both, and to help patients develop insight into their own behavior.

psychodynamic psychotherapy: therapy aimed at uncovering unconscious motives that underlie psychological problems.

free association: a psychotherapeutic technique in which the client takes one image or idea and says whatever comes to mind, regardless of how threatening, disgusting, or troubling it may be. This process is repeated until the client has made associations with all the images.

transference: process in psychotherapy when the client reacts to a person in a present relationship as though that person were someone from the client's past.

defense mechanisms: ways in which the mind protects itself from harmful, threatening, and anxiety-provoking thoughts, feelings, or impulses; they operate unconsciously, and they deny or distort reality in some way.

repression: the unconscious act of keeping threatening or disturbing thoughts, feelings, or impulses out of consciousness; the most basic of all defense mechanisms.

catharsis: the process of releasing intense, often unconscious, emotions in a therapeutic setting.

client-centered therapy: a form of humanistic therapy developed by Carl Rogers, which requires that the therapist hold unconditional positive regard for the patient.

unconditional positive regard: basic tenant of client-centered therapy; the therapist's genuine linking and empathy for the client, regardless of what he or she has said or done.

behavior therapies: therapies that apply the principles of classical and operant conditioning to treat psychological disorders.

token economies: a behavioral technique in which desirable behaviors are reinforced with a token, such as a small chip or fake coin, which can then be exchanged for privileges.

systematic desensitization: a behavioral therapy technique, often used for phobias, in which the therapist pairs relaxation with gradual exposure to a phobic object, generating a hierarchy of increasing contact with the feared object, ranging from mild to extreme.

flooding: an extreme form of *in vivo* exposure in which the client experiences extreme exposure to the phobic object.

cognitive therapy: any type of psychotherapy that works to restructure irrational thought patterns.

cognitive-behavioral therapy: an approach to treating psychological disorders that combines techniques for restructuring irrational thoughts with operant and classical conditioning techniques to shape desirable behaviors

group therapy: therapeutic settings in which several people who share a common problem all meet regularly with a therapist to help themselves and one another; the therapist acts as a facilitator.

support groups: meetings of people who share a common situation, be it a disorder, a disease, or coping with an ill family member.

integrative therapy: also called "eclectic," an approach to treatment in which the therapist is not loyal to any particular orientation or treatment, but rather draws on those that seem most appropriate given the situation.

mindfulness-based cognitive therapy (MBCT): an approach that combines elements of CBT with mindfulness meditation to help people with depression learn to not cling to negative thought patterns.

dialectical behavior therapy (DBT): a program developed for the treatment of borderline personality disorder, which integrates elements of CBT with exercises aimed at developing mindfulness without meditation.

PRACTICE STUDY QUESTIONS

1. _____ were among the first pharmaceuticals used to treat depression.
    a. SSRIs
    b. Tricyclics
    c. Benzodiazepines
    d. MAO inhibitors

2. Of these two drugs used to treat anxiety disorders, _____ have a higher risk of overdose than do _____.
    a. benzodiazepines; barbiturates
    b. barbiturates; benzodiazepines
    c. SSRIs; tricyclics
    d. MAO inhibitors; SSRIs

3. The phenothiazines help diminish the _____ symptoms of schizophrenia.
    a. negative
    b. positive
    c. catatonic
    d. entire set of

4. The use of traditional antipsychotics caused unpleasant side effects including a condition called _____ which consists of repetitive, involuntary movements of the jaw and tongue.
   a. agoraphobia
   b. tardive dyskinesia
   c. beta blocking
   d. disorientation reflex

5. _____ is used as a last resort treatment for people with severe depression that have not responded to other forms of therapy.
   a. Prefrontal lobotomy
   b. Token economy
   c. Electroconvulsive therapy
   d. Systematic desensitization

6. Mayberg and colleagues found that people with depression had _____ activity in Area 25 of the brain.
   a. overactivity
   b. depressed activity
   c. no
   d. none of the above are correct

7. _____ is the most prominent person in Humanistic therapy and developed _____ therapy.
   a. Freud; free association
   b. Rogers; client-centered
   c. Skinner; token economy
   d. Beck; cognitive

8. _____ pairs relaxation with gradual exposure to a phobic object.
   a. Free association
   b. ECT
   c. CBT
   d. Systematic desensitization

9. Asking a person with arachnophobia to hold three hairy tarantulas at once is an example of:
   a. free association.
   b. systematic desensitization.
   c. flooding.
   d. client-centered therapy.

10. _____ is used to change both thoughts and behavior.
    a. CBT
    b. ECT
    c. Systematic desensitization
    d. Free association

11. Medication compliance is often difficult for people with _____ because of the negative side effects associated with the medication used to treat the disorder. Many stop taking their medications which results in more difficulty for the person.
    a. schizophrenia
    b. phobias
    c. depression
    d. catatonia

12. _____ therapy combines CBT with methods of systematic desensitization and relaxation for treating PTSD.
    a. ECT
    b. Prolonged exposure
    c. Drug
    d. Mindfulness

13. _____ is used to treat borderline personality disorder and it integrates elements of CBT with exercises aimed at developing mindfulness without meditation.
    a. DBT
    b. Prolonged exposure
    c. Drug
    d. Mindfulness

14. The SSRIs and tricyclics show comparable effectiveness in treating depression.
    a. true
    b. false

15. No tricyclics are effective for treating anxiety disorders.
    a. true
    b. false

ANSWERS TO PRACTICE STUDY QUESTIONS

1. d
2. a
3. b
4. b
5. c
6. a
7. b
8. d
9. c
10. a
11. a
12. b
13. a
14. a
15. b